The Signature of America

Books by Charles Hamilton

The Signature of America (1979)

The Book of Autographs (1978)

Big Name Hunting: A Beginner's Guide to Autograph Collecting
    (with Diane Hamilton, 1973)

Scribblers and Scoundrels (1968)

The Robot That Helped to Make a President (1965)

Lincoln in Photographs (with Lloyd Ostendorf, 1963)

Collecting Autographs and Manuscripts (1961)

Braddock's Defeat (1959)

Men of the Underworld (1952)

Cry of the Thunderbird (1950)

The Signature of America

A FRESH LOOK AT FAMOUS HANDWRITING

by Charles Hamilton

HARPER & ROW, PUBLISHERS

NEW YORK, HAGERSTOWN, SAN FRANCISCO, LONDON

TO MY WIFE, DIANE

FIRST EDITION

Designed by Sidney Feinberg

Library of Congress Cataloging in Publication Data

Hamilton, Charles, 1913–
   The signature of America.
   1. Autographs—Collections.   2. United States—
History.   I. Title.
Z42.H25   1979   929.8   79-1666
ISBN 0-06-011794-X

79 80 81 82 83 10 9 8 7 6 5 4 3 2 1

CONTENTS

A Note From the Author

Look into this book and I'll take you on a rollicking excursion into the secret past and present of America.

My unwitting collaborators whose signatures ornament these pages, ofttimes appended to letters that should have been burned, are all famous Americans—from prigs and perverts to poets and Presidents.

If you ever wanted to be a Peeping Tom but lacked the temerity, here's your chance to pry into the private affairs of a host of celebrities and, at the same time, discover how more than fifteen hundred of them penned their monikers.

HEROES OF
1 THE OLD WEST

Buffalo Bill

Ned Buntline (E. Z. C. Judson)

Buffalo Bill was hitting the bottle. A quart a day, at least. His famous Wild West Show was in trouble because its buckskinned star was usually too drunk to smash the little balls with his rifle during the evening performance.

"Bill," said his manager, Nate Salsbury, "you're drinking more shots than you're firing. But I've got a plan."

That evening Buffalo Bill was tipsier than ever, but as he galloped around the circus ring he managed to break every one of the balls tossed into the air. He was again the crack shot of the plains and the crowd roared its approval.

Later Nate explained, "I simply substituted a double-barreled shotgun for Bill's rifle and made the balls twice as big."

Buffalo Bill's rough and ready penmanship was never affected by boozing. His script was so bad to start with that it took more than just a bottle of whiskey to make it worse.

Bill was a product manufactured out of the whole cloth by Ned Buntline (E. Z. C. Judson), the dime novelist. Buntline wanted a real live hero for his dreadfuls, a man he could make famous and then feature on the Broadway stage. He traveled out West to find a good-looking and articulate buffalo hunter who was willing to be romanticized, be turned into a folk hero, and face the footlights.

He discovered just the man he wanted under a wagon, greasing a wheel—William F. Cody. "From now on," said Buntline, "you're 'Buffalo Bill.'"

Perhaps because of his hazy past, lost in the fictions of Buntline, Buffalo Bill's letters seldom mention his earlier "adventures." Hundreds of his notes have passed through my hands, nearly all of them about circus matters, family affairs and his health. The variety of his letterheads, many of them in color, is amazing. They capture the splendor and excitement of the old West just as Buffalo Bill recreated it in his celebrated Wild West Shows.

Acting with Cody in his show or on the stage were some of the most interesting heroes of the West (or in some cases, the near West). There was the crazy "Wild Bill" Hickok, who got fired from Buffalo Bill's Broadway play for shooting blanks at

MILLER & ARLINGTON WILD WEST SHOW CO., INC. PRESENT

THE MILITARY PAGEANT
PREPAREDNESS "BUFFALO BILL" COMBINED WITH THE
(HIMSELF) 101 RANCH SHOWS

ROARING BATTERIES OF BIG FIELD GUNS (COL.WM.F.CODY) A STIRRING SCENE IN THE BUFFALO BILL
WITH REAL U.S. ARMY ARTILLERISTS THE SADDLE CHARGE! 101 RANCH SPECTACLE PREPAREDNESS
BUFFALO BILL. PERFORMANCE. BUFFALO BILL

GEORGE ARLINGTON, JOS. C. MILLER, EDWARD ARLINGTON,
GENERAL MANAGER. DIRECTOR. GEN'L AGENT.

Handwritten letter of Buffalo Bill about Washington, D.C.: "This is an awful town for me."

---

the legs of the walk-on actors. There was a host of noted Indians, including Sitting Bull, Rain-in-the-face (who is said to have cut out Tom Custer's heart at the Little Big Horn) and Iron Tail, a Sioux chief whom Buffalo Bill called "the finest man I ever knew, bar none."

But the real stars of Cody's show, next to Buffalo Bill, were Annie Oakley and her husband, Frank Butler. Annie was a pretty little girl from a farm in Pennsylvania, a dead shot who could knock a freckle off your nose. Sitting Bull called her "Little Miss Sure Shot."

Only a few letters of Annie Oakley survive and those of her marksman husband are even rarer. I once owned a letter written by Annie a year before her death in 1926. She was then confined to a wheelchair in a nursing home.

"Some friends came to see me," she wrote, "and they asked if I could still shoot.

"'Push me out into the garden and give me my rifle,' I said."

Annie described what took place. The visitors offered to toss a coin in the air for her to shoot at. Annie suggested a dime, but her friends felt a silver dollar would be easier for the crippled lady to hit. They compromised on a fifty-cent piece. Someone pitched it up.

Rain-in-the-face

Paris July 6th 89

Editor Enc

Dear Sir I am very Thankful for the very kind and flatering notice you gave me in your paper.

To be Considered a lady has always being my highest ambation. again Thanking you and with best wishes to your Esteemed wife I am Thankfuly

Annie Oakley

Buffalo Bills Wild West

Paris France

Handwritten letter of Annie Oakley, Paris, 1889: "To be considered a lady has always being [been] my highest ambation."

Calamity Jane, her mark

With almost the same movement, the sixty-five-year-old Annie raised her rifle and fired. The coin flew spinning off, and her friends picked it up a moment later with a slug embedded in the eagle's breast.

An elderly woman visited me a few years ago and after we had chatted awhile about Buffalo Bill and Annie Oakley, both of whom she had known intimately, she hurled a thunderbolt at me. "I had a whole trunkful of Annie's letters, written to me over the years, but when I sold my home I couldn't take them along so I burned them."

Normally I can take such bad news without flinching. But I was so stricken over the destruction of Annie's letters, no doubt full of wonderful anecdotes of the old West, that I said, "From a financial point of view, you would have done better to burn your house and sell the letters."

Of Calamity Jane (Martha Jane Burke) only a single signature has survived, an X in the form of a brace of crudely drawn pistols.

From Buffalo Bill and his friends it is but a step back to Daniel Boone and Kit Carson and the other pioneers who opened America's frontier. Boone's signature is as hard to find as a hostile Shawnee hiding in a copse. Although Boone was famous in his own day—Lord Byron put him into some rhymes—he signed very few documents and wrote fewer letters. Virtually everything from his quill that survives concerns financial or land transactions. The same is true of his associate

Kit Carson

Henry Wells, president of Wells-Fargo Express Company

Simon Kenton, who could barely write his name, and the noted Indian fighter Kit Carson, whose signature turns up only on a few photographs (as "Kit" Carson) and some routine military documents from Taos, New Mexico (signed "C. Carson").

What a pity that these men who led lives of high adventure never set down their deeds on paper!

Scarce, too, are letters of Henry Wells, William G. Fargo, Alexander Majors, John Butterfield and Ben Holladay, the "speed merchants" of their day, who opened the old West with the pony express and the stagecoach. The few documents left by these developers of the frontier are charged with romance.

Simon Kenton

Handwritten letter of crack shot Frank Butler about hunting: "Yesterday got 22 . . ."

Signed photograph of Kit Carson as United States brigadier general in the Civil War

Sir

You are hereby required to be ready to go on the intended Expedition against the Shawnese Your Service will be required as a field Officer agreeable to your late Recommendation made by the County Court in the mean Time Expect every exertion will be made by you to forward the Business ~~in the mean~~ *agreeable to the Orders here to issued relative to the Same*

I am Sir your most Obed't Serv't

Daniel Boone

Fayette Octob'r 25th 1782

To Lieut Col. Rob't Patterson

Letter of Daniel Boone, dictated and signed by him, 1782, about "the intended Expedition against the Shawnese"

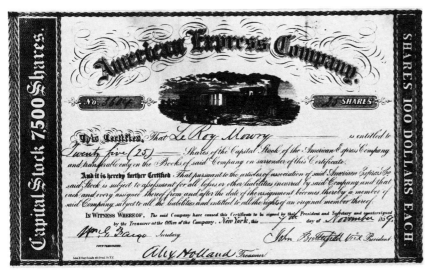

Stock certificate signed by William G. Fargo, secretary of Wells-Fargo Express Company and John Butterfield, pioneer expressman and founder of American Express

Receipt for a Colt revolver, filled out and signed by Alexander Majors, originator of the pony express

Check of the Oregon and California Rail Road Company signed by Ben Holladay, noted stagecoach operator

Squire Boone, Indian fighter and brother of Daniel Boone

Samuel Colt, inventor of the Colt revolver, the great weapon of the frontier

Isaac Shelby, pioneer and first governor of Kentucky

Moses Austin, Texas pioneer and colonizer

Moses Cleveland, Ohio pioneer

Joseph Virgo, fur trader at St. Louis

Julian Dubuque, Iowa pioneer

David Crockett, Tennessee frontiersman

William Clark, Western explorer with Meriwether Lewis

George W. Lillie, "Pawnee Bill," frontiersman
and circus owner

Meriwether Lewis, Western explorer with William Clark

Father Pierre J. De Smet, Indian missionary

John Sevier, pioneer and first governor of Tennessee

Manuel Lisa, fur trader at St. Louis; explored Missouri River

Auguste Chouteau, fur trader at St. Louis

Pierre Chouteau (senior and junior), fur traders

Rufus Putnam, Ohio pioneer; founded Marietta

James Robertson, Tennessee pioneer

Grenville M. Dodge, chief engineer, Union Pacific Railroad

Zebulon M. Pike, Western explorer; discovered Pikes Peak

Manasseh Cutler, Ohio pioneer

Manasseh Cutler

Nelson A. Miles, Indian fighter; captured Geronimo

*I remain
With great respect
Very Truly yours
Nelson A. Miles
U.S.A.*

Edward R. S. Canby, Indian fighter; murdered by Modoc Indians

Edw R Canby

George Crook, Indian fighter; opposed Sitting Bull and Geronimo

George Crook

O. O. Howard, Indian fighter; captured Chief Joseph

*O. O. Howard
Maj. Gen.*

MUCH-ADMIRED
AUTHORS **2**

Authors who go to parties of the cocktail variety quickly learn to accept graciously, or elude adroitly, the dreaded autograph album.

But an habitué of taverns, such as Truman Capote, has a different problem. He may be asked to sign bizarre objects. Two years ago in a bar, a man approached Capote, lowered his pants and asked the author for his autograph on a personal appendage.

Capote said later, "He was very drunk and very muscular, so of course I obliged."

Capote's letters are at present stowed away in the bureau drawers of society *dames*. The few that show up on the philographic (or autographic) market are not very revealing, but I have a hunch that a generation or two hence will witness the appearance of some exciting letters from this flowering thistle of literature.

Another holographically elusive author is Gore Vidal. I recently sold his personal telephone book at auction. It was a riotous disclosure of unexpected private phone numbers, including those of Jackie Onassis, Paul Newman, Tennessee Williams, Tony Perkins and Vincent Price. Informed of the sale, Vidal said, "Mr. Charles Hamilton is dealing in stolen goods," adding that the book of unlisted numbers had probably been pilfered by a guest who rented his flat in Rome.

Vidal's favorite quotation for autograph seekers is: "Live every day as if it were your last." When I was in the Air Corps during World War II, many pilots and gunners who daily faced death followed this classic advice, but their hangovers the next morning could not be alleviated by philosophic precepts.

The letters of the great limner in lavender Thomas Wolfe are full of vitality and read like excerpts from his famous novels. When the creative fervor was upon him, Wolfe turned out penciled epistles of ten or fifteen pages with ease, pouring forth his soul in profuse streams of unpremeditated art. No man ever put more of himself in his letters. They are almost embarrassing to read. Wolfe recounts his inner struggles in such detail that it is impossible not to share his fears and

Gore Vidal

J. D. Salinger

I have no secretary and my correspondence tends to go awry —

Sincerely

T. Capote

Truman Capote. Handwritten note signed

In appreciation.

William Faulkner
Oxford. Miss
3 June 1946.

William Faulkner

Sincerely yours

Winston Churchill

Winston Churchill, American author; wrote *The Crisis*

Winston S. Churchill

Sir Winston Churchill, British prime minister; honorary American citizen

Theodore Dreiser

Theodore Dreiser

exultations. His favorite topic, "you can't go home again," occurs in many variations.

Elusive and desirable are the letters of J. D. Salinger, who prefers the life of a recluse, and William Faulkner, who apparently had an aversion to correspondence. Several years ago I purchased from Faulkner's butler, Paul Pollard, several remarkable letters of the great novelist. In refusing to contribute to the National Association for the Advancement of Colored People, Faulkner wrote:

. . . I agree with your own two great men: Booker T. Washington and Dr. Carver. Any social justice and equality which is compelled to your people by nothing but law and police force, will vanish as soon as the police force is removed, unless the individual members of your race have earned the right to it. . . .

If the people of your race are to have equality and justice as human beings in our culture, the majority of them have got to be changed completely from the way they now act. Since they are a minority, they must behave better than white people. . . . They, not the law, have got to compel the white people to say, Please come and be equal with us.

If you run across a letter signed "Winston Churchill," it could have been written by one of two Americans: the author of such novels as *Richard Carvel* and *The Crossing*, or the British prime minister Sir Winston Churchill, by special act of Congress an honorary American citizen. Time has dealt harshly with the literary reputation of the novelist, but the letters of Sir Winston, an important author as well as a great statesman, are coveted articles of commerce.

The letters of Theodore Dreiser and Sinclair Lewis are abundant and moderately interesting. Dreiser's style is the most wooden of any author of importance since Fenimore Cooper. The same tautology that ensnarls his novels crops up in his letters. Still, Dreiser's comments on men and events are pertinent and forceful and I have yet to read a dull letter over his signature.

Tennessee Williams

Tennessee Williams

Meanwhile all the best!

Henry Miller

Henry Miller

Many authors decline to correspond with strangers. Some notable exceptions are John Steinbeck, who occasionally invested an hour or two in answering fan mail; Tennessee Williams, always a prolific patron of the mails; and Henry Miller, an indefatigable scribbler, whose dozens of pen pals hoard batches of letters in his labored but legible script.

H. L. Mencken, the "sage of Baltimore," was an apostle of brevity. His typed messages, pithy and clever, average only five or six lines. Two subjects could draw Mencken into a longer letter—beer and prohibition. Mencken relished the first and abhorred the latter. His comments on both could be viciously funny and were not intended for Sunday school reading.

H. L. Mencken

A most remarkable cache of Willa Cather's notes, photographs and personal memorabilia came to light when the novelist's heir visited me recently. From her I obtained many original manuscripts, including the only surviving page of *Death Comes for the Archbishop.*

"Miss Cather was, as you perhaps know, a lesbian," she told me. "Shortly before her death she asked her correspondents to send back the notes and messages she had written them over the years."

Cordially yours Willa Cather

Willa Cather

"Was she preparing a volume of her letters?"

"No; she was preparing a holocaust. She sat in front of a fireplace blaze and tossed letter after letter—hundreds of them—into the flames.

"It was as though Miss Cather wished to wipe out every evidence of her earthly existence."

Sincerely yours A. B. Toklas

Alice B. Toklas

A most intriguing odd couple were Gertrude Stein and Alice B. Toklas. Their Parisienne adventures form an exciting chapter in the history of culture, for there was not an author, artist or composer who did not court them. Miss Stein was profligate in her help to youthful devotees of the muses.

The letters of Gertrude Stein, often penned on stationery ornamented with her famous circular "a rose is a rose is a rose" design, are difficult to decipher and when deciphered difficult to understand. But after a few readings, her comments often

Gertrude Stein. Handwritten inscription in a copy of *Geography and Plays* (1922) to a friend "whose interest in my work has touched me profoundly"

Thomas Wolfe. Conclusion of a handwritten letter signed about his first book, *Look Homeward, Angel* (1929): "I shall always feel that something I wrote made its way out into the great jungle of the world, and found a friend there."

Willa Cather. First page of the original manuscript of *Death Comes for the Archbishop*

take on a rich and beautiful meaning.

Always a delight are the letters of James Thurber, most of which were typed and signed with a huge penciled signature during his later years, when he was nearly blind. Thurber's left eye, which he lost in a childhood accident, was glass. Whenever Thurber went on a spree, he took along a series of three glass eyes and inserted them progressively: slightly bloodshot, very bloodshot, and the final eye, a resplendent full-color American flag. I recently owned a letter in which Thurber declined to endorse some Scotch whisky. "It is well known that I am an old rye drinker and that my second choice is Bourbon. . . . I told the late Harold Ross that no likeness of me would ever appear in the *New Yorker's* ads, holding a beer or whisky glass, reclining alone or with a gal in the back of a Pontiac, or trying on a hostess gown at Bests. . . . Now that I'm fifty-eight all Scotch tastes to me like what I call Burglar's Uncle." Thurber is much venerated in his hometown of Columbus, Ohio, where

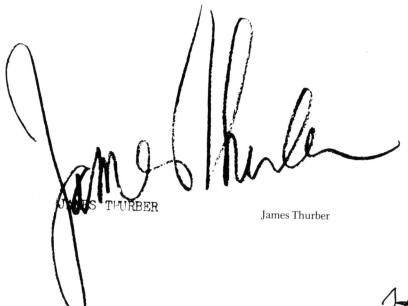

James Thurber

Yrs truly
Henry Adams

Henry Adams

Edgar Rice Burroughs

John Burroughs
Oct. 24th 1904

John Burroughs

Sincerely yours,
Paddy Chayefsky

Paddy Chayefsky

a grateful citizenry has named a grotesque high-rise in his honor.

The eccentric and unpredictable Norman Mailer is often regarded as America's greatest living author. His letters, only a very few of which have come my way, are plate-glass windows into his mind.

Many years ago a slight, elderly man carrying a cane entered my gallery and asked if we had a letter of Eleonora Duse. I recognized Erich Maria Remarque at once and after he bought a letter of Duse for his wife, Paulette Goddard, we spent over an hour discussing the characters in his books.

Finally I said, "How do you think your *All Quiet on the Western Front* compares with Crane's *The Red Badge of Courage?*"

"Crane's book is the greatest war novel ever written," he replied, "despite the fact that Crane had no firsthand experience of war."

I asked Remarque for his opinion of other war novelists—Tolstoy, Barbusse, Empey and Hemingway—as I worked my way up to the big question: "What's your opinion of Mailer's *The Naked and the Dead?*"

Remarque's face stiffened. I could see that he looked upon Mailer as a competitor.

"Mailer writes well and knows his subject," he said, "but he is too explicit, much too explicit.

"After all, one of the greatest tools a writer has is the reader's imagination. Mailer has not learned to use this tool."

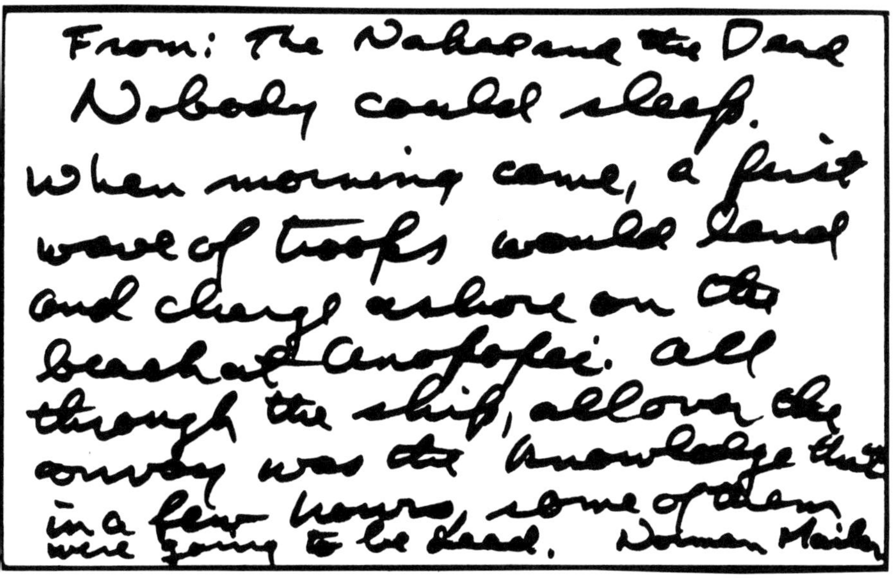

From: The Naked and the Dead
Nobody could sleep. When morning came, a first wave of troops would land and charge ashore on the beach at Anopopei. All through the ship, all over the convoy was the knowledge that in a few hours some of them were going to be dead. Norman Mailer

Norman Mailer. Handwritten quotation signed from *The Naked and the Dead*

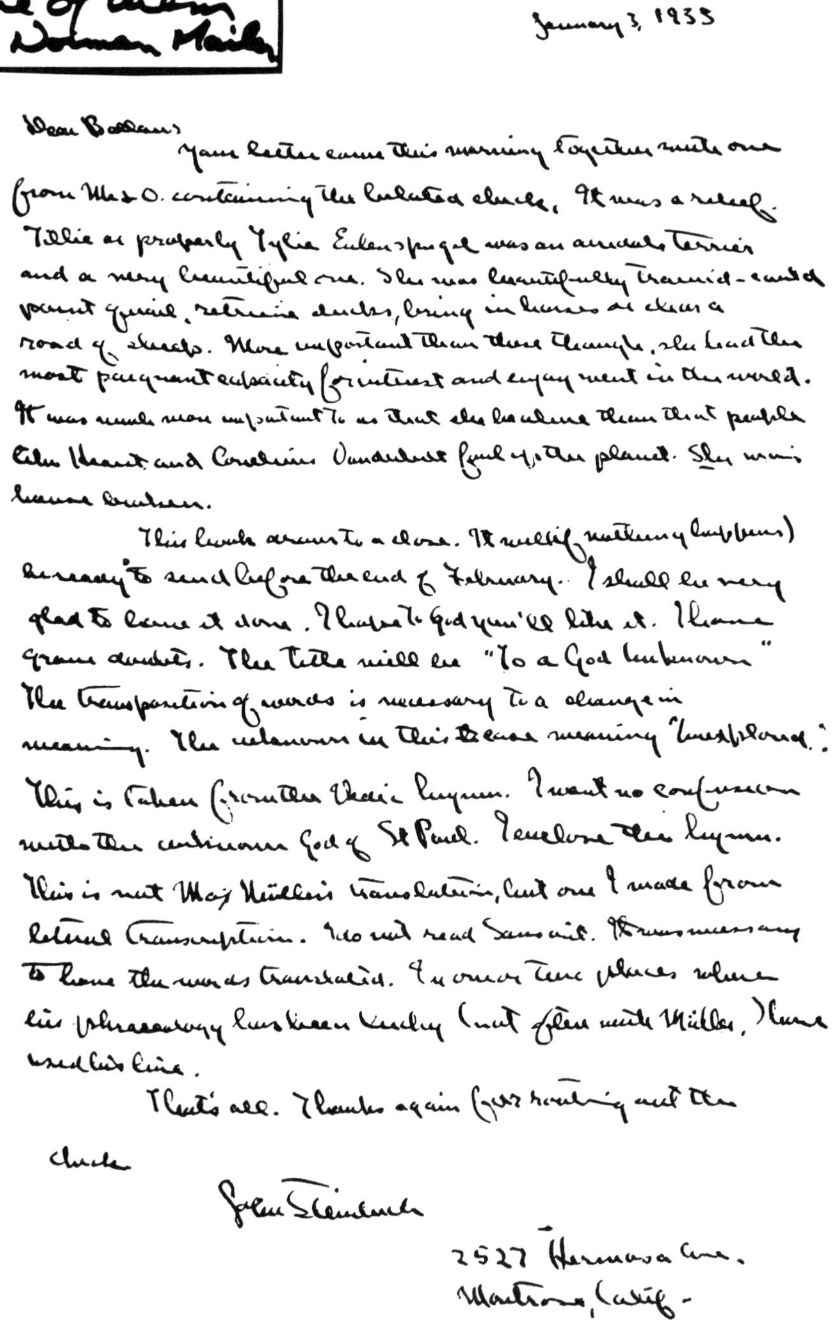

January 3, 1933

Dear Ballou:

Your letter came this morning together with one from Mrs O. containing the belated check. It was a relief.
Tillie or properly Tylie Eulenspiegel was an airedale terrier and a very beautiful one. She was beautifully trained—could point quail, retrieve ducks, bring in horses or drive a band of sheep. More important than these things, she had the most poignant capacity for interest and enjoyment in the world. It was much more important to us that she be alive than that people like Hearst and Cornelius Vanderbilt fouled up the planet. She was house broken.

This book draws to a close. It will (if nothing happens) be ready to send before the end of February. I shall be very glad to have it done. I hope to God you'll like it. I have grave doubts. The title will be "To a God Unknown" The transposition of words is necessary to a change in meaning. The unknown in this case meaning "Unexplored." This is taken from the Vedic hymn. I want no confusion with the unknown God of St Paul. I enclose the hymn. This is not Max Müller's translation, but one I made from literal transcription. I do not read Sanscrit. It was necessary to have the words translated. In one or two places where his phraseology has been lucky (not often with Müller,) I have used his line.

That's all. Thanks again for sending out the check

John Steinbeck

2527 Hermosa Ave.
Montrose, Calif.

John Steinbeck. Handwritten letter signed to his publisher Robert Ballou about his new book *To a God Unknown:* "I hope to God you'll like it. . . . The unknown in this case meaning 'Unexplored.'"

Malcolm Cowley

James Branch Cabell

Erskine Caldwell

Saul Bellow

L. Frank Baum

Pearl S. Buck

Sherwood Anderson

Maxwell Anderson

With best wishes to you and all our comrades I am sincerely yours, Ambrose Bierce. September 23, 1913.

Ambrose Bierce

Sincerely,

Peter Benchley

Peter Benchley

Sidney Howard

Lillian Hellman

DON'T EVER ACCEPT ADVICE ABOUT THE STATE OF YOUR PERSONAL HONESTY FROM OTHERS. ONLY YOU CAN KNOW HOW HONEST YOU ARE. AND ANYWAY, IT'S NONE OF THEIR BUSINESS. BESIDES, THEY MIGHT ALWAYS HAVE ULTERIOR MOTIVES. ALWAYS BE A LITTLE MORE HONEST WITH YOURSELF THAN YOU THINK YOU CAN AFFORD.

AFFECTIONATELY,

James Jones. Advice to a young boy

Sarah Orne Jewett

Stephen Leacock, Canadian humorist

My only advice would be not to
take yourself seriously as a writer--not to think of yourself as a writer--not to cultivate yourself to be a writer.
If you can write, write. If you can't, don't.
                        Sincerely.

Robert Benchley. Advice to a writer

Arthur Miller

O. Henry

Christopher Morley

Anaïs Nin

Joseph Hergesheimer

O. Henry (William Sydney Porter). Variant signatures

Fannie Hurst

Glen Ellen, Calif.,
March 1, 1911

I come of old American
stock, tracing back to an
American residence long prior
to the French & Indian Wars. All
my forefathers fought for
liberty. I am still fighting
for it, wherefore I sign
myself,
        Yours for the Revolution
        Jack London

Anita Louise

Richard Wilbur

Jack London. Autograph note signed about his ancestors

"... and nobody, nobody knows what's going to happen to anybody besides the forlorn rags of growing old, I think of Dean Moriarty, I even think of Old Dean Moriarty the father we never found, I think of Dean Moriarty."

ON THE ROAD
Last Page

Jack Kerouac

Jack Kerouac. Handwritten quotation from his book *On the Road*

Katherine Anne Porter

Katherine Anne Porter

Herman Wouk

Herman Wouk

Ernie Pyle

Ernie Pyle

John Buchan

John Buchan (Scotch-Canadian)

Jacqueline Susann

Jacqueline Susann

G. Santayana

George Santayana

Dorothy Thompson

Dorothy Thompson

S. S. Van Dine

S. S. Van Dine

Thornton Wilder

Thornton Wilder

"Ellery Queen" Manfred L. Lee

"Ellery Queen"
(Frederic Dannay)

Ellery Queen (Manfred Lee and Frederic Dannay)

Margaret Mitchell

John Dewey

James Baldwin

Always sincerely yours,

Maxwell Perkins

P. G. Wodehouse

Zane Grey

MacKinlay Kantor

John P. Marquand

Joseph C. Lincoln

For Burt Britton
There we are + there
we go don't we

William Saroyan
Fresno December 25 1974

William Saroyan. Self-portrait signed

Best wishes,

Edward Albee

Edna Ferber

Zona Gale

(Just because I
smile Alot
doesn't mean I
don't also
weep)

Erica Jong

"Terror writes
Poetry,
Hope, prose."

Erica Jong. Self-portrait signed

A BRACE OF TALL
PRESIDENTS **3**

In the winter of 1789, at the capitol in New York, a group of Indian leaders from the Western frontiers assembled to meet the new great chief, President George Washington.

As the President shook hands, he exchanged a few words with each, occasionally more than a few words, for Washington had known many of the chiefs during the Revolution and he seldom forgot a face. The interpreters were volleying pleasantries in the Indian tongues between the President and his guests.

As one old chief shook the President's hand, he said in Shawnee, "I once had the honor of saving the life of the great white father."

Washington searched his face. "I must apologize for not remembering you."

"We never met."

"Then how is it you saved my life?"

"It happened at the defeat of the rash white chief [Braddock] near Fort Pitt about thirty-five summers ago" (July 9, 1755).

"I thought I knew every Indian scout with Braddock's forces," said Washington.

"I was not with the British chief. I was with the young French chief [Captain Beaujeu] who was killed at the first fire. I was in the woods above the narrow way in which you and the other long knives were trapped.

"I was directing the fire of the warriors who were cutting down your soldiers like a herd of deer in the snow. Suddenly I saw a tall young British warrior riding up and down trying to rally the soldiers into whose ranks we were driving death.

"I called three of my best shots to my side. 'See that tall chief on the white horse? Kill him.'"

The President listened attentively. The Shawnee chief was describing what had happened at Braddock's defeat when Washington had two horses shot from under him and four bullets through his coat.

"My warriors took very careful aim. They fired. When the smoke from their muskets cleared, the tall chief's horse was

George Washington. Signature at age 23, at the time of Braddock's defeat (1755)

I *George Washington Commander in chief of the armies of the United States of America*
do acknowledge the U N I T E D S T A T E S of AME-
RICA, to be Free, Independent and Sovereign States, and
declare that the people thereof owe no allegiance or obedience to George the Third, King of Great-Britain; and I re-
nounce, refuse and abjure any allegiance or obedience to him;
and I do *swear* ——— that I will to the utmost of
my power, support, maintain and defend the said United
States, against the said King George the Third, his heirs and
successors and his or their abettors, assistants and adherents,
and will serve the said United States in the office of *Com-
in chief as aforesaid* ⸪ which I now hold, with fidelity,
according to the best of my skill and understanding.

Sworn before me
Camp at Valley Forge
May 12th 1778
Stirling Major General

G Washington

George Washington. Oath of allegiance to the United States,
filled out and signed as commander in chief of the Continental army

---

down and he already had his foot in the stirrup of another
mount.

"I was amazed that he was not hit. It seemed as though the
Great Spirit had turned aside the bullets in their flight.

"'What is the matter with you?' I said to my braves. 'If you
cannot shoot any better than that, I will send you home to
make moccasins with the old squaws. *I want that man dead!*'

"My warriors reloaded and this time they took a long while
to aim. The tall chief was galloping first to the right, then to the
left, in his efforts to save the long knives from rout.

"When the smoke cleared from the second volley, I could
not believe what I saw. The white chief was still alive, un-
wounded. His second mount was down and he was searching
for another horse.

"Suddenly I knew what I must do. 'Carry the word to the
others,' I said to my marksmen, 'that no one is to shoot at the
tall young chief, for the Great Spirit is protecting him this day
and saving him for some wonderful destiny.'"

Washington's signature at the time of Braddock's defeat,
when he was only twenty-four, was tall and imperial like the
young officer himself. It had a stately, aristocratic appearance.
Later in his life it grew in elegance and beauty.

If an autograph seeker had been present on that bloody
afternoon at the Monongahela and cared to defy bullets and
scalping Indians, he could have filled an album with illustrious
names. The woods were full of future generals. There was
Thomas Gage, later commander of the British at Bunker Hill;

By the President.

George Washington. Signature as President (1790)

---

and Revolutionary generals-to-be Walter Stewart, Adam Stephen, Hugh Mercer, Charles Lee and Horatio Gates. The buckskinned fighters included Daniel Boone, Christopher Gist, George Croghan, John Finley and the future General Daniel Morgan.

During my long career in the world of autographs, hundreds of Washington letters have passed through my hands and I still feel the same pounding of the heart whenever I hold a letter touched by his pen. His notes are rich in wisdom and urbanity, expressed in impeccable English and always interesting. He never wrote a letter that did not add to his stature.

One of the greatest letters of this great man ever to come my way was written to Henry ("Light Horse Harry") Lee, then governor of Virginia. Washington described the assaults on his character and his view of the presidency. Noting the "arrows of malevolence, barbed and well-pointed" fired at him, Washington speaks of himself as one of the nation's "public servants, for in this light I consider myself, whilst I am an occupant of office; and, if they were to go further and call me their slave I would not dispute the point.

"But in what will all this abuse terminate? The result, as it respects myself, I care not; for I have a consolation within, that no earthly efforts can deprive me of, and that is, that neither ambitious nor interested motives have influenced my conduct."

When this letter was knocked down at my auction on September 28, 1967, for the enormous price of twenty-five thousand dollars, the bidders and spectators spontaneously burst into applause. I felt it was a tribute to the letter and its writer, not to the price it fetched.

Abraham Lincoln was no aristocrat. He sprang from the soil and so did most of his jokes. Years ago I had the pleasure of selling at auction a slightly naughty tale, a masterpiece of spoonerisms, written out and doubtless intentionally left unsigned by Lincoln. Whether he composed it or merely copied it for a friend I don't know, but it bears the unmistakable touch of his bawdy humor:

George Washington. Signature at age 17

George Washington. Lottery ticket signed at age 36

He said he was riding *bass-ackwards* on a *jass-ack*, through a *patton-cotch*, on a pair of *baddle-sags*, stuffed full of *binger-gred*, when the animal *steered* at a *scump*, and the *lirrup-steather* broke, and throwed him in the *forner* of the *kence*, and broke his *pishing-fole*. He said he would not have minded it much, but he fell right in a great *tow-curd*; in fact, he said it give him a right *sick* of *fitness*—he had the *molera corbus* pretty bad— He said, about *bray dake* he came to himself, ran home, seized up a *stick* of *wood* [sic] and split the *axe* to make a light, rushed into the house, and found the *door* sick abed, and his *wife* standing open— But thank goodness she is getting right *hat* and *farty* again—

On another occasion I was briefly the custodian of a remarkable letter about Lincoln in which the writer told of meeting "The Honest" and listening to his salty conversation. Of General McClellan, whose inactivity galled him, Lincoln said: "McClellan doesn't realize that you can't fertilize a field with a fart." I have often thought that it is a great misfortune that Lincoln and Mark Twain, author of *1601*, the classic tale of explosive flatulence, never sat face to face, for their merriment as they bartered ribald jokes would have fractured the chandeliers in the White House.

George Washington. Handwritten letter signed, Mount Vernon, 1786, mentioning Lafayette

Abraham Lincoln. Handwritten letter signed to General Meade, asking the suspension of execution of a deserter "until further orders." Lincoln wrote hundreds of such notes, and needless to say, no further orders ever came from him.

Lincoln's letters never even hint at the bawdy. His clear, crisp style made him a master of the short letter. Seldom do his presidential notes run more than ten lines and the average is about five or six. Lincoln said what he had to say and then put down his pen.

Unlike Washington's, Lincoln's handwriting developed little during his lifetime. It was a homey, honest script, untouched by flourish or adornment. But of all the autographs that survive the past, those most avidly sought by historians and philographers are Lincoln's.

Abraham Lincoln. Vulgar tale written out and deliberately left unsigned

With malice toward none; with charity for all; with firmness in the right, as God gives us to see the right, let us strive on to finish the work we are in; to bind up the nation's wounds; to care for him who shall have borne the battle, and for his widow, and his orphan— to do all which may achieve and cherish a just and a lasting peace, among ourselves, and with all nations,

Abraham Lincoln. Last paragraph of the original manuscript of Lincoln's Second Inaugural. "With malice toward none; with charity for all . . ."

THEY COURTED
THE ANGELS 4

Joseph Smith, as mayor of Nauvoo, Illinois

Angels are a vanishing species. Very few have appeared on earth since Biblical days. William Blake spotted one or two perched in trees, but the really big discovery was made by a New York farm boy named Joseph Smith.

On the evening of September 21, 1823, Smith went to bed as usual; but during the night he was startled by the appearance of an angel, who told him about a book written upon golden plates. This marvelous volume, said his celestial visitor, recorded the ancient history of America and "the fulness of the everlasting gospel."

The angel, Moroni, revealed to Smith where he might find the plates and, after further visitations, gave him the key to translate the weird characters incised upon the golden tablets.

Young Joseph, only eighteen, copied the "caractors" and with the aid of a pair of magic glasses, Urim and Thummim, translated them from behind a curtain. Two friends of Smith, Martin Harris and Oliver Cowdery, recorded *The Book of Mormon* at the dictation of Smith and another friend, Sidney Rigdon.

Opponents of Mormonism claim that Smith and Rigdon heisted the whole book from an unpublished romance by an aspiring author, the Reverend Solomon Spaulding.

Smith's letters and documents, set down in a crabbed script, reveal a limited education but an astute mind. Not many papers from his pen survive.

Far more prolific was the flamboyant Brigham Young, who succeeded to the Mormon presidency after Smith was murdered by a mob in Carthage, Illinois, on June 27, 1844. Young's letters—about military affairs, politics, religion, Indians and his vast real estate holdings in Salt Lake City—turn up frequently.

Sidney Rigdon

Oliver Cowdery

Martin Harris

Caractors

The characters on the golden tablets, copied by Joseph Smith

Truth will previl.
The Kingdom of God or nothing.

Brigham Young.

Brigham Young. Autograph quotation signed

Joseph Smith. Handwritten authorization to use the "sterotipe plates and coppy right" of *The Book of Mormon*

Nauvoo City Feb. 24th 1842
Ebenezer Robinson is intitled
to the use of the sterotipe plates
and Coppy right for the printing
fifteen Hundred Books of
Mormon   Joseph Smith
Witness N K White

Less spectacular than Smith's angel were the "glows" of Mary Baker Patterson Glover Eddy. (Three-fifths of her long name was acquired from her trio of husbands.) During a fever when she was twelve, Mary turned to God. "I prayed; and a soft glow of ineffable joy came over me. The fever was gone."

The first "glow" was followed by others and in 1870 Mrs. Eddy published a pamphlet, "The Science of Man," in which she wrote: "I affix for all time the word *Science* to *Christianity*." Five years later came *Science and Health*, the bible of the Christian Science religion.

Mary Baker Eddy

Joseph Smith

Brigham Young

John Taylor

Milton Woodruff

Lorenzo Snow

Heber J. Grant

David O. McKay

Sincerely your brother,
Joseph Fielding Smith.

Joseph F. Smith

Harold B. Lee

Presidents of the Mormon Church

Many years ago I read _Science and Health_ and on glancing over my copy of the book with the marginal annotations I jotted in it at the time, I see that I was impressed by the native wisdom and common sense of Mrs. Eddy. Her letters, however, do not bear out this impression, for they are rambling and emotional, lacking the vigor of her classic work on mental healing. Critics of Mrs. Eddy claim that she cribbed her ideas and most of her book from Phineas Quimby, a proponent of mental healing. Mrs. Eddy had been a patient of Quimby, who died in 1866.

The mother church in Boston is fiercely vigilant in its efforts to suppress the unauthorized publication of Mrs. Eddy's letters, most of which are insipid instructions to her students. I once received a menacing letter from the church's lawyer after I published in a catalogue portions of several Eddy letters thanking a journalist for correcting the grammar and style of one of her essays.

Twenty-five years ago I sat in the study of a Syracuse, New York, autograph dealer, the late Elmer Heise, and denounced as a forgery a letter of Mrs. Eddy he had just offered to me.

After a brief discussion, Heise accepted my opinion. Then he put his arachnoid legs on his desk and leaned back reflectively in his chair.

John D. Lee

John D. Lee, Mormon leader

Hyrum Smith

Hyrum Smith, Mormon leader; brother of Joseph Smith

Whitefield

George Whitefield, colonial evangelist

Elias Hicks, Quaker minister

Jonathan Mayhew, Boston minister

Henry Ward Beecher, Brooklyn minister; antislavery leader

William Miller. Founded Millerites (or Adventists), who expected the second coming of Christ in 1843 or 1844 and gathered on hills to await him

Elizabeth Ann Seton. Founded Sisters of Charity; canonized

Cardinal James Gibbons, Baltimore religious leader

REV. M. J. DIVINE, Ms.D., D.D.
(Better known as FATHER DIVINE)

Father M. J. Divine, Negro evangelist

Billy Graham

Aimee Semple McPherson

Hosea Ballou, clergyman; leader in Universalism

T. De Witt Talmage, minister in Dutch Reformed Church

William White, Philadelphia clergyman

"This is not the first time I have been stuck with something of Mrs. Eddy," he said. "When I was young and new at this autograph business, I bought a collection of letters of Mrs. Eddy of a most shocking and confidential nature. They revealed that she was conducting a business in abortions. Rather foolishly, I now realize, I featured these letters in a catalogue, referring to this very private activity of Mrs. Eddy as 'an abortion racket.'

"Hardly was the ink dry on the press run when I had a visit from several attorneys representing the Christian Science church. Their arguments were persuasive. I was to surrender the letters to them and destroy every copy of the catalogue or they would press suit against me and put me out of business."

"Did you keep photographs of the letters?" I asked.

"I didn't dare. I gave the lawyers the letters and obediently destroyed every catalogue."

"Surely you kept one copy as a souvenir?"

"Not one," said Heise. "I was too scared."

When I was a freshman in college, I owned a crystal set with headphones, and I often lay in bed at night listening to it. It received only one program—the Four-Square Gospel broadcast of Aimee Semple McPherson. I was fascinated by her spectacular "cures." One Sunday I visited the Four-Square Gospel to watch her performance. I remember only one remark of the slender lady in the flowing white gown, spoken when the ushers took up a collection.

"I hate the metallic clink of coins. Do let me hear the soft, soothing rustle of bills."

Today it would require the rustling of quite a few bills to buy one of Aimee's letters!

the great truth that is opening the eyes of the true seeker, and opening the blind eyes to behold the things that make us blest. I hope to hear of you in the field gathering the golden grain, sowing the seed and reaping a rich reward.

Billy Sunday

Mary Baker Eddy. Last page of a handwritten letter to a student: "I hope to hear of you in the field gathering the golden grain, sowing the seed and reaping a rich reward."

Mary Baker Eddy. Last two pages of a handwritten letter to A. McLellan, Pleasant View, 1904: "Sometimes the spelling of words and the punctuation of my writings will leave my thought suddenly and I cannot trust myself on these points at present. Please let this be *strictly confidential.* I hope to be the master of this soon."

5 SOME REMARKABLE WOMEN

Belle Boyd. Postwar signature

They called her the "Cleopatra of the Secession," but she had a big hook nose, a hatchet face, a complexion like an army saddle and beady little eyes. Despite this defective natural equipment, Belle Boyd used her youth and keen mind and exuberant personality to con Union officers into revealing military secrets that were of great value to Stonewall Jackson. The Confederate general wrote Belle a note thanking her for "the immense service that you have rendered your country."

Twice Belle was arrested by Union officers. They knew exactly who she was and what she was doing, but evidently they had spunk water for brains. The Yankees refused to hang an eighteen-year-old girl. They let her go both times and she kept on giving the rebels information that cost the lives of thousands of Union soldiers.

I once owned Belle's original receipt for five hundred dollars in gold to carry dispatches to England. She didn't get far. The Yankees intercepted her ship and Belle had to burn the dispatches.

Many years ago I sold at auction the last two letters ever written by the famous spy. Scribbled in pencil in a cramped hand to her daughter, they told of Belle's struggles to succeed on the stage. Her last note, written the day before she died and postmarked on the day of her death (June 11, 1900), was a pathetic recital of her troubles: "I feel like a criminal not sending you money. But I have only been able to play the one night and sent you all I had out of it over expenses—two dollars."

Two other Civil War spies merit mention—Pauline Cushman, a beautiful actress who served the Union cause, and Rose Greenhow, a Washington society woman who aided the Confederacy. Rose was sent on a secret mission to England, where she wrote a book about her experiences. On the voyage home, a few hundred yards off Wilmington, the rebel ship carrying Rose was shelled and sunk. The spy, a good swimmer, set out for shore in a rowboat. Strapped around her pretty little waist was two thousand dollars in gold, most of it royalties from her book. The boat capsized and Rose plummeted to the bottom of the sea like a cast anchor.

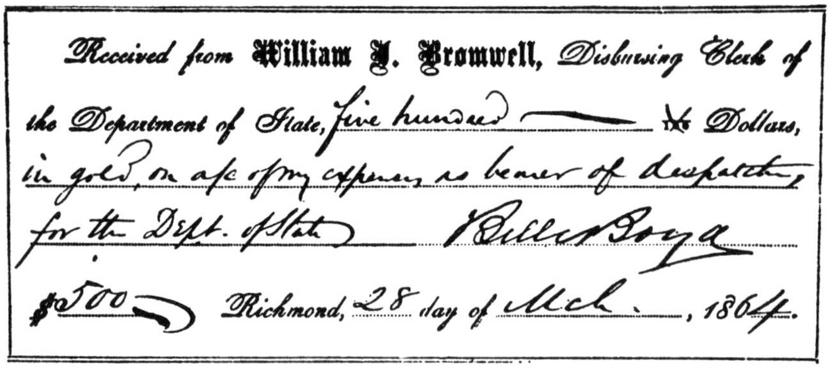

Received from **William J. Bromwell**, *Disbursing Clerk of the Department of State, five hundred — Xx Dollars, in gold, on a/c of my expenses as bearer of despatches for the Dept. of State* Belle Boyd

$500 *Richmond, 28 day of Mch., 1864.*

Belle Boyd. Receipt signed for $500 in gold

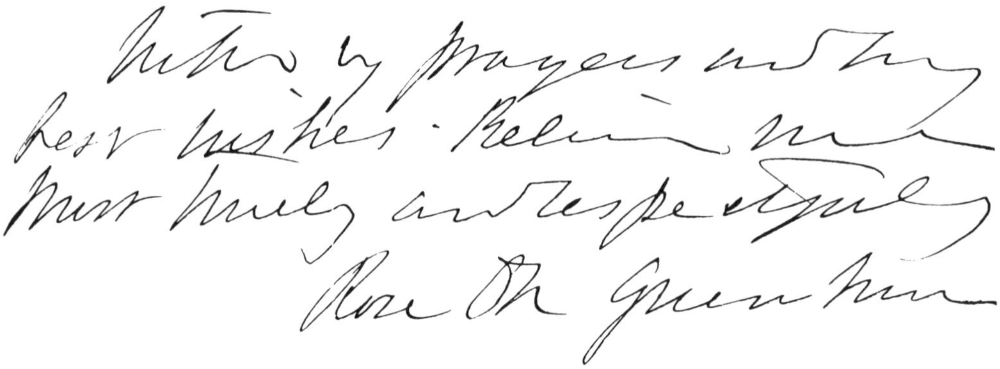

[handwritten letter conclusion]

Rose (O'Neill) Greenhow. Handwritten conclusion of a letter to Jefferson Davis: "With my prayers and very best wishes. Believe me most truly and respectfully Rose ON Greenhow"

Letters of Belle Boyd, Pauline Cushman and Rose Greenhow are very rare and much coveted. The first two sometimes turn up in the form of signed cards, indited long after the war for admirers of the dashing ladies.

Every war has an eccentric character immortalized by a credulous poet in search of a hero. The Civil War gave us Barbara Fritchie, a crazy old woman who probably screamed obscenities from her window at the rebel troops as they marched by. The incident was embellished by the newspapers. They told of Barbara waving an American flag.

> "Shoot, if you must, this old gray head,
>   But spare your country's flag," she said.

Then, according to the poet John Greenleaf Whittier, Stonewall Jackson bellowed something to his troops that sounded like: "Who touches a hair of yon gray head/Dies like a dog! March on!"

Stonewall Jackson's widow, Mary, commented on this celebrated incident in an unpublished letter written in 1913 and lent to me by Nancy L. McGlashan: "I am glad to have . . . testimony to the falsity of that miserable 'Barbara Fritchie' *myth*. Whittier's poem is a great favorite in Northern school books and it is too aggravating to be told that Stonewall Jackson has been made more famous by the story of 'Barbara' than in any other way! O the wonder of such ignorance!"

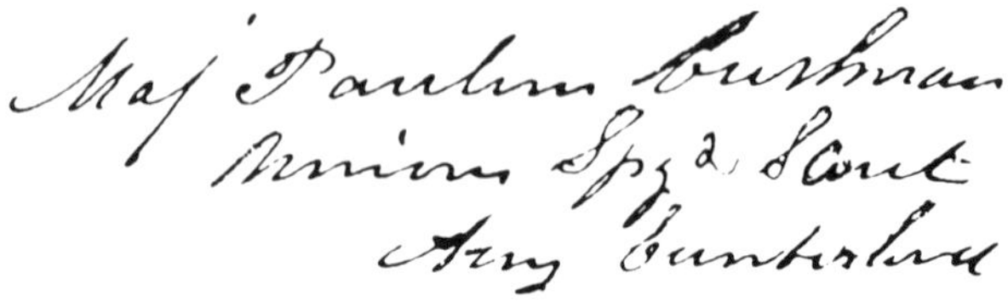

Maj Pauline Cushman Union Spy & Scout Army Cumberland

Major Pauline Cushman, Army [of the] Cumberland

Barbara Fritchie

Barbara Fritchie

Clara Barton Pres Red cross

Clara Barton, president of the Red Cross

Brother I hope your health are very good and that we may soon have you with us once more I must end my letter as I am suffering with a violent headache

Do not for get to pray for a poor sinner sometime

Very pray......

M. E. Surratt

I for got to tell you that Henny Bearg is Marred

Dorothea L. Dix

april 12th 1853

Mary E. Surratt. Handwritten conclusion of a letter signed

Dr. Mary E. Walker

Rose Greenhow. Signed photograph

Barbara signed most documents with an X, a pleasant way to avoid the laborious scribbling of her name. Only a few actual signatures survive.

The derringer ball that John Wilkes Booth fired into Lincoln's head on the night of April 14, 1865, eventually claimed the life of another innocent person. The second victim was Mrs. Mary Surratt, in whose rooming house the conspirators had plotted the murder of the President. After a farcical trial during which the principal evidence against Mrs. Surratt was that her son, John (later exonerated), had fled the country, she was sentenced to death and hanged.

Just one letter of Mrs. Surratt has ever come my way, a rather rambling epistle in which she asks her correspondent to pray for her, "a miserable sinner."

A dedicated and picturesque group were the Civil War nurses, headed in the North by Clara Barton, founder of the American Red Cross. So sparse were hospital supplies during the war that at Antietam Clara was forced to use corn husks for bandages. Miss Barton's war letters often deal with the search for wounded and missing soldiers. Scarcer are the war letters of nurse Dorothea Dix and surgeon Mary E. Walker, who was captured and imprisoned by the Confederates. A year after the Civil War ended, Dr. Walker was presented with the Congressional Medal of Honor. In a sense, this coveted award to Dr. Walker honored all the valiant women of the conflict.

In 1917 the Congress of the United States, apparently then composed mainly of microcephalics and antifeminists, revoked the award on the frivolous grounds that "nothing was found in the records to show the specific act or acts for which the decoration was originally awarded." This gratuitous insult to Dr. Walker belittled all the courageous women not only of the Civil War but of all American wars.

One of the most astounding mental achievements in history was that of Laura D. Bridgman, the first blind deaf-mute who learned to read and write. Her teacher, Samuel Gridley Howe, devised a "blind alphabet" for her, consisting of raised letters. Laura's notes, written in pencil, are fairly common and available for modest prices. More costly are those of Helen Keller, also a blind deaf-mute, whose script startlingly resembles that of Laura Bridgman. Miss Keller was aided by Alexander Graham Bell and her teacher, Anne Sullivan, and learned not only to read and write, but to "lip-read" by placing her fingers on the lips and throat of the speaker. Her letters are attractively written and poetically expressed, rare beauty from a realm of darkness. To her friend Polly Thompson, Helen wrote:

It saddens me to leave you. It seems as if I had just a taste of the sweet homecoming, but that is only an appearance—a cloud floating in a love-bright sky. . . . When I am far off, in the body, my soul will often be at your side among the birds singing their love because you make them know they are safe, or in the deep-grassed apple orchard. . . .

A Adams

Abigail Adams, First Lady; wife of John Adams

Helen Keller. Handwritten note signed

Mr. Anagnos is away and I am unable to get a printed ticket; but I have written two for you which will do just as well.
    Lovingly yours
        Helen Keller

Please excuse this hastily written note.
        Helen

Helen Keller. Photograph inscribed and signed

Lucretia Mott.

Lucretia Mott, Quaker antislavery leader

Yours always very truly
Lucy Stone

Lucy Stone, suffragist

Perfect Equality of rights for
women — civil & political — is
the demand of
yours sincerely
Sept. 17. 1912 — *Susan B. Anthony*
Rochester — N. Y.

Susan B. Anthony. Handwritten quotation signed

M Washington

Martha Washington, First Lady

D P Madison

Dolley P. Madison, First Lady

Eleanor Roosevelt

Eleanor Roosevelt, First Lady

Letters of the leaders in the fight for women's rights are avidly sought by historians. Notes from the pens of Susan B. Anthony, Mary A. Livermore, Lucy Stone and Lucretia Mott, usually couched in ringing language, are eloquent protests against a world that has improperly placed men above women. The favorite quotation of Miss Anthony, bold advocate for woman suffrage, was written out hundreds of times and states the goal of the feminist leaders: "Perfect Equality of rights for women—civil & political—is the demand of yours sincerely, Susan B. Anthony."

There are many First Ladies who are legends—Martha Washington, Dolley (that's the way she spelled it) Madison and Mary Lincoln, for example. The brilliant and amiable Eleanor Roosevelt wrote countless thousands of letters, many of them with sage observations on politics and morals.

The most spectacular signed portrait I ever saw of any celebrated woman was one of Eleanor Roosevelt, owned by my artist friend Robert W. Gill, who served for a time as her secretary. When Bob resigned, Mrs. Roosevelt presented him with a huge studio photograph set in a large white mat on which the great lady wrote: "To Robert W. Gill, with fondest regards, Eleanor Roosevelt." Bob then painted a stark-naked and very suggestive portrait of the dignified Mrs. Roosevelt and placed it in the inscribed mat. For years the portrait hung over his mantel and amazed and delighted all who viewed the native charms and intimate inscription of the famed First Lady.

Susan B. Anthony. First page of a handwritten letter about the suffrage movement

Rochester n. j. aug 28/87

Darling niece Rachel

Mrs Blake has again written me about the Constitutional Convention – (Centennial) to be held in Phila. earnestly desiring the National should make some demonstration there – –

I have just replied to her – That any personal display – in the procession – was out of the question – since I should be in the West – Mrs Sewall just opening a new school year – and scarce of you State Vice Presidents would be able to go to Phila – But continued – – If an able & eloquent Statesman

Mary A. Livermore

Melrose, Mass.

Mary A. Livermore, suffragist and temperance reformer

Frances E. Willard

Frances E. Willard, temperance leader; conducted prayer groups in saloons

Carrie Chapman Catt

President

Carrie Chapman Catt, suffragist

Mary Lyon,

Mary Lyon, educator; founded Mount Holyoke College

R L Gratz

Rebecca Gratz, Philadelphia philanthropist

Yours very truly,
Henrietta Szold
Sec'y to the Publication Com.

Henrietta Szold, Zionist leader; founded Hadassah

Faithfully
Jane Addams.

Jane Addams, social worker; founded Hull House

Margaret Sanger
Oct 25 /29

Margaret Sanger, birth-control movement leader

Executive Mansion,
Washington, 186

Oct 24th

Capt C. H. Tompkins

Will please give,
Thomas C. Kelly,
something to do, in
your Department —
that he is capable
of doing I understand
there have been some
vacancies in your
Department, the

First page of a handwritten letter of Mrs. Abraham Lincoln
signed vertically at the top

Wash. D. C. Mar. 6/95.

Opportunities must be
utilised when they come,
not at our pleasure.
Belva A. Lockwood

Attorney-at-Law, 619. F. St.

Belva A. Lockwood. Distinguished lawyer; candidate for
President in 1884 and 1888. Handwritten quotation signed

Wallis Windsor

Wallis, Duchess of Windsor

Amelia Bloomer
Council Bluffs
Iowa

Amelia Bloomer. Suffragist; popularized "bloomers"

Emily Post

Emily Post

I pray that things will work
out for you — as I said — I would have
helped you if I could — I hate to put
an end to your Dream — but I think you
were happy for a miracle that just won't
happen in the twentieth century —
May you and your family stay as happy
as you are with each other — and I am sure
God will be kind to you
Very Sincerely
Jacqueline Kennedy

Last page of a handwritten letter signed of Jacqueline
Kennedy to a begging stranger in England: "I pray that
things will work out for you . . . I would have helped you if I
could"

UNEXPECTED
ARTISTS **6**

A spindling man wearing a bowler sat hunched over his desk, on which were more than a dozen bottles of colored ink. Meticulously the thin man dipped his pen and carefully he formed an uncial initial in red, blue and gold, to which he added a rhymed message in tiny black script.

The artist was Eugene Field, a poet whose every epistle was a calligraphic masterpiece and whose original manuscripts were often wrought with utmost cunning and then amusingly illustrated.

You might not suspect that the poet of childhood was also an amateur artist, yet he was one of a cohort of authors who loved to sketch.

Field's friends James Whitcomb Riley and Mark Twain also dabbled in art. Riley had longed to be an American Rembrandt and, by way of getting started, had toured the Indiana countryside painting on barns the name and virtues of Lydia E. Pinkham's patent medicines. His avocation of scribbling Hoosier verses blossomed with the publication of a few homespun poems in 1877 and launched Riley on a great literary career.

Mark Twain, better known to academicians as Samuel L. Clemens, was a delectably inept artist. His sleeping cat looks like a bundle of rags and the cartoonist Thomas Nast was unable to resist the temptation to make fun of it. Some of Mark's drawings were even worse and are to art what Bloodgood H. Cutter's comically bad verses (a target of Mark Twain's amiable ridicule) are to poetry.

O. Henry often put a humorous twist to his letters by adding a caricature or two in the margins. His self-portraits show a pudgy, sophisticated elf, but O. Henry was really at his best when he portrayed his friends. He had a flair for dramatic detail. After a New Year's revel with a former stirmate, the outlaw Al Jennings, which left both with hangovers, the author drew a sketch of Al taking the temperance vow.

Jennings studied it. "But my hair is red, Bill."

"A thousand pardons, colonel," said O. Henry. "We'll fix that." And O. Henry heated up a stick of sealing wax and

Eugene Field. Sketch of himself with a lady friend

Sinclair Lewis. Self-portrait

1907

O. Henry. Sketch of the outlaw Al Jennings

George Gershwin. Self-portrait

Ezra Pound

Ernest Thompson Seton

Ellis Parker Butler

applied it to the drawing, almost exactly duplicating Al's blazing red hair.

Reminiscent of Mark Twain's are the sketches of Sinclair Lewis and F. Scott Fitzgerald. Even worse are the grotesqueries of Ezra Pound, whose letters in scatological Poundese often contain sketches that are closer to hieroglyphics than art.

Booth Tarkington, creator of Penrod, had a knack for illustrating letters. Faulkner's forays into art are as adroitly crafted as his prose. The illustrations he made for his early novel *The Marionettes* suggest the chaste lines of Aubrey Beardsley.

The prodigal George Gershwin had a remarkable talent for sketching and painting portraits. A few quick lines in pencil or pen often preserved the likeness of a chance acquaintance, and not one of the composer's close friends escaped his gentle humor. Gershwin sometimes turned his pen on himself with hilarious results.

Occasionally an author or a musician added a tiny sketch to his signature as a sort of trademark. Ernest Thompson Seton, expert on woodcraft, put a bear paw under his name. Ellis Parker Butler, author of *Pigs Is Pigs*, wrote out for me when I was a boy a verse lampooning his famous tale of proliferating guinea pigs:

> Pigs is pigs in Flushing
> And pigs is pigs in Cork.
> But pigs ain't pigs in butchershops
> 'Cause their pigs is pork.

UNEXPECTED ARTISTS 39

Liberace

W. C. Fields. Self-portrait, 1911, when Fields was famed as a juggler

Booth Tarkington

Charlie Chaplin. Symbolic drawing of himself

And he signed his full signature followed by a piglet with a corkscrew tail. Most elaborate of all such trademarks is that of Liberace, who appends to his moniker a grand piano adorned with a candelabrum.

The Hollywood comedian Ben Turpin and the youthful W. C. Fields were sharp critics of their own looks. Late in life, Fields grew to hate autograph seekers and his fierce cry to album-bearing urchins—"Get away from me, you little bastards"—became a legend along Sunset Strip.

Harpo Marx's zany antics with a pen enliven many of the otherwise pedestrian albums kept in Hollywood during the "good old days." Charlie Chaplin, an American by adoption, drew symbolic portraits of himself. Lionel Barrymore took his art seriously. He specialized in etching and turned out landscapes with professional skill. Each year at Christmas he etched his own card and mailed it out to friends.

Among Presidents, two stand out as artists: Theodore Roosevelt, whose delightfully illustrated letters to his children are American classics, and Dwight D. Eisenhower, who strove in watercolor and oil. Ike's paintings, reproductions of which he sent at Christmas to his staff, are quite as neatly turned as those of his two great European rivals Sir Winston Churchill and Adolf Hitler. There is a certain pompous flavor to the work of all three, but Hitler holds the enviable—or is it unenviable?—position of being the only one of this celebrated triumvirate whose paintings have been extensively forged.

And after you
Have spent the Mon
ovie's hoping, too,
Our Car will run...
In fact it ran
All right yestreen...
As I began—
You are a Queen.

* We know that it is
fixed today,
The question is, how
long 'twill stay!

Love to Stripey!

SEA
GULL

William Rose Benét. Handwritten poem with a drawing of a cat *on you get on at football.*

We have found no bear. I shot a deer; I sent a picture of it to Kermit.

A small boy here caught several wild-cats. When one was in the trap, he would push a box towards him, and it would get into it, to hide; and so he would capture it alive. But one, instead of getting into the box, counted the hair of the small boy!

We have a great many hounds in camp; at night they all gaze solemnly into the fire.

Theodore Roosevelt

Theodore Roosevelt. Two pages from an illustrated letter to his children, written as President, with his signature

WHEN the frost is on the punkin and the fodder's in the shock,
And you hear the kyouck and gobble of the struttin' turkey-cock,
And the clackin' of the guineys, and the cluckin' of the hens,
And the rooster's hallylooyer as he tiptoes on the fence! —
O, it's then's the times a feller is a-feelin' at his best,
With the risin' sun to greet him from a night of peaceful rest,
As he leaves the house, bareheaded, and goes out to feed the stock —
When the frost is on the punkin and the fodder's in the shock!

Very truly Yours,
James Whitcomb Riley,
Indiana,
1888.

James Whitcomb Riley. Last stanza of his famous poem "When the Frost Is on the Punkin," with a sketch of a farmyard

O. Henry. Self-portrait (at top right), shaking hands with his friend J. P. Crane

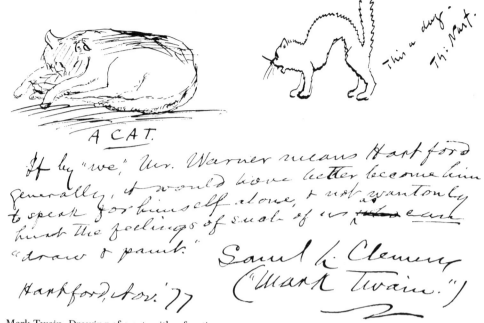

A CAT.

Mark Twain. Drawing of a cat, with a facetious comment on Charles Dudley Warner's jesting criticism of Twain's artistic ability; sketch by Thomas Nast

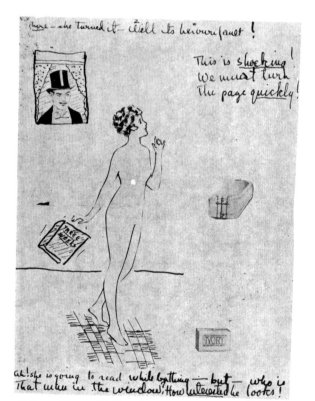

F. Scott Fitzgerald. Sketches, with annotations, made for a girl friend when Scott was at Princeton

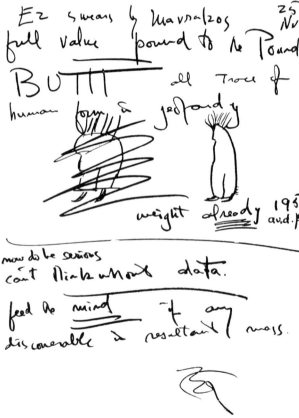

Ezra Pound. Illustrated letter, signed with his weird initials

Little Boy Blue.

The little toy dog is covered with dust
    But sturdy and staunch he stands,
And the little toy soldier is red with rust
    And his musket moulds in his hands.
Time was when the little toy dog was new
    And the soldier was passing fair,
And that was the time when our Little Boy Blue
    Kissed them and put them there.

"Now don't you go 'til I come", he said,
    "And don't you make any noise!"
So, toddling off to his trundle bed,
    He dreamt of the pretty toys.
And as he was dreaming, an angel song
    Awakened our Little Boy Blue —
Oh, the years are many — the years are long —
    But the little toy friends are true!

Aye, faithful to Little Boy Blue, they stand —
    Each in the same old place,
Awaiting the touch of a little hand,
    The smile of a little face.
And they wonder — as waiting these long years through
    In the dust of that little chair —
That our Little Boy Blue
    Since he kissed them and put them there.

Eugene Field. Original manuscript of "Little Boy Blue," with two sketches by the author

Booth Tarkington. Self-portrait in an irate mood on the first page of a handwritten letter

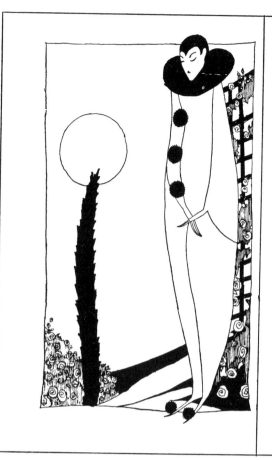

a colonnade, and the nine white columns of the colonnade are nine muses standing like votive candles before a blue mountain, they are nine candles flaming quiet circles. on the ceiling of a marble pavilion where a young man, surrounded by slaves, lies sleeping, and the sky behind the pavilion is a curtain of purple velvet painted with stars in heavy gold. Do you not see how the sky sags with the weight of the

7

William Faulkner. Illustration and manuscript page from his youthful novel *The Marionettes*

Always wear a Smile

Ben Turpin. Self-portrait

This is supposed to be me at the piano Harpo drew it Chico Marx

Harpo Marx. Sketch of his brother Chico, signed by Chico

Emmett Kelly. Self-portrait

Bill Robinson. Self-portrait

Alfred Hitchcock. Profile self-portrait

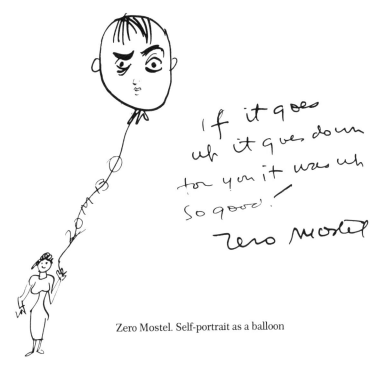

Zero Mostel. Self-portrait as a balloon

Enrico Caruso. Sketch of himself with three friends. Caruso
is in the lower left with an enormously high collar.

THE WITCH
HUNTERS 7

In February 1692, a terrible calamity struck Salem Village, Massachusetts. It was worse than a disastrous hurricane, worse than a terrible plague. It was a loathsome disease of the mind. It hit first a few hysterical girls and the simple folk of Salem Village, spread quickly to Boston and environs and soon infected the minds of the clergy and the bench. It was the discovery that predatory "witches" were loose in Salem.

Search the annals of human folly and you will find few things more vile than the mental erosion that afflicted virtually every powerful man in Massachusetts. All were out to kill witches, to destroy the power of the devil.

Chief among these pious malefactors was the bigoted and self-righteous Reverend Cotton Mather. He was a classical scholar of enormous erudition, with Latin and Greek coming out of his ears, but his Harvardized mind was inhabited with warlocks and witches. Mather fueled the witch mania with his sermons and pamphlets. He was a prolific author, widely admired in his own day. His writings on witchcraft provide a wonderful opportunity to study his aberrant mind, but I find his other books, including the famed *Magnalia Christi Americana*, unreadable.

Many documents survive in Mather's printlike script. His original sermons are indited on tiny sheets, in almost microscopic letters, so that he could conceal them in his palm during fire-snorting tirades against sinners.

With Mather and other subscribers to the injunction "Thou shalt not suffer a witch to live" stirring up the populace, it was not long before the governor himself, Sir William Phips, was bilked into believing the wild tales about witches. Phips could have risen above the madness and refused to sign the witchcraft bill, but he succumbed quietly and put his signature to the most infamous document in American history.

The witch hunt was now at its zenith and every bent old crone in Massachusetts was fair game for the gallows. Fingers of accusation were pointed out of nowhere and suspected witches were seized and tried. I once sold a moving letter of Mary Easty, condemned as a witch and under sentence of death, in which she pleaded to the court for clemency, not for

Cotton Mather. Handwritten account of an adventure with a "devil," revealing that Mather was at least slightly unhinged: "While I was preaching at a private fast (kept for a possessed young woman)—on Mark 9. 28. 29.—ye Devil in ye Damsel flew upon mee, & tore ye leaf, as it is now torn, over against ye Text; Nov. 29, 1692."

Increase Mather, father of Cotton, a believer in witches and president of Harvard

Sheriff George Corwin. Announcement of the execution of Bridget Bishop, recording that Corwin had caused "ye said Brigett to be hange by the neck untill shee was dead"

John Hathorne. Legal deposition signed, 1684

Witchcraft judges, including Bartholomew Gedney (bottom left) and Jonathan Corwin (bottom right)

Cotton Mather. Handwritten letter signed

herself but for other suspected witches. It was an act of nobility lost in a world of lunacy. Mary Easty was hanged and no mercy was shown to those for whom she pleaded.

Several of the witchcraft judges merit special attention. There was John Hathorne, forebear of the author of *The Scarlet Letter*, and Samuel Sewall, whose naïve diary is one of the still readable documents of the colonial era. Five years after the witchcraft mania died down, Sewall admitted his folly and took "the blame and shame" for the condemnations. Until the end of his long life he set aside one day each year for meditation and prayer in repentance.

Sewall's letters, often full of gossip, are written in a bold, open script, a delight to read after one has toiled through the minuscule hand of Mather.

At the height of the witch hunt, a Boston merchant, Robert Calef, questioned the guilt of some of the alleged witches. Cotton Mather threatened to take him to court and Mather adherents still claim that Calef never said or wrote anything or was only a youth in 1692. But Calef made his point. According to New England law, when any person had committed a capital offense as the agent of another, the instigator of the crime had to be produced in court before sentence was passed.

"Produce the devil before you condemn another witch," said Calef.

At the same time, several overzealous Matherites went so far as to put the finger on the governor's wife, accusing her of sorcery, and as suddenly as it had started, the madness was over.

Nineteen victims were dead, hanged or strangled.

Perhaps we should be grateful that they were not, in the European fashion, burned to death.

A Bill against Conjuration, Witchcraft and dealing with evil and wicked Spirits.

For more particular direction in the Execution of the Law against Witchcraft.

xbr. 14. 92:   *William Bond Speaker*

Read several times in Council, Voted, Ordered to be Engrossed and pass into an Act. die predict.

And is consented unto

I William Phips

First and last paragraphs of the notorious witchcraft bill "A Bill against Conjuration, Witchcraft and dealing with evil and wicked Spirits," signed by Governor William Phips

Robert Calef. Handwritten dedication in his book *More Wonders of the Invisible World* (1700)

Judges John Hathorne and Jonathan Corwin. First and last portions of the examination on a witchcraft charge of Rebecca Nurse, a feeble, old lady of seventy-one who was, at the time, confined to bed. Rebecca was found guilty and hanged on July 19, 1692.

HUMAN
8 MONEYBAGS

Jay Gould

Henry Ford

John Jacob Astor, fur trader

"Here's a nickel," said the multimillionaire Jay Gould to his young secretary, Edward W. Bok. "Get three apples for me from the sidewalk vendor across the street. They'll do for my lunch."

Edward crossed the street. The three-for-a-nickel apples were moldy and withered, so he got the finer two-for-a-nickel fruit.

Gould was furious at the extra cost. "In the future," he said, "do as you are told. If you hope to be successful in life you must learn frugality."

Gould was not only parsimonious but pious. Whenever he cheated a man, he made it a point to pray for forgiveness at church on Sunday. If you have read the story of Gould and his moneybags, you will realize what a twinge it must have cost God to forgive such overweening deceit and avarice.

All Gould's letters deal with one subject—money. His name turns up frequently on stock certificates and contracts. He never put his signature to anything that didn't represent a profit.

The same may be said of Henry Ford. My father, who was a lumber salesman and a friend of Buick and Chrysler, once tried to sell Ford some wooden blocks for holding cars in place during shipment. My father later said, "Ford was the tightest and hardest man I ever met." This meanness shows up in Ford's letters. It also shows up in his activities, for he published an anti-Semitic magazine in Dearborn, Michigan, and was soundly thumped when he tried to buy his way into the United States Senate. Ford's autograph in any form is very rare. He was as close-fisted with his signature as with his pennies.

John D. Rockefeller, Sr., handed out bright new dimes to children, but he usually made it a point not to give away his autograph. I once acquired a group of John D.'s letters to an old schoolmate. The notes were warm and friendly but with just a touch of reserve. I finally understood what the reserve meant. Despite the fact that his old comrade was in very modest circumstances, the billionaire assiduously avoided any men-

John D. Rockefeller, Sr.

Stephen Girard

William B. Astor, son of fur trader

Commodore Cornelius Vanderbilt

John Jacob Astor, grandson of fur trader

Moses Myers, Jewish merchant in Virginia

Marshall Field

J. C. Penney

Edward H. Harriman, railroad magnate

Henry Rutgers, benefactor of Rutgers College

Aaron Lopez, Jewish merchant in Rhode Island; Revolutionary War patriot

tion of money and no doubt lived in fear that his former schoolmate would hit him for a fifty-dollar loan.

Most interesting and appealing of early millionaires was John Jacob Astor, fur trader and founder of the Astor fortune. His letters, penned in fluent German or stumbling English, discuss fur-gathering ventures on the frontier. No deal was too small for Astor and he personally supervised every aspect of his vast financial empire.

If you ever find yourself in Philadelphia and have a moment to cast an eye around, you will discover many evidences of the generosity of Stephen Girard, the French-born millionaire. Girard got his wealth mostly from banking and shipping, but he also dealt in illegal opium. I recall a lengthy letter of Girard in which he explained to a sea captain, in great detail, how to smuggle a cargo of opium into the United States.

Andrew Carnegie, the doughty little Scotsman whose steel empire spanned the world, gave away most of his money long before his death.

"Why are you giving your money away?" he was asked.

"The man who dies rich dies disgraced," said Carnegie.

Mark Twain, consort of millionaires, once decided to poke fun at Carnegie's generosity. "Dear Sir and Friend," he wrote to him. "You seem to be in prosperity. Could you lend an admirer $1.50 to buy a hymn book with? God will bless you. . . . P.S. Don't send the hymn book; send the money; I want to make the selection myself."

J. P. Morgan, Sr., the banking tycoon of Wall Street, started assembling wealth and autographs in his youth. His first autograph collection, an uninspiring (and still incomplete) assemblage of signatures of Methodist-Episcopal bishops, cost him nothing but postage, but before he died in 1913 the fierce-eyed and acquisitive Morgan had invested millions in art, rare books and autographs. His collection was the greatest in America. Many of his treasures are now on display at the Metropolitan Museum of Art in New York. The J. Pierpont Morgan Library, a bequest to the people at Morgan's wish, is

J. PAUL GETTY

J Paul Getty

J. Paul Getty

John Harvey Kellogg

John Harvey Kellogg

N Biddle

Nicholas Biddle, banker

Philip D Armour

Philip D. Armour

New York Dec 8th 1864

My dear Stevens
Yours of 6th inst.
I am willing to pay the $50 to Bassett provided he will agree to send us very early two copies of every document published for committees of ways & means & finance committee — both when first reported & when printed as passed. —
You can pay him if you think it safe to do so in advance — but the whole thing is useless unless we can depend upon it being faithfully carried out
Yours truly
Pierpont Morgan

J. Pierpont Morgan, Sr. Handwritten letter signed about getting advance copies of proposed government bills

one of the cultural nuclei of the world. Curiously, Morgan's own autograph is something of a rarity and I suspect many of his letters were thrown out because the recipients couldn't read his signature.

Once a great power in financial circles, Henry H. Rogers will someday probably be remembered only because he was a friend and benefactor of Mark Twain. After the failure of Twain's publishing company and the Paige typesetting machine, in both of which Twain had sunk all his money, Rogers helped the aging humorist to dig out of the ruins and pay his creditors.

A critic said to Twain, "Why do you associate with Rogers? His money's tainted."

"It's twice tainted," replied the author. " 'Tain't yours and 'tain't mine."

Jay Cooke

Jay Cooke, banker

Bernard M Baruch

Bernard M. Baruch

A. W. Mellon

Andrew W. Mellon

*Sincerely yours
Aristotle Onassis*

Aristotle Onassis, Greek tycoon

*with my thanks & best wishes the offering
Andrew Carnegie*

Andrew Carnegie

[signature: Peter Cooper]

Peter Cooper, locomotive inventor; founded Cooper Union

[signature: Leland Stanford]

Leland Stanford

[signature: F. W. Woolworth]

Frank W. Woolworth

[signature: Du Pont de Nemours]

Pierre Du Pont de Nemours, founder of Du Pont fortune

[signature: Haym Salomon]

Haym Salomon, Jewish merchant in Philadelphia; helped to finance Revolutionary War

[signature: Alex. T. Stewart]

Alexander T. Stewart, New York merchant

My respects and best wishes
to the Drake Well
Museum Association,
Titusville Penn

[signature: Howard Hughes]

Howard Hughes. Handwritten note signed (genuine)

[signature: W H Vanderbilt]

William H. Vanderbilt, son of commodore; president of New York Central Railroad

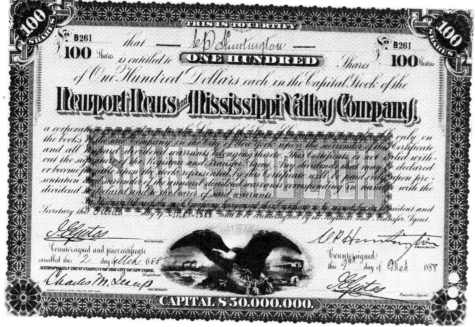

Collis P. Huntington, California railroad builder; signed stock certificate

[signatures: Mathias Bush, Michael Gratz, Barnard Gratz]

Mathias Bush, Michael Gratz and Barnard Gratz, Jewish colonial merchants in Philadelphia

LEADERS OF
9 THEIR PEOPLE

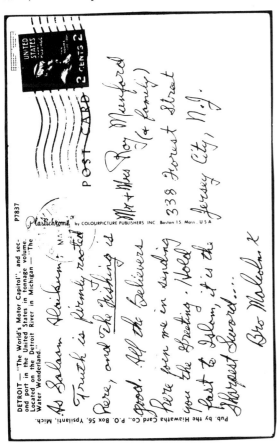

Malcolm X. Handwritten postcard signed: "Hold fast to Islam, it is the Sharpest Sword . . ."

I was seated in my office when suddenly a shadow fell across my desk. I looked up to discover a huge, muscular black man framed in the doorway like a life-size portrait of Othello.

"Here's something which may interest you," he said, pulling from his coat pocket a small file of papers. "The last speech ever made by Malcolm X."

I studied the typescript, larded with corrections in a clear, childlike hand. The pages were splotched with peculiar rust-colored stains. I glanced at my visitor, who, taking back the papers, confirmed my suspicions.

"Blood," he said. "Malcolm X's blood. He was holding these pages when he was gunned down by three Black Muslims."

I tried to buy this dramatic souvenir of the great Negro orator, but even as we discussed its sale, my visitor clutched the manuscript tighter and backed away as though in fear that he might succumb to my offer. I could scarcely blame him, for this was the most remarkable relic of black history I had ever held in my hands.

The few letters and notes of Malcolm X that have come my way were alive with that fire of intensity that marked the man. Malcolm X led a seamy life, part of it in prison, and his impassioned oratory carried a very special message to dwellers of the ghetto. In Detroit he cried out, "We didn't land on Plymouth Rock, my brothers and sisters. Plymouth Rock landed on us."

Malcolm X's spiritual heritage began nearly two centuries ago on the mysterious island of Haiti, land of zombies and voodoo, where a slave named Toussaint, nearly fifty years old, unexpectedly emerged from obscurity, took command of a small army of Haitians and startled the world with his military genius. In a few years Toussaint L'Ouverture was dictator of Haiti, a brilliant administrator and skilled diplomat as well as a great soldier. He was betrayed and destroyed by the man he most resembled—Napoleon I.

Toussaint set a model of flamboyance for his black successors by wearing a yellow madras handkerchief knotted around his head and, on state occasions, a baroque blue uniform with gleaming gold buttons and braid and enormous, glittering

Le Général en Chef.

Toussaint L'Ouverture

Salut et fraternité

Henri Christophe

With best wishes,
Ralph J. Bunche

Ralph J. Bunche

J. J. Roberts, first president of Liberia

Congresswoman
Shirley Chisholm

Shirley Chisholm

Fredk Douglass

Frederick Douglass. Variant signature

Frederick Douglass,
1877

Frederick Douglass. Variant signature

epaulets. His stationery as general was very ornate and his extravagant signature with three dramatic dots at the end has long intrigued historians.

The successor of Toussaint (after he killed Dessalines) was the spectacular black Caesar, Henri Christophe, a brilliant and powerful slave who rose by brute strength to become King Henri I. Christophe built a great stone citadel, La Ferrière, to shut out his enemies, but when his army revolted he shot himself with a silver bullet. Christophe was the original of Eugene O'Neill's Emperor Jones. His letters as general and later as king are signed with a mighty signature, daring and inpudent. One glance at this powerful scrawl, which seems to embody two great bullets in the paraph—the flourish after the signature—could have sufficed to terrify his enemies. Most of Christophe's epistles, like those of Toussaint, deal with military affairs.

In America, in the year 1838, another slave, named Frederick Bailey, ran away from his Baltimore master and, cleverly posing as a courier, escaped to New York, where he took a new name—Frederick Douglass. One of the most exciting orators of his day, Douglass often withstood a bombardment of curses and eggs to make his point. To read his letters is to adventure into the mind of a great leader.

"Are you aware," a black man asked me, "that Douglass's handwriting was truly a reflection of his personality? Just as in his speeches he moved from whimsy to fury to humor to pathos, with wonderful skill, so in his script he varies the handwriting according to his mood. Sometimes it is bold and vigorous, sometimes cramped and furtive."

"An excellent analysis," I said. "I've noticed that Douglass used three or four scripts and these variants always puzzled me until now."

Few manuscript relics of early America carry the horrifying impact of slave bills of sale. They record the days when black men and women were sold at auction like cattle, often in the same lot as cattle. Hundreds of slavebills have passed through my hands and I can never touch them without a little shudder. Study these old documents, more degrading to the slave

9 June 1794 — Rec'd of B Dandridge One hundred and seventy nine dollars & seventy three Cents to purchase Sundries & pay sundry bills as rendered & acc'd this day when I leave the President's service

$179 73/100

Sam'l Fraunce

Samuel Fraunce, friend and steward of George Washington; founded Fraunce's Tavern. Handwritten receipt for purchases made the day he left Washington's service

In a composite nation like ours, made up of almost every variety of the human family, there should be, as before the Law, no rich, no poor, no high, no low, no black, no white, but one country, one citizenship, equal rights and a common destiny for all.

A Government that cannot or does not protect the humblest citizen in his right to life, liberty and the pursuit of happiness, should be reformed or overthrown, without delay.

Fredk Douglass

Washington D.C. Oct 20. 1883.

Frederick Douglass. Handwritten credo signed: ". . . one country, one citizenship, equal rights and a common destiny for all."

NAVIGATION & TRADING CO., INC.

Marcus Garvey
President

Marcus Garvey

Booker T. Washington

Booker T. Washington

owners than to the slaves, and you will understand every word ever spoken or written by the great Negro leaders, such as Frederick Douglass, Marcus Garvey and Martin Luther King, Jr.

Almost like a reincarnated Toussaint was the feisty and brilliant Marcus Garvey. A short man with coal-black features in which glowed eyes of fire, Garvey electrified his fellow Negroes by urging an "Africa for Africans." Garvey declared himself provisional president of the new Africa in 1921, appointed dukes and knights, outfitted in plumes and cockades, for his far-off domain and even chartered a boat (which never sailed) to take the first contingent of Harlemites to the Dark Continent.

Among Garvey's business enterprises was the Negro-operated Black Star Line, which in four years accumulated a mysterious deficit of half a million dollars. Garvey was tried and sent to prison for fraud. His dream of an empire of black supremacy collapsed and he died, forgotten, in London in 1940.

From the Negro Elysium he envisioned, filled with black angels and saints (the whites were devils), Garvey may today be smiling with satisfaction to look down and discover that the once worthless Black Star certificates which sent him to the Atlanta penitentiary are today valued at many times their face value, for they bear Garvey's scarce, sought-after signature. Even rarer are letters of Garvey.

Almost as uncommon are letters of Elijah Muhammad, founder of the Black Muslims, who wrote rarely, except on urgent business.

Often regarded as an Uncle Tom by more militant blacks, Booker T. Washington holds a special place in America's heart. His autobiography, *Up from Slavery*, is a model of restrained prose by a remarkable man who understood, as did Martin Luther King, Jr., the art of transforming fierce enemies into fast friends. Washington's letters are the most abundant of any great Negro leader. From the president's office of the Tuskegee Institute poured forth a flood of letters reporting on the progress of the institute and pleading for more funds.

In the placid tradition of Booker T. was Martin Luther

Best Regards

Adam C Powell

Adam Clayton Powell

King, Jr., a Baptist minister who adopted the passive resistance tactics of Mahatma Gandhi to win support for the blacks. King was awarded the Nobel Peace Prize in 1964. On April 3, 1968, he delivered one of his greatest speeches, reaffirming his disdain of would-be assassins and concluding with the ringing words, "I have been to the mountaintop"; less than twenty-four hours later he was dead, cut down by an assailant's bullet.

King's letters are very scarce and most of them were signed for him by a battery of secretaries hired just to answer the sacks of mail that poured in from those who hated King and those who loved him. King's full handwritten letters are worth almost as much as those of another martyr in the black cause, also slain by an assassin—Abraham Lincoln.

Far more militant than King was Adam Clayton Powell, the noted congressman around whom seethed perpetual controversy. Powell occasionally dropped in to chat with me when I had a gallery at Fifty-third Street and Madison Avenue. For a man who was keenly interested in philography, Powell certainly bequeathed very few of his own signatures to posterity.

A handsome, athletic man, Powell always had with him a beautiful girl, at each visit a different one. Once he was studying a framed document on my walls while I studied the young lady at his side.

"I admire your taste, Congressman," I said.

Powell, who was examining a document of George Washington, turned to me, slightly puzzled, and then suddenly his eyes twinkled and a little smile of understanding flickered over his face.

With Best Wishes

Martin Luther King

Martin Luther King, Jr.

Marcus Garvey. Stock certificate signed

MEMPHIS RIVERMONT

Mt Hebron Baptist Church
Pittsburg Kansas

My Dear Brothers & Sisters

It is a great priviledge
to have an opportunity to greet you.
It has been my good fortune to
meet your pastor, Rev Joseph Howze.
He has been a real help to
the struggling workers of Memphis by
his presence and by his aid in the
March. May God bless all of you
and may you have success in all of
your endeavors

Martin Luther King, Jr.

200 West Georgia at Riverside Drive · Memphis, Tenn. 38103 · Phone (901) 525-0125

Martin Luther King, Jr. Handwritten letter signed, mailed just before his assassination

THE SUPREME WISDOM

By Allah in person to we the
Lost-found Nation of Islam
in the Wilderness of
North America.

Can you qualify?
You can.

Get on to your Own Kind.

The Problem:
Allah has declared that
we must return to our
Native Land and People
or be destroyed.

Will we accept Allah
And return to our Own?

4847 South Woodlawn Avenue
Chicago 15, Illinois

June 29, 1957

TO THE BELIEVERS IN TEMPLE NO. 21
80 Clifton and Jackson
Jersey City, New Jersey

As-Salaam-Alaikum:

In the Name of Allah, the Beneficent, the Most Merciful, Master of the Day of

Requital, Thee do we serve and to Thee Alone do I submit and seek

refuge.

Dearest Beloved Laborers and Muslims in General in Temple No. 21:

We have received your donations in the amount of $190.00 for new

transportation for me, your leader, who has declined in favor of the new drive

for new Temples and Schools or put the fund in Treasure for the Convention of

1958, whatever you say.

Many, many thanks for your wonderful donations and may Allah bless

each and every one who gave with all of the good things in life. We can make

the present cars do until next year or longer, so please let me know just what

you would like to do with the money. I will await your decision.

My best love and wishes to you all for success as I say unto you,

As-Salaam-Alaikum:

Your brother,

Elijah Muhammad

Elijah Muhammad. Typed letter signed

In Consideration of the Sum of Five
Thousand Dollars to me paid as follow,
I have this day bargained & Sold unto
E. Stadman a negro man named
Isaac. black aged 33 years and
Lewis a man aged 22 years Copper
Colour. I warrant said negros Isaac
& Lewis Sound in body and mind
& Slaves for life and title good
This 24th day of July 1863

Abxdr Williams (Sic)

Wm Amis
T W Evans

HUMAN
10 MONSTERS

Professor John W. Webster

$$\Delta \epsilon \alpha \tau \eta$$

P.M. Parker:
Use good judgment. You are the loser. Do This. Secure 75-$20 gold certificates - U.S. Currency - 1500 dollars - at once. KEEP THEM ON YOUR PERSON. Go ABOUT YOUR DAILY BUSINESS AS USUAL. LEAVE OUT POLICE AND DETECTIVES. MAKE NO PUBLIC NOTICE. KEEP THIS AFFAIR PRIVATE. MAKE NO SEARCH. fullfilling these terms with the transfer of the currency will secure the return of the girl.
FAILURE TO COMPLY WITH THESE REQUESTS MEANS - NO ONE WILL EVER SEE THE GIRL AGAIN. except the angels in Heaven
The affair must end one way or the other within 3 days. 72 HRS. YOU WILL RECEIVE FURTHER NOTICE,
But the terms Remain the Same.
FATE
If You WANT AID AGAINST ME ASK GOD NOT MAN.

William Edward Hickman. Handwritten ransom note to Marion Parker's father

William Edward Hickman

A Harvard professor, witness at a trial, squirmed under a relentless battering of questions by the prosecuting attorney.

The defense cut in: "May I remind my distinguished colleague that he is addressing a Harvard professor?"

"Yes, I know. We hanged one the other day."

The prosecution was alluding to Dr. John W. Webster, a rather ordinary Harvard geologist but an extraordinary murderer.

In a dispute over a loan—the geologist had borrowed twice on the same collateral, his collection of minerals—Webster cudgeled his fellow professor Dr. George Parkman to death in his laboratory on November 23, 1849, then carved him up. Webster burned several of the body parts in his assay furnace and hid others in a tea chest and his privy. Some mysterious stains that appeared on the walls a few days later, plus the probing of a clever janitor, brought the murder to light and Dr. Webster was arrested, tried and hanged.

The butchered remains of the victim were recovered and buried, except for the head, which was never found.

I like to think that somewhere in the old buildings at Harvard there awaits discovery, perhaps by a freshman coed, of Dr. Parkman's skull.

Dr. Webster was a prolific correspondent and most of his letters mention his prized collection of minerals.

Much rarer are the letters of the Sunday school teacher Lizzie Borden, who did, or did not, chop up her parents with an ax on August 4, 1892. A jury exonerated Lizzie, but my opinion, after reading the trial minutes very carefully, is that the jury should all have been taken out and hanged for their not-guilty verdict. Anyhow, the old jingle assumes her guilt:

> Lizzie Borden took an ax
> And gave her mother forty whacks;
> And when she saw what she had done
> She gave her father forty-one!

The gallery of human monsters would be incomplete without William Edward Hickman, an honor student and pride of his Sunday school in Los Angeles, who in 1928 held little

Lizzie Borden. Handwritten note signed

Albert De Salvo, the "Boston Strangler." Handwritten postscript from a letter

Bruno Richard Hauptmann

Marion Parker, murder victim

Albert De Salvo

Richard F. Speck

Nathan F. Leopold, Chicago murderer

Marion Parker for ransom and swapped her dismembered body for a pile of banknotes; and Bruno Richard Hauptmann, who kidnapped and murdered curly-headed Charles Lindbergh, Jr., in 1932, then collected a ransom from his father, the famous aviator. Some people claim there is doubt about Hauptmann's guilt, but such persons cannot have read the evidence.

While in stir, Hauptmann refused to sign autographs but endorsed many checks for one dollar, sent to him by devious collectors who sought his signature. These grisly souvenirs occasionally turn up on the philographic market.

Before me at this moment lies a collection of letters of the "Boston Strangler," Albert De Salvo, who terrorized the women of Boston with a series of brutal rapes and mutilation murders. Writing from prison, where he was later stabbed to death, the strangler tells a pen pal: "Boston people are sex pots. They all love there sex. Most broads are just waiting to get so-called raped. . . . I'm 39 years old . . . but I'm getting more of a sex drive than I have ever had!"

De Salvo's letters to his pen pal, Roy, whom he later addressed as "Rose," are filled with raunchy, pornographic details and take us on an amazing journey into the mind of a psychopath. Such letters intrigue collectors and are sought for their psychiatric fascination.

There is a bizarre combination of poet and killer in Charles

H. Judd Gray

H. Judd Gray, murderer

Charles Manson. Signature as a prisoner

Charles Manson. First page of a handwritten letter

I'm going to pray for you, Rosina, that you find alot of friends in this world and that you find someone to love, who can be with you and share his life with you.

Goodbye, Rosina, and thank you for caring. Take care.

Yours Truly
David B.
(Sam)

David Berkowitz, "Son of Sam." Last page of a letter to a sympathizer

Manson, the cult leader who induced a small harem of wild and devoted women to butcher senselessly the movie actress Sharon Tate and several of her friends. Writing in pencil from prison, Manson pours out his undigested dreams and visions in a childlike scrawl. His fantasies outsoar the confines of punctuation and grammar. He is a William Blake run amok with a bloody dagger in his hand.

Could the bottom be the top [Manson writes], or is the cercel [circle] with out center for ever. I play with out madness in dull sleep with walking dead & minds mouthing meannlyness [meaningless] words from men long in graves of King james & Engling [England's] mother sent her children to my cross & prays to death of a million marters in who's name praze a fool for only a fool could keep the center of his mind under the spinning world less a hole be put in his head by Sain men looking for them selves in side my own eyes are hot & hide from my voice because its vibrations is concitered [concentered] out burst . . .

Who can read such strange lines without marveling at the wild chemistry of this madman's mind?

Not long ago I looked over half a dozen handwritten letters of David ("Son of Sam") Berkowitz, who methodically slew or seriously crippled a whole host of young men and women with a rifle. The evidence of Berkowitz's schizophrenia was apparent in his letters; on a single page his handwriting and spelling would suddenly change completely, as though another person had picked up the pen.

Berkowitz's letters from prison are full of grief and repentance. A deep current of religious fervor runs through them. Berkowitz believes himself beyond saving—not even worth saving—and he is certain that his next journey will be through the gates of hell.

Why do historians study or collect the letters of human monsters like Charles Manson, Albert De Salvo and David Berkowitz?

It is the eternal fascination of evil and the excitement of violence that draws philographers into the quest. And the more monstrous the killer, the more valuable and desirable are his letters!

Dear Mrs. Channel,

Please pray for me. Pray to Jesus that I get well and can overcome the demon forces that have a hold on me.

I would like to go to a mental hospital where they can perhaps treat me more humanly than a prison. I know that I am no cold blooded killer and I don't hate girls.

I want to be forgiven of my sins and be with Jesus when I die. However, I still feel that the demons have a strong hold on me but the doctors are helping me. Please pray that I go to a hospital, please. It will be better for me, I know it.

Also, Mrs. Channel please write District Attorney Gold, 360 Adams St., Brooklyn, N.Y. 11201 and tell him what you know. I know it would help me.

I am reading my Bible and praying for help.

love
David B

David Berkowitz. Handwritten letter signed about "the demon forces that have a hold on me"

I'm the Son of Sam and I killed six people
David Berkowitz
Marcy, N.Y.

David Berkowitz. Handwritten confession signed

SON OF SAM

David Berkowitz. Signature as "Son of Sam"

THE MASTER
11 MECHANICS

Ambition, Imagination, and 17 hours work day

Thomas A. Edison

Thomas A. Edison. His prescription for success

In the writing of Autographs there is no end.

Alexander Graham Bell

Alexander Graham Bell

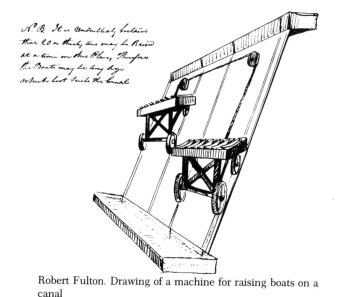

N.B. It is undoubtedly certain that 20 or thirty tons may be Raised at a time on this Plan, therefore the Boats may be any size which best suits the Canal

Robert Fulton. Drawing of a machine for raising boats on a canal

Thomas A. Edison's latest invention, the phonograph, worked perfectly, except for one small defect. It couldn't say "sugar."

So Edison applied his genius—"ninety-nine percent perspiration and one percent inspiration"—to the problem and, after two years and more than a thousand experiments, solved it.

Edison was indefatigable. His average workday was seventeen hours long. He kept voluminous handwritten records of his experiments, penned scores of fascinating letters and mailed out autographs by the thousands to his admirers.

I recall a letter in which Edison wrote gleefully to a friend that Mrs. Edison was out of town. "While the cat's away," he added, "the mice will *work*."

Although Edison's laboratory notes are hastily set down in pencil, his holograph letters are beautifully penned, and always conclude with an artistic signature which, in its day, was a celebrated trademark.

Edison's persistence and stamina were shared by many other inventors—Robert Fulton, Eli Whitney, Alexander Graham Bell and Robert H. Goddard, among others.

Fulton was a prolific correspondent. Some of his letters and manuscripts are adorned with sketches. His fertile mind was always churning. Whenever a new idea struck him, he whipped off an enthusiastic letter to his friend and fellow inventor Thomas Jefferson, who had devised a multiple letter signer, the polygraph. Fulton could have benefited from Jefferson's machine to sign his extensive mail, some of it bitter complaints that too much recognition was accorded to Oliver Evans and John Fitch, rival steamboat inventors. For his part, Fitch invested a great deal of paper and ink in attempts to win the acclaim he felt he had earned.

Samuel F. B. Morse began his great career as an artist. His portrait of the aging Lafayette is an American classic. The inspiration for the electric telegraph came to Morse in 1832 while he was on board a ship returning from Europe to America. He drafted a preliminary sketch of his invention while still at sea, but it was twelve years before he tapped out on a wire from Washington, D.C., to Baltimore the historic message "What hath God wrought!"

Eli Whitney, inventor of cotton gin

Oliver Evans

Thomas Jefferson

Cyrus W. Field

Orville Wright

Wilbur Wright

Samuel P. Langley

Glenn H. Curtiss

Michael I. Pupin, physicist and electrical inventor

Morse was a modern Leonardo, caught up in the patent squabbles of the nineteenth century. He was an associate of Cyrus W. Field in laying the first transatlantic cable, helped to found Vassar College and was enthusiastic in promoting the work of young authors. Morse wrote many provocative letters, often on photography, in which field he was an ardent pioneer. Nearly every letter of Morse provides a fresh excursion into a great creative mind.

The subject of aviation has always intrigued me and one of my boyhood heroes was the German glider pilot and inventor Otto Lilienthal, who was killed in a freak accident in 1896. By his astute study of birds' wings, Lilienthal paved the way for the first successful heavier-than-air craft flown at Kitty Hawk on December 17, 1903, by Orville and Wilbur Wright.

The late Colonel Richard Gimbel, who bequeathed his superb collection of aeronautica to Yale, was himself a distinguished balloonist and pilot. We often spent hours chatting about the colonel's adventures and the history of aviation.

"You'll never know what love really is," he once confided, "until you make love in the basket of a balloon floating silently through the clouds a mile above the earth."

I once asked Gimbel, "Why was Glenn Curtiss able to fly a replica of Samuel P. Langley's aircraft when Langley could never make it work? After all, the pontoons Curtiss put on it couldn't help to make it airborne."

"Of course not," said Gimbel. "The fact is that although Langley had successfully flown a model plane, his man-carrying craft would never in a million years have got off the launching ramp without crashing. The wing structure needed modification."

The colonel made a sketch showing Langley's wing design and explained why it would not work.

"By an infringement of the Wright brothers' wing patent," he continued, "Curtiss, who loathed the Wrights, made Langley's machine fly.

"The Smithsonian Institution, of which Langley had been secretary, naturally supported Langley's claim and at once proclaimed him the real inventor of the first successful airplane. The Wrights were furious and took their original Kitty Hawk plane out of the Smithsonian, where it was on display, and sent it to France for exhibit. After all, the French were really the first to appreciate the Wrights.

"Years later, the Smithsonian people finally admitted that Langley's plane was a turkey and Orville gave them his original aircraft as a permanent exhibit."

Langley's letters are hard to find, except for brief typewritten notes sending his autograph. Notes of the Wright brothers, especially Wilbur, who died of typhoid fever in 1912, are very scarce and, like those of Glenn Curtiss, are nearly always about aviation.

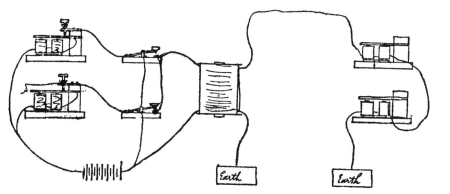

Alexander Graham Bell. Sketch of wiring for a telephone

David Rittenhouse, inventor of telescope improvements

Thomas A. Edison. Two pages from a laboratory notebook in Edison's rapid script

Eli Terry and Seth Thomas, clockmakers

Robert Fulton. Steamboat stock certificate signed

George Eastman

Sincerely yours,

Wernher von Braun

Simon Lake, developer of submarine

George W. Pullman

Robert Fulton. Handwritten memorandum signed on the cost of operating steamboats

John Fitch. Handwritten statement signed about the lack of financial recognition for inventing the steamboat

Santos-Dumont

Alberto Santos-Dumont, Brazilian inventor of early airplane

I wrote to Dr. Adams regarding the nitroglycerin powder, and the motor belonging to Clark College.

In addition, I would like very much if the two sectional-threaded breach blocks could be sent to Clark College, Worcester Mass, Physics Department. Mr. Deer's brother (D. W. Deer) who packed the apparatus will know where they are; I think they are in Box 9.

I shall be glad to pay expenses connected with packing and sending these. They will weigh together about three or four pounds.

I hope everything is going well at the Observatory, and suppose you have settled down to peace basis by this time.

Sincerely yours,
R. H. Goddard

Robert H. Goddard. Handwritten letter signed about materials for building a rocket

Jas. B. Eads

James B. Eads, inventor of diving bell

Hiram S. Maxim.

Hiram S. Maxim. Machine-gun inventor; also devised an early aircraft

Charles Goodyear

Charles Goodyear, developer of vulcanizing process

with compliments of Washington A. Roebling

Washington A. Roebling, builder of Brooklyn Bridge

C. H. McCormick

Cyrus H. McCormick, inventor of reaper

Charles P. Steinmetz

Charles P. Steinmetz, electrical wizard

5 West 22d St
Nov. 7, 1871

Dear Sir,

In reply to yours of Nov. 6th I am compelled to say you have asked an impossibility. I have not painted a portrait for more than 30 years, and have no facilities in materials, or place for such a purpose. I have no studio, nor canvas nor colors suitable for taking a portrait. You must, therefore, excuse me if, I am under the necessity of refusing your request.

With kind wishes
I am Yr. Ob. serv!
Saml. F. B. Morse.

James W. Hale, Esq.
69 Wall St.
New York

Answer to my request that the Professor would sketch my portrait MM

Samuel F. B. Morse. Letter about his work as an artist: "I have not painted a portrait for more than 30 years."

Orville Wright. Inscribed and signed photograph of the first powered flight, December 17, 1903

Hartford Conn. July. 3/93.

Chas. W. Fee.

St. Paul. Minn.

Dear Sir.

In reply to your favor of May 4th (which was mislaid for a time) I would say that I conceived the idea of my Machine Gun in 1861. & the first gun was made in 1862. Since which time I have taken out six (6) different patents for various improvements I have made in this gun —

Yours respectfully R. J. Gatling

South Framingham May 9 1853

Messrs Sohier & Lowell

gents I have recd your favor of the 6th and will in Boston and attend to it in the course of this week.

Yours truly

Elias Howe

Elias Howe, inventor of sewing machine

R. J. Gatling, inventor of machine gun

Rue du Theatre francais N° 4

12 Thermidor year 8

Dear Sir

I send you a Sketch of a Plan that I believe is new in this Country. The Idea originated with Franklin. This is sufficient to procure it attention. I have done no more than apply it to the circumstances france is now in. The letter addressed to Sir Robert Smith is in Answer to one he wrote to Mr. Milbank respecting the iron Bridge at Sunderland. I send it because it is referred to in his plan and also a perspective painting of the Bridge.

As for myself I have no object in view in this Country otherwise than its own prosperity. My intention is to return to America as soon as I can pass the Sea in safety. The letter to Sir Robt and the view of the Bridge I shall want again. The plan I make you a present of, wishing you would endeavour to bring it into practice, which is the only motive I have in sending it

yours with esteem

Thomas Paine

Thomas Paine, patriot and author; inventor of the steel bridge. Handwritten letter signed, August 31, 1799, probably to Thomas Jefferson, a fellow amateur inventor

HITCHHIKERS
ON PEGASUS **12**

The poet with the soiled bow tie took a swig of whiskey and put his glass down on the bar.

"What'll you have?" he asked the stranger next to him. "Sonnets, ballads, triolets—only a dollar. You name the subject. How about a little ode to the lady friend?"

Everybody, or almost everybody, knew the poet. He was Maxwell Bodenheim of Greenwich Village, once the darling of the critics, now a seedy, alcoholic rhymester, bumming drinks, living in sordid poverty, often sleeping in the subway. He was to wind up mugged and murdered.

Today the penned-to-order verses of Bodenheim are worth many times the modest price he asked. His letters, too, are prized by those who remember with nostalgia bohemian life in the Village.

Poets have always had a tough time. Vachel Lindsay peddled his *Rhymes to Be Traded for Bread* from door to door like a modern troubadour. Later, dogged by poverty, he killed himself. Suicide was almost a tradition among poets. Sara Teasdale, lyric poet and Lindsay's paramour, drowned in her bathtub. George Sterling, brilliant sonneteer of Carmel, California, took his own life. The letters of these tragic figures occasionally show up, but except for those of Lindsay, the pride of Springfield, they are not much collected.

Edwin Arlington Robinson confessed that his income from the poems that made him famous was only five hundred dollars a year. You would have to invest double that sum today for a mere transcript of his poem "Richard Cory." Poe was paid just fifteen dollars for "The Raven." Richard Gimbel, who owned the only complete manuscript of the poem, carried a one-hundred-thousand-dollar insurance policy on it.

The colorful life of Amy Lowell is far more interesting than her saccharine imagist verses. Amy was a large woman, broad of beam, who fancied herself a reincarnation of Keats. Her two-volume biography of Keats is a classic reference work. Amy smoked great black cigars. Whenever she wanted a man she strolled down to the Boston waterfront, made her selection from the roistering stevedores and plunked down a five-dollar fee. Her letters, regrettably, are uninteresting and have little appeal for philographers.

Maxwell Bodenheim

Sara Teasdale

Edgar Allan Poe. Inscription to Elizabeth Barrett Browning in a copy of *The Raven and Other Poems* (1845). Mrs. Browning (then Miss Barrett) was fetched by Poe's assonance and alliteration and thought the line "And the silken sad uncertain rustling of each purple curtain" from "The Raven" was one of the most beautiful verses in English

Amy Lowell

Thy yearnings yet elude
Our quest and scrutiny,
Tho mortals echo thee
Thy moan in solitude
For dreams that are not nor shall
ever be.

George Sterling.

George Sterling. Handwritten stanza signed

N. P. Willis

Geo. H. Boker

George H. Boker

Ezra Pound. Conclusion of a letter: "in fraternal affexshun E.P."

Laurence Ferlinghetti. Self-portrait signed

Richard Cory

Whenever Richard Cory went down town
We people on the pavement looked at him.
He was a gentleman from sole to crown,
Clean favored and imperially slim.

And he was always quietly arrayed,
And he was always human when he talked;
But still he fluttered pulses when he said
"Good morning", and he glittered when he walked.

And he was rich — yes, richer than a king —
And admirably schooled in every grace:
In fine, we thought that he was everything
To make us wish that we were in his place.

So on we worked, and waited for the light,
And went without the meat, and cursed the bread;
And Richard Cory, one calm summer night,
Went home and put a bullet through his head.

Edwin Arlington Robinson

Edwin Arlington Robinson. Handwritten transcript signed of his famous poem "Richard Cory"

Anne Rutledge

Out of me unworthy and unknown
The vibrations of deathless music!
"With malice toward none, with charity for all."
Out of me the forgiveness of millions toward millions,
And the beneficent face of a nation
Shining with justice and truth.
I am Anne Rutledge who sleep beneath these weeds,
Beloved in life of Abraham Lincoln,
Wedded to him, not through union,
But through separation.
Bloom forever, O Republic,
From the dust of my bosom!

Edgar Lee Masters

Oct 2-1939
N.Y.C.

Edgar Lee Masters. Handwritten transcript of his famous poem "Anne Rutledge" from *Spoon River Anthology*

John Hall Wheelock

Lucy Larcom

Rose H. Thorpe

Joseph Rodman Drake

Edwin Markham

Some poets have trafficked in their own manuscripts. Edgar Lee Masters copied out the whole of *Spoon River Anthology* for five hundred dollars. Edwin Markham's fee for replicating "The Man with the Hoe" was fifty dollars. John Hall Wheelock once told me he usually asked fifty dollars for transcribing his famous poem "Earth." He waited for my reaction and I could think of nothing to say except, "That's pretty cheap—less than a dollar a line."

Allen Ginsberg and Gregory Corso now put their manuscripts on the market almost before the ink is dry. Several years ago I received a dealer's catalogue that offered not only holograph verses of Ginsberg but intimate personal relics in abundance, including some pubic hairs selectively scissored by the poet for sale to his admirers.

The two leaders in the cult of unintelligibility, Ezra Pound and T. S. Eliot, rarely gave out autographs and never peddled their manuscripts. Pound's letters, typed by the poet himself, abound in scatological references and are signed with a variety of initials and flourishes. Weird neologisms, wild spellings and frenetic punctuation are characteristic of his notes. I once had a huge correspondence of Pound. To read the letters from start to finish in sequence was like falling into an intellectual bog and struggling to keep afloat. In one letter (1930) he wrote: "Gord! a GOOD moozik paper!!! sufferin bellybuttons of Jheezus!!!! Go find one. . . ." In another (1931) he posed for editorial meditation the subject "whether a nation that fails to provide me with 50 bucks a month ought to consider itself a nation or a shithouse."

Speaking of vast correspondences, I have for years been seeking the torrid love letters of Edna St. Vincent Millay to the

HOWL

AND OTHER POEMS

BY

ALLEN GINSBERG

' Unscrew the locks from the doors !
Unscrew the doors themselves from their jambs !'

FOR Robert Duncan in the hope that Howl seems more gracious mellow a lament to him as time goes by; or that it drops out of my own affection in the Future.

THE POCKET POETS SERIES : Number Four
The City Lights Pocket Bookshop
San Francisco

Allen Ginsberg

Allen Ginsberg. Presentation inscription in a copy of *Howl*, with two tiny sketches by Ginsberg

The moment of the rose & the moment of the yew tree are of equal duration.

T. S. Eliot
24. iv. 61

T. S. Eliot. Handwritten quotation signed

John Gould Fletcher

Edna St. Vincent Millay. Excerpt from a handwritten letter signed

William Carlos Williams. Early signature

William Carlos Williams. Signature late in life.

Horace Gregory

Be good and you will be lonesome.

Carl Sandburg

Carl Sandburg. Handwritten quotation signed (a remark originally made by Mark Twain)

poet George Dillon, for I hear exciting reports that these suppressed epistles are couched in passionate and intimate language.

Not long ago I acquired a large collection of letters written by William Carlos Williams, who admitted that when he was in medical school his initials had inspired the nickname "Water Closet." Williams's signature changed dramatically during his life, degenerating at the end to a shaky and almost unreadable replica. His letters are invariably revealing. After an accusation of anti-Semitism following a radio broadcast in 1957, Williams wrote to Helen F. Luskin:

Some of my very best friends in and out of the profession of Medicine are Jews. In fact I myself have some Jewish blood in my veins on one side and am vastly proud of it. But that doesn't make me selfconscious of the fact or blind to some of the characteristics of Jewry or blind to them through the ages and when a poet such as my friend Ezra Pound takes a public stand against usury and associates the race through the ages with it I am forced to go along with him. . . . Permit me to appeal to your intelligent understanding, under the circumstances, and as a tolerant Jew forgive me.

Turning back two centuries to the colonial era, there is little to say about our poets. Few manuscripts and letters survive.

Thou go not, like the quarry-slave at night,
Scourged to his dungeon, but, sustained and soothed
By an unfaltering trust, approach thy grave,
Like one who wraps the drapery of his couch
About him and lies down to pleasant dreams.

William Cullen Bryant.

William Cullen Bryant. Handwritten quotation signed from "Thanatopsis"

Park Benjamin

We need not lament their loss. If you have the hardihood, as I once did, to read Michael Wigglesworth's dreadful doggerel *Day of Doom* from beginning to end, then test your remaining strength on the verses of Anne Bradstreet. Somewhere along the line you will reach your breaking point.

The best poet of the Revolutionary era was Francis Hopkinson, author of the amusing "Battle of the Kegs" and also a composer and signer of the Declaration of Independence. Hopkinson's letters nearly always concern financial matters and his signature is readily obtainable on bank drafts issued by the fledgling American government. Of Philip Freneau, known as "the poet of the Revolution," I have seen but one document in the past twenty years.

Letters of the Hartford Wits, a literary group of the early nineteenth century, are abundant. Except for John Trumbull, whose *M'Fingal* is still navigable with effort, the Wits turned out epics and odes which serve no use today except as subjects for doctoral dissertations. I cannot speak for the graduate students who suffer this purgatory, but I would rather be flogged with red-hot scorpions than re-read Joel Barlow's *The Columbiad*. Barlow's letters, however, are quite another matter and many of them written when he was minister to France are extremely interesting, spiced with astute political observations.

The poetry of America really began with William Cullen Bryant's "Thanatopsis" (1817), written when the poet was only a youth. Scholars tell us that the Greek-derived word "thanatopsis" means "a view of death" and that Bryant was inspired to write his poem by a reading of the verses of Henry Kirke White and Robert Southey. But I prefer the explanation I heard many years ago. Bryant and his sister were strolling through a meadow when they came upon a dead cat. The poet observed, "He's deader *than a top, sis!*" And at that moment, the inspiration for the great philosophic poem came to him.

Bryant's letters and signed excerpts from his poems are very common. Often written in purple ink, they are extremely attractive and prized by collectors. A caution about the purple (aniline dye) ink. It fades when exposed to light. In my gallery

I remain ye Faithful friend
& fellow watchman in ye Lord
Michael Wigglesworth

Michael Wigglesworth

A Bradstreet   Anne Bradstreet

Philip Freneau   Philip Freneau

Maria Brooks   Maria Brooks

L. H. Sigourney —   Lydia H. Sigourney

Sarah J. Hale   Sarah J. Hale

The Bucket.

How dear to this heart are the scenes of my childhood!

When fond recollection presents them to view.

The orchard, the meadow, the deep tangled wild-wood,

And every loved spot that my infancy knew

And even the rude Bucket that hung in the well.

The old oaken bucket, the iron bound, bucket

The moss-covered Bucket, that hung in the well.

Samuel Woodworth.

Samuel Woodworth. Handwritten stanza signed from "The Old Oaken Bucket" (originally titled "The Bucket")

the boys i mean are not refined
They go with girls who buck and bite
they do not give a fuck for luck
they hump them thirteen times a night

one hangs a hat upon her tit
one carries a cross in her behind
They do not give a shit for wit
the boys i mean are not refined

They come with girls who bite and buck
who cannot read and cannot write
who laugh like they would fall apart
and masturbate with dynamite

the boys i mean are not refined
they cannot chat of that and this
they do not give a fart for art
they kill like you would take a piss

they speak whatever's on their mind
they do whatever's in their pants
the boys i mean are not refined
they shake the mountains when they dance

E. E. C.

E. E. Cummings. Handwritten poem signed

at the corner of Fifty-third Street and Madison Avenue, I once framed a sonnet of Bryant's with a portrait by Sarony and placed it in my window, where the sun could reveal its beauty. Three weeks later a man entered the shop and asked, "Why did you frame a blank sheet of paper with Bryant's photograph?"

I took the sonnet out of the window and, sure enough, it had totally vanished. The bright rays of the sun had sucked the ink right off the page.

The age of Bryant was an age of "gift albums," issued for Christmas sale and filled with sugary verses by poetasters. Some of these rhymesters permanently damaged the literary taste of the nation. Still vaguely remembered are Lydia H. Sigourney, George P. Morris, Maria Brooks, Park Benjamin, Sarah J. Hale (who wrote "Mary Had a Little Lamb") and Samuel Woodworth. The letters of them all are easily obtainable. However, a signed manuscript of "Mary's Lamb" or Woodworth's "Old Oaken Bucket" would certainly command a high price.

I breathed, a song into the air;

It fell to earth I knew not where;

For who hath sight so keen and strong,

That it can follow the flight of song!

Henry W. Longfellow

Henry W. Longfellow. Handwritten quatrain signed. Notice Longfellow's habit of breaking his letters, so that his manuscript has the appearance of fading.

In the Age of Sentiment it was considered an obligation of the poet to copy excerpts from his verses on request. Longfellow wrote out thousands of four-line quotations. So did Holmes and Lowell. So prolific in letters and poems were the New England writers that every year they wore out dozens of quills.

Despite the enormous output of the New England poets, their manuscript poems and letters are eagerly sought today. Early letters of Whittier and Longfellow are always interesting, unlike the pedestrian notes of their later years.

Of all the New England poets, I prefer Oliver Wendell Holmes, the perfect Renaissance man. Holmes was the head of the Harvard medical department. In 1842 he published his *The Contagiousness of Puerperal Fever*, five years before Semmelweis with great fanfare made the same disclosure about childbed fever. Holmes wrote the first psychological novel, *Elsie Venner*, and his breakfast-table essays are full of pungency and wit. Like Samuel F. B. Morse, Holmes was fascinated by photography; he invented a three-dimensional viewer in 1859, for which he coined the name stereoscope.

As a poet, Holmes is more readable than most of his contemporaries. His letters are extremely abundant and always replete with delicious humor.

Gregory Corso. Self-portrait signed

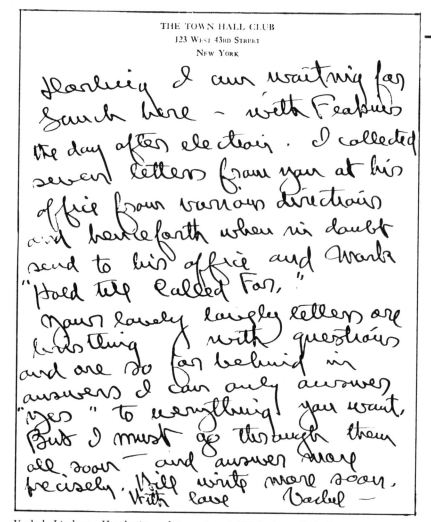

Vachel Lindsay. Handwritten letter signed "With love Vachel"

The Hartford Wits

Joel Barlow

Timothy Dwight

Lemuel Hopkins

David Hartley

David Humphreys

*What are the islands to me
if you hesitate,
what is Greece if you draw back
from the terror
and cold splendour of song
and its chorus sacrifice?*

"H. D."

Hilda Doolittle (H.D.). Handwritten stanza signed

War is for everyone, for children too.

Robert Frost

Robert Frost. Line of poetry signed

R. Alsop

Richard Alsop

*Christ's troop, Mary's guard, God's own men,
Draw your swords and strike at Hell and strike again
Every steel-born spark that flies where God's battles are
Flashes past the face of God and is a star.*

Joyce Kilmer.

Brooklyn, N.Y.
June 20, 1913.

Joyce Kilmer. Handwritten quatrain signed

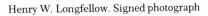

John Trumbull

John Trumbull

William Cullen Bryant. Signed photograph

Henry W. Longfellow. Signed photograph

Henry W. Longfellow.

William Cullen Bryant
March 20, 1862

Grace Greenwood

Hannah F. Gould

John Pierpont

Thomas Buchanan Read

My Loyalty is still the same
Whither I win or loose the game
True as a Diall to ye Sunn
Altho It bee not Shind upon

Benj. Tompson

Benjamin Tompson (colonial poet). Handwritten quatrain
signed

Emma Willard

John Greenleaf Whittier

Sarah Helen Whitman, friend of Poe's

Always truly Yours

Oliver Wendell Holmes. Early signature

Frances S. Osgood

Joseph Hopkinson

Henry Timrod

Joaquin Miller

Fitz-Greene Halleck

I am,
Affectionately,

John Hay. Variant signatures

Irwin Russell

T. Buchanan Read

Thomas Buchanan Read. Variant signature

Yours always
Bret Harte

·Bret Harte

Edith M. Thomas

Edith M. Thomas

Build thee more stately mansions, O my soul,
As the swift seasons roll!
Leave thy low-vaulted past!
Let each new temple, nobler than the last,
Shut thee from heaven with a dome more vast,
Till thou at length art free,
Leaving thine outgrown shell by life's unresting sea!

Oliver Wendell Holmes.
Beverly Farms. Mass.
August 11th 1885.

Oliver Wendell Holmes, Sr. Handwritten stanza signed from his celebrated poem "The Chambered Nautilus"

Yours very sincerely
Emma Lazarus.

Emma Lazarus. Wrote "Give me your tired, your poor . . ."

She prowled around my steps by day,
And from my dreaming hours,
Still drove the fancied joy away,
And blighted all its flowers.

1831.

W. Gilmore Simms

William Gilmore Simms. Handwritten quatrain signed; Simms was also an important novelist.

Ah, let us hope that to our praise
Good God not only reckons
The moments when we tread his ways,
But when the spirit beckons!

J. R. Lowell.

29th Jan. 1871.

James Russell Lowell. Handwritten stanza signed

Richard Henry Wilde

Richard Henry Wilde

'Twas the night before Christmas, when all through
    the house
Not a creature was stirring, not even a mouse;
The stockings were hung by the chimney with care,
In hopes that St. Nicholas soon would be there;
The children were nestled all snug in their beds,
While visions of sugar-plums danced in their heads;
And Mamma in her 'kerchief, and I in my cap,
Had just settled our brains for a long winter's nap;
When out on the lawn there arose such a clatter,
I sprang from the bed to see what what was the matter.
Away to the window I flew like a flash,
Tore open the shutters and threw up the sash.
The moon, on the breast of the new-fallen snow,
Gave the lustre of mid-day to objects below,
When, what to my wondering eyes should appear,
But a miniature sleigh, and eight tiny rein-deer,
With a little old driver, so lively and quick,
I knew in a moment it must be St. Nick.
More rapid than eagles his coursers they came,
And he whistled, and shouted, and called them by name;
"Now, Dasher! now, Dancer! now, Prancer and Vixen!
On, Comet! on, Cupid! on, Donder and Blitzen!
To the top of the porch! to the top of the wall!
Now dash away! dash away! dash away all!"
As dry leaves that before the wild hurricane fly,
When they meet with an obstacle, mount to the sky;
So up to the house-top the coursers they flew.

With the sleigh full of Toys, and St. Nicholas too.
And then, in a twinkling, I heard on the roof
The prancing and pawing of each little hoof —
As I drew in my head, and was turning around,
Down the chimney St. Nicholas came with a bound.
He was dressed all in fur, from his head to his foot,
And his clothes were all tarnished with ashes and soot;
A bundle of Toys he had flung on his back,
And he look'd like a pedlar just opening his pack.
His eyes — how they twinkled! his dimples how merry!
His cheeks were like roses, his nose like a cherry!
His droll little mouth was drawn up like a bow
And the beard of his chin was as white as the snow;
The stump of a pipe he held tight in his teeth,
And the smoke it encircled his head like a wreath.
He had a broad face and a little round belly
That shook, when he laughed, like a bowl full of jelly.
He was chubby and plump, a right jolly old elf,
And I laughed, when I saw him, in spite of myself;
A wink of his eye and a twist of his head,
Soon gave me to know I had nothing to dread;
He spoke not a word, but went straight to his work,
And fill'd all the stockings; then turned with a jerk,
And laying his finger aside of his nose,
And giving a nod, up the chimney he rose;
He sprang to his sleigh, to his team gave a whistle,
And away they all flew like the down of a thistle.
But I heard him exclaim, ere he drove out of sight,
"Happy Christmas to all, and to all a good night."

Clement C. Moore,
1862, March 13th originally written
many years ago.

Clement C. Moore. Handwritten manuscript of "A Visit from
St. Nicholas," better known as "The Night Before Christmas"

The oriole weds his mottled mate;
    The lily's bride o' the bee:
Heaven's marriage-ring is round the earth—
    Shall I wed thee?

Bayard. Taylor,

Bayard Taylor. Handwritten stanza signed

1835.
Finished Feb 18th
Portrait in Oil.

Clement C. Moore

Original unpublished pen-and-ink portrait of Clement C. Moore by the celebrated American artist Henry Inman. Identified in Inman's hand as a sketch for a portrait in oil, 1835, the portrait is signed by Clement C. Moore

'By the rude bridge that arched the flood,
Their flag to April's breeze unfurled,
Here once the embattled farmers stood,
And fired the shot heard round the world.

R.W. Emerson.

Ralph Waldo Emerson. Handwritten quatrain signed from his poem "Concord Bridge"

Learn that the loveliest weed which holds.
Its smile fee-simple o'er the clod —,
A lovelier faith than yours unfolds,
To comfort man, revealing God.

Paul. H. Hayne.

Paul Hamilton Hayne. Handwritten stanza signed

"He died with the glory of faith
in his eyes,
And the glory of love in
his heart"
                              The Fool

Robert W. Service

Robert W. Service (Canadian). Two lines signed

Alan Seeger.

Alan Seeger

Yours sincerely
Delmore Schwartz

Delmore Schwartz

Ella Wheeler Wilcox

Ella Wheeler Wilcox

A poem should not mean
But be.
                    Archibald MacLeish
          Archibald MacLeish
          Pulitzer Prize Winner 1933

Archibald MacLeish

Marianne Moore
i.e. Marianne Craig Moore

Marianne Moore

Home, Sweet Home!

1

'Mid pleasures and palaces though we may roam
Be it ever so humble, there's no place like home!
A charm from the sky seems to hallow us there
Which, seek through the world, is ne'er met with elsewhere!

Home, home, — sweet, sweet home!
There's no place like home! there's no place like home!

11.

An exile from home, splendor dazzles in vain!
Oh, give me my lowly thatch'd cottage again!
The birds singing gaily that came at my call! —
Give me them, with the peace of mind dearer than all!

Home, home, — sweet, sweet home!
There's no place like home! there's no place like home!

John Howard Payne./

John Howard Payne. Handwritten transcript signed of "Home, Sweet Home!"

thanx

Laurence Ferlinghetti

--- All the arts lose virtue
Against the essential reality
Of creatures going about their business among the equally
earnest elements of nature. (Roan Stallion - page 88)

— Inscribed for William David Hennessy, Jr.
Sincerely,
Robinson Jeffers.

Tor House, Carmel, California. — July, 1934.

Robinson Jeffers. Handwritten quotation signed

Sidney Lanier

Conrad Aiken

Randall Jarrell

Wallace Stevens

Sincerely,

MacKinlay Kantor

MacKinlay Kantor

Up in the mountains, its lonesome
all the time,
(Soft wind blowin' thru' the
sweet-potato vine.)
Up in the mountains, its lonesome
for a child
Whippoorwills a-callin', when the
sap runs wild.

Stephen Vincent Benét

& you while still
Yours very sincerely
Elinor Wylie.

Elinor Wylie

Stephen Vincent Benét. Handwritten stanza signed

CRAZY CURRENCY 13

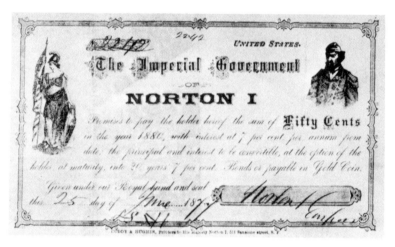

Norton I. Bank note for fifty cents signed

A paunchy, bearded man, wearing a plumed hat and a blue uniform with enormous epaulets and glittering brass buttons, descended from a rickety bicycle and walked with regal step into a haberdashery on Market Street in San Francisco.

"We should like a necktie," he announced.

The shopkeeper produced one.

"We require a silken cravat," said the visitor, whom the merchant had instantly recognized as the self-proclaimed Emperor Norton I.

The second tie pleased the "emperor" and he tendered a five-dollar bill bearing his own portrait and signature. It was a tradition among shop owners in the San Francisco of the 1860s and 1870s to accept the currency of the colorful emperor (formerly the rice merchant Joshua Norton) and the shopkeeper gave Norton his purchase and change.

Today that five-dollar note is worth fifty times its face value!

The Emperor Norton I, who peppered San Francisco with eccentric proclamations, was welcome everywhere. His flamboyant costume, to which he often added an enormous sword, amused and delighted the citizenry. Even the restaurateurs honored his paper money—which, after all, was not so foolish, for today historians zealously seek examples as mementos of the most colorful and lovable of San Francisco's old-time characters.

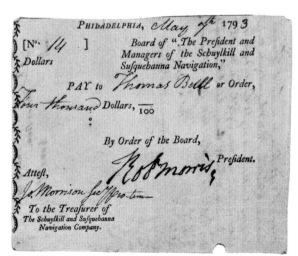

Robert Morris. Private currency issued by the Schuylkill and Susquehanna Navigation Company, signed by Morris as president

John Morton. Colonial bank note signed

Joseph Smith. Kirtland Safety Society Bank note for ten dollars signed by Smith (left) as cashier and Sidney Rigdon, Smith's counselor and spokesman, as president

John Hart. New Jersey colonial bank note signed

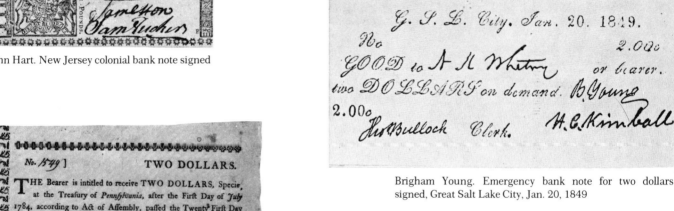

Brigham Young. Emergency bank note for two dollars signed, Great Salt Lake City, Jan. 20, 1849

David Rittenhouse. Pennsylvania bank note signed

Less successful in getting his currency accepted was Joseph Smith, the Mormon leader. In fact, when Smith issued his crisp and beautifully engraved Kirtland Safety Society Bank notes, guaranteed with his personal signature, there was a lot of grumbling that the notes were not backed by anything except the assurances of an insolvent prophet.

Word got to Washington that there was some "wildcat" currency around in Kirtland, Ohio, and a bank examiner came to see Smith, who assured the examiner that he would willingly redeem his currency with more of the same. This is precisely what our government does today, but in the late 1830s, when paper money had to be backed by silver or gold, the examiners looked askance at such peculations. Smith was charged with fraud and fled to Illinois.

A few years later, after the prophet was murdered by a mob, Brigham Young, his successor, reissued some of Smith's currency, adding his own signature. The supply was not sufficient to meet the demand, so Young signed special bank notes for nominal amounts.

Today the currency of Smith and Young is treasured by philographers and examples fetch prices well into the hundreds of dollars.

Peyton Randolph. Colonial bank note signed

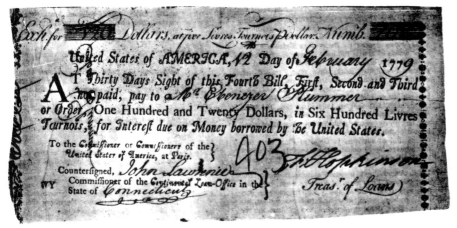

Francis Hopkinson. Revolutionary sight draft signed

You've heard the expression "not worth a Continental" and perhaps you've wondered just what a Continental was and how much it was worth.

A Continental was a bank note issued by the Continental Congress (1775–1783), or one of the colonies in rebellion, backed by no more security than a ragged, ill-equipped army of Revolutionary troops. Two hundred years ago these Continentals weren't worth fifty cents a bushel. Today many of them bring more than a hundred times their face value.

A whole galaxy of famed patriots put their personal signatures on these pictorial bank notes, each of which bore the awesome warning "Death to Counterfeit." Some of the signers of the Declaration of Independence were also set to the task of signing Colonial or Continental notes—John Hart, Francis Hopkinson, John Morton, Robert Morris. The noted leader from Virginia Peyton Randolph signed thousands. So did David Rittenhouse, clockmaker and patriot of Pennsylvania. Some of the early Pennsylvania currency, long before the Revolution, was run off on the press of the most famous printer who ever lived—Benjamin Franklin.

Like other fledgling nations, the young Republic of Texas in the mid 1830s struggled to keep afloat on a sea of paper currency and bonds. Recruited for the task of signing were some of the most devout patriots of those stirring times. Sam Houston personally affixed his enormous autograph to the "land script" issued by Texas. Two great leaders of Texas, Stephen F. Austin and David G. Burnet, also signed ornate bonds of the Lone Star republic.

The beauty and rarity of most early American bonds and bank notes, as well as the great names penned on them, make them an exciting pictorial record of our nation's first adventures in high finance.

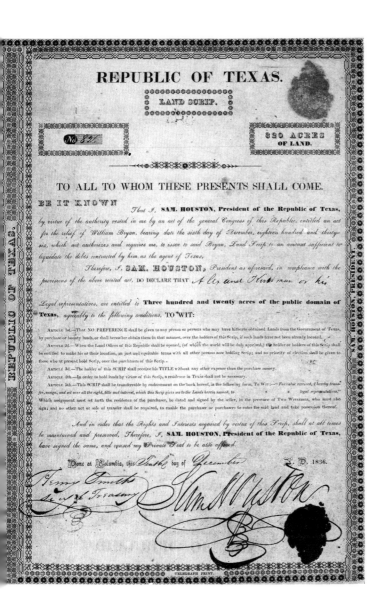

Sam Houston. Texas land script signed

Stephen F. Austin. Texian loan certificate signed

THE GUNSLINGERS **14**

With a butcher knife in his left hand and a revolver in his right, Billy the Kid cautiously edged into the dark room where Sheriff Pat Garrett was waiting to ambush him.

"Quién es?" asked Billy.

Garrett answered with two quick shots and Billy crumpled to the floor.

The twenty-one-year-old desperado, a fast draw who according to his own admission had slain one man for each year of his life—"and that ain't countin' niggers and Injuns"—was dead.

Later Garrett was asked if he ever got scared while tracking down Billy.

"Scared? Well, I should say so. I went out figuring I'd be shot at, and I knew there was a good chance I'd be killed."

"Sheriff," he was told, "a lot of cowpokes say Billy was really a coward and you should have shot it out with him in a fair fight. They say a courageous man would not have gunned him down in the darkness."

Replied Garrett: "There is not one of these brave mouth-fighters that, if the Kid were on their track, would not have set the prairie on fire to get out of his reach and, in their fright, extinguished it again as they ran!"

In a biography of Billy the Kid, whose real name was William H. Bonney, Garrett noted that Billy "wrote a fair letter." I wonder what's become of all the fair letters he wrote. Only two apparently survive, treasured in the Indiana Historical Society among the papers of New Mexico's governor General Lew Wallace.

Billy was a dead shot, but many of his gunslinging feats are obvious exaggerations. The Colt revolver, that redoubtable weapon of the West, simply could not perform with the accuracy often ascribed to it. Even when fired from a fixed mount, the Colt shows at fifty yards a strike spread of several inches.

The most notorious bandit of the West (Missouri) was Jesse James, a sullen, paranoid, inept robber who suffered from conjunctivitis and should have been called "Blinky" James. So disliked was this surly thief that one of his band threatened to

Sheriff Pat Garrett. Handwritten document signed, certifying that Garrett arrested a fugitive. This document was penned less than three months after Garrett shot and killed Billy the Kid on the night of July 14, 1881.

yours Truly
Robert. N. Ford
K. C., Mo

Robert N. Ford

kill him, shoving a revolver under his chin, another called him a rattlesnake to his face and a third, Robert Ford, shot him down from behind. James's legendary reputation was built up by the *Police Gazette* and other sensational newspapers. James's letters are rare and only a few survive. Several interesting ones have come my way. The first, signed with his hideout alias, Thomas Howard, was mailed to me by an elderly woman in California. I replied with a huge offer of two thousand dollars, the value at the time of four or five Washington letters. With my offer I enclosed a check. Three weeks passed, then six weeks, and no answer came from California, nor was my check cashed. Finally I heard:

My husband and I had thought that the letter of Jesse was worth only a few dollars and your check for $2000 bewildered us. We called a family conference and after a debate decided to send back your check and keep the letter, since it was so valuable. But it was hard to give up $2000. So I held the check for a few weeks more and we called a second conference. This time, after a lot of discussion, we concluded to give up the letter and we have cashed your generous check.

Very Respectfully
P. F. Garrett

Pat Garrett

Santa Fe
Jan." 1st 1881
Gov." Lew Wallace
Dear Sir
I would like to see You for a few moments if You can spare time
Yours Respect."
W. H. Bonney

Billy the Kid. Handwritten letter signed with his real name, W. H. Bonney, to Governor Lew Wallace, requesting a meeting. Billy was considering the possibility of surrendering if granted a pardon.

Dr. Bates. Pleas read this letter & hand it to Mrs Flood & oblg . JWJames

Jesse James. Handwritten note signed

OATH OF OFFICE.

I, *Charles A. Wells*, do solemnly swear that I will faithfully execute all lawful precepts, directed to the Marshal of the United States for the Western District of Arkansas, under the authority of the United States, and true returns make and in all things well and truly, and without malice or partiality, perform the duties of Deputy Marshal of the Western District of Arkansas during my continuance in said office, and take only my lawful fees, so help me God.

C. A. Wells [S.S.]

Sworn to and subscribed before me this 13 day of May 18 90.

"Hanging Judge" Parker. Oath of office for a marshal, signed as witness

In another letter of James, which I acquired more recently, the outlaw expended six penciled pages in a truculent blast against the Pinkertons and one Samuel Hardwick for the bombing of Jesse's home, which blew off his mother's right arm and killed James's half-brother. "I want the law to take its course and spair Clay Co. [Clay County, Missouri] of a mob that will be bloody and desperate. . . . Strain every nerve to have the midnight assassins punished."

A few years ago, I authenticated for the owner a letter in which James vehemently denied the charge of horse-stealing:

I & Frank [James] have been lied on & persecuted enough. We cannot stand every thing. What did you mean by telling . . . that we stole Dr. Gates horse. Do you suppose if we were thieves we would steal a horse from one that has been so kind to mother as Dr. Gates has . . . No . . . they are no men in Mo. who scorn horse thieves more than we do. If you value your life you had better retract your Slander.

Jesse's brother, Frank, an alcoholic whose favorite epistolary request was "bring a pint of good whiskey," gunned down an unarmed bank cashier during the celebrated Northfield (Minnesota) Raid, a bumbled attempt at bank robbery by the James and Younger brothers. Frank later allowed his fellow bandits, the Youngers, to take the rap for him.

Captured shortly after the attempted Northfield robbery, Cole Younger and his brothers, Jim and Bob (who later died in prison of his wounds), were sentenced to life imprisonment. Cole and Jim were pardoned in 1901 as a result of the unrelenting efforts of Cora Lee McNeill, Jim's sweetheart, who wrote hundreds of letters to public officials urging their release from prison.

Unlike many Western outlaws, whose reputations were built up largely by lurid tabloids, Cole Younger furnished "facts" (mostly grandiose lies) about his life to his early biographers, Appler, Buel and Connelley. Cole even wrote a short autobiography, which is almost pure fiction.

Jim Younger was more literate and not at all boastful, a sensitive, poetic man, who, after his release from prison, found employment selling tombstones. Unable to face life without

Virgil Earp (brother of Wyatt). Bill for boarding Tombstone prisoners, 1881, written and signed by Earp. Doc Holliday was one of the prisoners.

Allan Pinkerton

Jesse James. Last page of a handwritten letter signed: "If you value your life you had better retract your Slander."

Very Respectfully
Bob Younger

Bob Younger

Cole Younger

Cole Younger

Jim Younger
Stillwater
Minn

Jim Younger

Cora, who had married during his imprisonment, Jim finally decided to put a bullet in his head. In a dramatic farewell letter to Cora, October 18, 1902, published here for the first time, the outlaw explained why he was going to shoot himself:

A life sentence behind prison bars can tie knots in a man's soul, make scars that constantly burn, unless he is strong enough to try to make the adjustment. . . .

I am a ghost, the ghost of Jim Younger, who was a man, although not an extra good one. Walking around here, people might suppose that I am alive, but legally I am as dead as Caesar. The fact is I believe there is nothing left for me but the soul I started out with. In the library at Stillwater I read and sent for nearly everything that was ever written and published about the soul and its manifestations.

I would like to win at something. If the world would let me be Jim Younger, I'd start again under all handicaps and beat them before I'd quit, but I am non-existant, I am dead, and there will be no moaning when I cross the bar.

It was under the tutelage of the ruthless William C. Quantrill, an ex-schoolteacher turned guerrilla, that the James and Younger brothers learned how to rob and kill. The only letters that exist of this brutal bandit-soldier, scourge of the border

Sheriff William Tilghman

Frank James. Handwritten letter signed to his nephew: ". . . ask Charlie to come and bring me a pint of good whisky"

states during the Civil War, are a few gossipy notes to his mother. I can imagine nothing more exciting and revealing than a letter of Quantrill describing his murderous raid on Lawrence, Kansas, in 1862.

Of great rarity are letters of the Dalton brothers, the only bandits ever to attempt the simultaneous robbery of two banks. All of the would-be thieves were killed in the ensuing fight of Coffeeville, Kansas, except Emmett Dalton. "The doctors picked buckshot out of me for weeks after the robbery," he said later.

The sheriffs of the frontier were as tough as the outlaws and sometimes tougher. Most of them have galloped into legend with six-shooters blazing. There was the psychotic James Butler ("Wild Bill") Hickok, of whom detractors say, "He never shot a man except in the back." Hickok's dull letters to his wife are apparently the only scribblings from his pen that remain.

Sheriff William M. Tilghman of Dodge City also wrote many letters to his wife. "I owe my life to the fact that I am one-sixteenth of a second faster on the draw than the men I fight," he told Theodore Roosevelt. "This shade of advantage is due to the fact that I represent the law."

At sixty, Tilghman took a job as marshal of Cromwell, Oklahoma, a wide-open boom town. He was gunned down in the street.

The exploits of Wyatt Earp and Bat Masterson have inspired dozens of scenarios. Both folk heroes lived well into the twentieth century and occasionally used the typewriter for their correspondence. Yet scarcely a letter of either survives.

Emmett Dalton

Grat Dalton. Signature as "Deputy" (at top)

Bat Masterson

Very sincerely,
Wyatt S. Earp.

Wyatt S. Earp

Mr. J.D. Calhoun
Lincoln Neb
　　　　Dear Sir

　　　　　I have noticed that you have 160 acres of land advertised for sale in Franklin co. Neb please write at once and let me know the lowest cash price that will buy your land. give me a full description of the land &c.
　　　　I want to purchase a farm of that size provided I can find one to suit I will not buy a farm unless the

land is nice. I will start on a trip in about 6 days to northern Kan & western Nebraska and if the description of your land suits me I will look at it & if it suits me I will buy it from the advertisement in Live[?] Journal I suppose your land can be made a good farm for Stock & growing please answer at once

Respectfully,
　　Thos. Howard
　　No. 1318 Lafayette St.
　　　St. Joseph
　　　　Mo
March 2nd 82.)

Jesse James. Handwritten letter signed with his hideout moniker, Thomas Howard. Jesse was interested in buying a farm and possibly intended to retire from the robbery business.

Wyatt S. Earp. Handwritten letter signed (at top center)

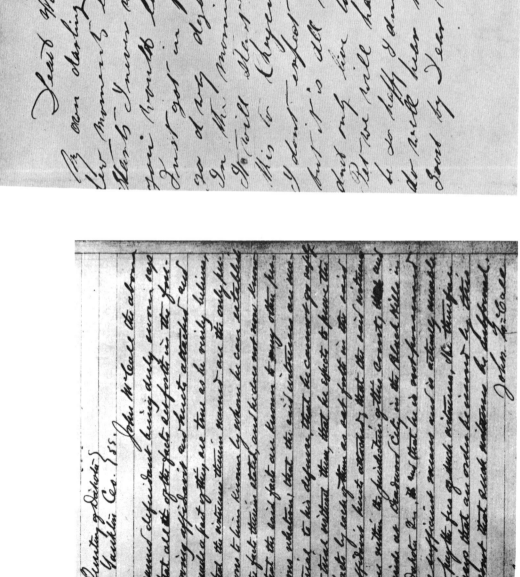

James Butler ("Wild Bill") Hickok. Handwritten letter signed to his wife

Jack McCall. Affidavit signed at his trial for the murder of Wild Bill Hickok, whom McCall shot in the back of the head while Hickok, then marshal of Abilene, was playing poker in Deadwood City on August 2, 1876. The poker hand Hickok was holding—aces and eights—was thereafter known as "The Dead Man's Hand." On his second trial, McCall was found guilty and hanged.

Cole Younger. Handwritten letter signed (in top left margin) to Cora McNeil, about the "Lull affair," a shootout involving the Youngers

William C. Quantrill. Handwritten letter signed

SING
A PATRIOTIC **15**
SONG

"There is something challenging to tunesmiths in the simple lyrics of 'America the Beautiful,'" a composer once told me. "At least seventy have already put the verses to music, despite the fact that the setting of Samuel A. Ward is now standard, and I predict that seventy more will try in the next fifty years."

Katharine Lee Bates, a professor of English at Wellesley, wrote the poem after climbing Pikes Peak in 1893 and gasping in awe at the panorama. In 1929, when I was fourteen and inspired by patriotism, I wrote to Miss Bates and asked her to copy out the verses for me. In reply I got a signature cut from a check and a letter from her sister: "I am very sorry to tell you that Miss Bates died a few weeks ago, I know that she would gladly have written out the poem for you. My own daughter, who is just your age, is most unhappy that she never asked her famous aunt to copy out 'America the Beautiful.'"

"America the Beautiful" is a moving and tender love song to a great country and should be our national anthem, but the members of Congress were doubtless all drunk on that day in 1931 when, after a brief debate, they voted to make the bellicose "Star-Spangled Banner" the national anthem of the United States. I doubt if more than a dozen of those worthies could sing it and hit the high notes. They should have tried to sing the song before taking a vote.

"The Star-Spangled Banner" was written aboard ship to the accompaniment of bursting shells. As Francis Scott Key, a Baltimore attorney, watched the embattled flag of Fort McHenry, under bombardment by the British during the War of 1812, he composed the hostile words and set them to an old drinking tune, "The Anacreontic Song."

Only three manuscript copies of "The Star-Spangled Banner" are known to exist. A fourth manuscript by Key has vanished. If it turns up in your attic, don't part with it for less than two hundred thousand dollars.

The blood-churning patriotic march "The Stars and Stripes Forever" was also composed on board a vessel. John Philip Sousa wrote me in 1929: "The inspiration for 'The Stars and Stripes Forever' came to me as I was pacing the deck of a steamship on which I was returning to America some thirty

John Philip Sousa. Four bars from "The Stars and Stripes Forever" signed

The Star-spangled banner.

O Say! can you see by the dawn's early light
What so proudly we hail'd at the twilight's last gleaming
Whose broad stripes and bright stars, through the clouds of the fight,
O'er the ramparts we watch'd were so gallantly streaming?
And the rocket's red glare - the bomb bursting in air
Gave proof through the night that our flag was still there!
O Say, does that star-spangled banner yet wave
O'er the land of the free & the home of the brave? —

F S Key

Francis Scott Key. Handwritten copy of the first stanza of
"The Star-Spangled Banner" signed

years ago. I hurried to my stateroom and set down the entire march in a few minutes." Later, Sousa recalled, he walked up and down the deck "with a mental brass band playing the march fully a hundred times during the week I was on the steamer."

The rosy-cheeked Baptist minister Samuel Francis Smith, who looked like a Kewpie doll that had been tippling, holds the all-time record for copying out verses. How many times he wrote out his great hymn "America" ("My country, 'tis of thee"), I won't venture to guess. Certainly thousands. He never turned down an applicant, observing, "We ought to gratify as many as we can in this short life of our pilgrimage."

Smith originally wrote the verses for a children's choir in 1831, using the tune from an old German hymn which also happens to be the music of "God Save the Queen [King]," the British national anthem. Smith lived for sixty-four years after this youthful effort and always set down the date of composition as 1832, but the earliest printed copies disclose that "America" was sung at the Boston Sabbath School Union on July 4, 1831.

The two great marching songs of the Civil War were both written by Northerners. In 1859, while traveling with a minstrel troupe, Daniel Decatur Emmett of Mount Vernon, Ohio, dashed off a little "walkaround," a sort of perambulatory interlude, which he called "Dixie's Land." The words were based on the standard lament of Southern musicians stranded in the North during the winter: "I wish I was in Dixie land," meaning south of the Mason-Dixon line, especially New Orleans. The Confederate soldiers took the song as their rallying march and when Lee surrendered on April 9, 1865, a conciliatory Lincoln waved to the cheering Northern throngs from the balcony of the White House and called out, "Will the band please strike up 'Dixie's Land'?"

Yankee Doodlefuly Yours

Geo. M Cohan

George M. Cohan

Kate Smith

Kate Smith

In December 1861, during a visit to the campfires of McClellan's army, Julia Ward Howe wrote the "Battle Hymn of the Republic," a stirring martial hymn sung to the tune of "John Brown's Body." The Union troops pounced upon it as their own and modern authors still quarry its great lines for book titles. Mrs. Howe occasionally wrote out a few lines from her hymn for admirers and such quotable fragments come high on the philographic market.

When the United States entered World War I in 1917, George M. Cohan, the jaunty little Yankee Doodle Dandy of Broadway, composed a rousing song to honor our expeditionary force. Belted out by the army's sweetheart, Nora Bayes, "Over There" quickly became the anthem of the war.

At the very time when Cohan was writing "Over There," another composer, Irving Berlin, was putting the finishing touches on the great song of World War II, "God Bless America." Berlin laid his song aside for two decades until 1938, when Kate Smith introduced it over the radio on an Armistice Day program.

Perhaps, one of these days, a sober Congress will convene and change our national anthem to "God Bless America" or "America the Beautiful." Then I, and millions of vocal dropouts like me, will be able to sing our anthem and also relish the beauty and meaning of the words.

Irving Berlin

Irving Berlin. Youthful signature

Irving Berlin

Irving Berlin. Signature in old age

America the Beautiful

O beautiful for spacious skies,
  For amber waves of grain,
For purple mountain majesties
  Above the fruited plain!
    America! America!
  God shed His grace on thee
And crown thy good with brotherhood
  From sea to shining sea!

O beautiful for pilgrim feet,
  Whose stern, impassioned stress
A thoroughfare for freedom beat
  Across the wilderness!
    America! America!
  God mend thine every flaw,
Confirm thy soul in self-control,
  Thy liberty in law!

O beautiful for heroes proved
  In liberating strife,
Who more than self their country loved,
  And mercy more than life!
    America! America!
  May God thy gold refine
Till all success be nobleness
  And every gain divine!

O beautiful for patriot dream
  That sees beyond the years
Thine alabaster cities gleam
  Undimmed by human tears!
    America! America!
  God shed His grace on thee
And crown thy good with brotherhood
  From sea to shining sea!

Katharine Lee Bates

Katharine Lee Bates. Complete handwritten manuscript of "America the Beautiful" signed

America!

My country, 'tis of thee,
Sweet land of liberty,
Of thee I sing;
Land where my fathers died,
Land of the pilgrims' pride,
From every mountain side
Let freedom ring.

Let music swell the breeze,
And ring from all the trees
Sweet freedom's song;
Let mortal tongues awake,
Let all that breathe partake,
Let rocks their silence break,
The sound prolong.

My native country — thee,
Land of the noble, free,
Thy name I love;
I love thy rocks and rills,
Thy woods and templed hills,
My heart with rapture thrills
Like that above.

Our fathers' God, to Thee,
Author of liberty,
To Thee we sing;
Long may our land be bright,
With freedom's holy light,
Protect us by Thy might,
Great God, our King.

Written in 1832.

S. F. Smith.

Samuel Francis Smith. Handwritten transcript of "America"
("My country, 'tis of thee") signed

Battle Hymn of the Republic

Mine eyes have seen the glory of the coming of the Lord:
He is trampling out the vintage where the grapes of wrath are stored
He hath loosed the fateful lightning of his terrible swift sword:
His truth is marching on.

I have seen Him in the watchfires of a hundred circling camps;
They have builded Him an altar in the evening dews and damps;
I can read His righteous sentence by the dim and flaring lamps,
His day is marching on.

I have read a fiery gospel, writ in burnished rows of steel:
"As ye deal with my contemners, so with you my grace shall deal;
Let the Hero, born of woman, crush the serpent with his heel,
Since God is marching on."

He has sounded forth the trumpet that shall never call retreat;
He is sifting out the hearts of men before His judgment seat:
Oh! be swift, my soul, to answer Him! be jubilant, my feet!
Our God is marching on.

In the beauty of the lilies Christ was born, across the sea,
With a glory in his bosom that transfigures you and me:
As he died to make men holy, let us die to make men free,
While God is marching on.

Julia Ward Howe.

Julia Ward Howe. Handwritten copy of "Battle Hymn of the Republic" signed

Dan D. Emmett. First page and music, written out and signed, of
"I Wish I Was in Dixie's Land"

George M. Cohan. Words and music of the chorus of
"Over There" written out and signed

SOUTH OF
16 THE BORDER

Francisco ("Pancho") Villa

Maximilian. Signature as emperor of Mexico

Pancho Villa liked to be his own chauffeur. It gave the ex-bronco buster and guerrilla fighter a feeling of power to sweep through the streets at forty-five miles an hour. At eight o'clock in the morning on July 23, 1923, he guided his big gray Dodge touring car, with three armed passengers and a rifled body-guard on each running board, through Calle Gabina Barrera in Parral, Chihuahua.

Villa was ready for would-be assassins. He carried a pistol in the holster at his left hip.

Suddenly a bullet shattered the windshield and eight men firing rifles and revolvers poured from an adobe hut in the street. Villa's bodyguards fell at the first blast. All the occupants of the car were riddled, even the driver. But Villa would not die. Blood gushed from his chest and mouth as the assassins pumped bullet after bullet into his body. The man with the bronze-colored skin seemed made of bronze. Finally he managed to pull his pistol and fire. One of the assassins fell just as Villa slumped forward in death.

Like most men of violence, Villa was not prodigal with the pen. He spent long hours behind his big roll-top desk fumbling with papers, but seldom put his florid signature on anything. In more than a quarter of a century, all that have come my way are a few typewritten passes for American reporters. But for thirty years I have pursued a great handwritten letter of Villa, penned in prison and seeking his freedom. Three decades ago a dealer listed it for twenty-five dollars and my telephoned order came only seconds too late. The last time the letter surfaced I offered a thousand dollars for it, but before I could get a yes or no the owner had archly vanished. Someday I will own that exciting letter and when I do I will relish and savor it as one does an embrace from a woman long coy and elusive.

No death can be sweet, but the execution of Maximilian, emperor of Mexico, was as festive and pleasant as a judicial murder can be. When Benito Juárez seized power in 1867, his first move was to condemn to death the puppet ruler, Maximilian, whom the French had placed on the "throne" of Mexico. Four thousand soldiers gathered around the square where the emperor was to be shot. Maximilian bade farewell to his friends, embracing many of them. As he faced the firing squad, he turned to the officer in charge.

"Poor fellows," he said. "They have an unpleasant task." From his pocket Maximilian took six twenty-dollar gold pieces and spoke his last words. "Please give one to each man after I am shot."

Maximilian waved away the blindfold and placed his hand over his heart.

The volley that killed Maximilian also destroyed his beautiful wife, Carlota, who was in France seeking help for her beleaguered husband. Carlota became hopelessly insane and lived another sixty years in a fancy lunatic asylum, actually a chateau.

The letters of Maximilian have always appealed to me because of his tragic career. They crop up in two forms: penned in German and signed as Archduke Ferdinand of Austria, and in Spanish as emperor of Mexico, signed "Maximilian." Most of his letters in Spanish were dictated, but they are couched in eloquent language, with every sentence flower-bedecked.

Carlota's letters are very rare. After the age of twenty-seven she signed nothing at all. Carlota is the sweetheart of philographers who long for storybook romance.

The turbulent history of Mexico is replete with drama. My own favorite among all the characters who peopled this stage of sunburned cacti and adobe huts is Antonio Lopez de Santa Anna. His career is one long series of plots and counterplots, intrigues and deceptions, victories and defeats. At Vera Cruz on December 5, 1838, Santa Anna was struck in the left leg by a cannonball. As the blood poured from his wound, then believed to be fatal, Santa Anna wrote with his own hand a gallant and beautiful letter in which he told of his great love for Mexico. I once owned this bloodstained "farewell" missive.

Most of Santa Anna's letters are very dramatic. He has been severely criticized by historians for "slaughtering" the survivors of his assault on the Alamo on March 6, 1833. Consider that Santa Anna was making a frontal attack on a well-fortified position against determined Americans whose intent was to kill as many Mexicans as possible before their fort was taken or they were captured. Santa Anna warned the defenders by running up the "no quarter" flag. The carnage among the Mexicans was terrible, as expected, and Santa Anna was certainly within his rights to execute the few survivors who had continued to shoot down his troops until the very moment they were seized.

Among South American patriots, Bernardo O'Higgins continues to fascinate historians. His autograph letters are scarce and invariably relate to military affairs.

Not long ago I had a visit from a statuesque and imperial dueña who carried under her arm a huge roll of papers that resembled a bazooka.

"I have here," she said in impeccable English, "a few family papers that may interest you."

Together we spread them out. Of special fascination to me was a collection of letters and military commissions signed by Simón Bolívar, the great liberator.

Carlota

Antonio Lopez de Santa Anna

Simón Bolívar

Agustín de Iturbide, Mexican soldier and emperor

Antonio Lopez de Santa Anna. Portrait, inscribed and signed

Al honorable Juez, Mr Charles Andrews
Suestmo J. J.—
A. L. de Sta Anna

Nassau Febrero
15 de 1871

Bernardo O'Higgins. Handwritten note signed

Miguel Hidalgo, Mexican revolutionist; defeated and shot

Mariano Arista, Mexican general; president of Mexico

"My forebears fought with Bolívar," explained my visitor, "and since we were clearing out a few old things, I thought these might be of value."

As I chatted with the dueña about Bolívar, I studied her carefully. The ghost of a former radiance still clung to her face. I got the impression that she was a lady of noble birth who needed money badly and was forced to part with her family heritage.

I made a high offer and she accepted it. While I was writing the check, she said, "It is hard to part with these old papers."

Her eyes were glistening with tears.

As she left, I said, "You will be glad to know that there are many Americans who greatly admire Bolívar and who will treasure and care for these documents just as you have."

Of all South American autographs since the Spanish conquest, Bolívar's are the most prized. His letters reveal a keen understanding of military and civil affairs, for Bolívar was as much at home behind a desk as on a battlefield.

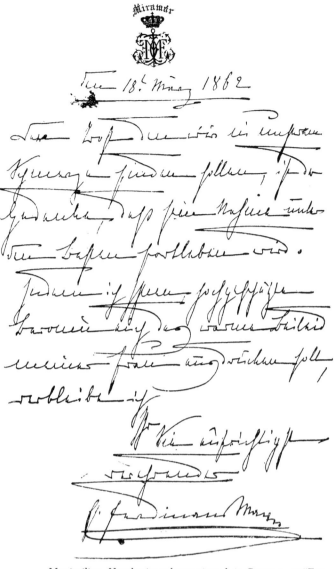

Maximilian. Handwritten letter signed, in German, as "Ferdinand Maximilian Joseph"

Anastasio Bustamante, Mexican general and president

Benito Juárez, president of Mexico

José de San Martin

Bernardo O'Higgins, Chilean liberator

Miguel Miramón, Mexican soldier; supported Maximilian; captured and shot

Guadalupe Victoria, Mexican leader and first president

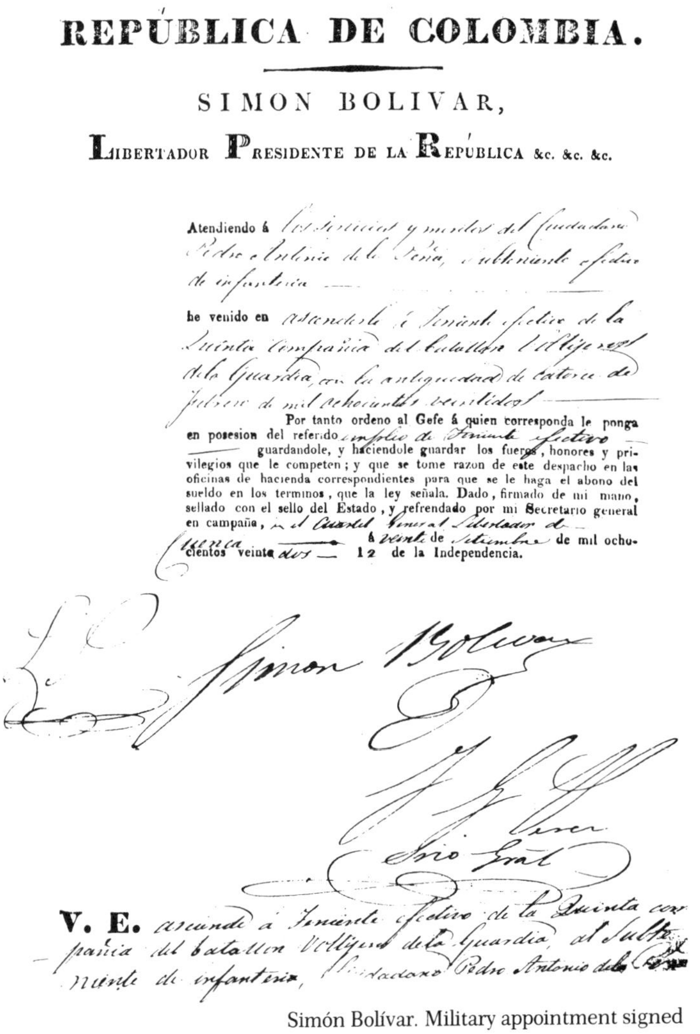

REPÚBLICA DE COLOMBIA.

SIMON BOLIVAR,

LIBERTADOR PRESIDENTE DE LA REPÚBLICA &c. &c. &c.

[handwritten and printed military appointment document in Spanish]

Porfirio Díaz, Mexican president

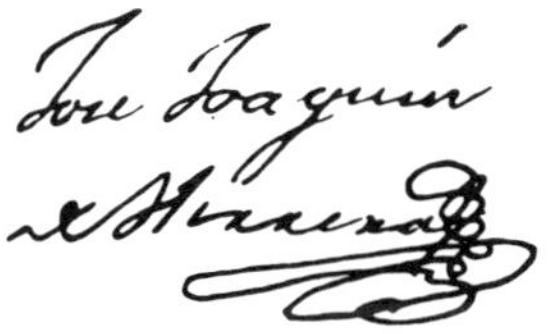

José Joaquín Herrera, Mexican general under Santa Anna

Simón Bolívar. Military appointment signed

Antonio José de Sucre, South America liberator; first president of Bolivia; assassinated

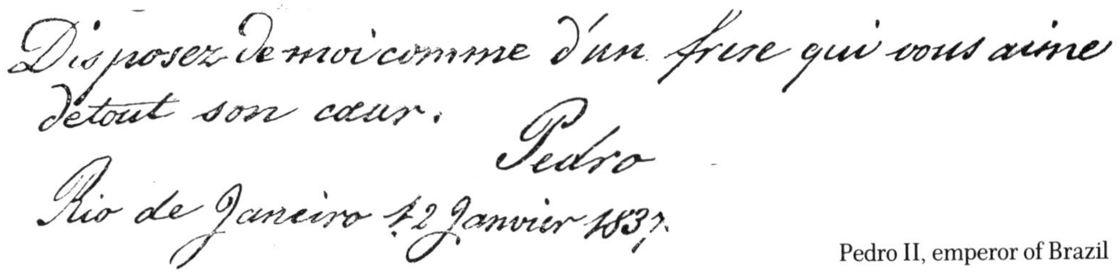

Francisco de Paula Santander, Mexican general; president of New Granada (Colombia)

Pedro II, emperor of Brazil

THE MUSIC
MAKERS **17**

L'Oiseau de Feu

Igor Stravinsky. Musical excerpt signed from his famous
L'Oiseau de Feu

"It's an outrage," said my college friend, a student of advanced mathematics and music at U.C.L.A. "Look at these pages, all scribbled on in ink." He handed me a worn library copy of Stravinsky's *The Rites of Spring*. "What's more, a lot of the musical notes are tampered with. There should be a heavy fine for mutilating library books."

As I looked at the slender tome, I noticed something familiar about the handwriting and it took me several seconds to place it.

"Why, these are Stravinsky's own corrections," I said. "This book is priceless."

A simple explanation was forthcoming. Stravinsky was at that time, in the mid 1930s, a visiting professor at U.C.L.A. He had checked out this classic work and annotated it, afterward returning it to the library for general circulation.

I urged my friend to have the precious volume placed in the rare book room.

Stravinsky's letters and manuscripts, which turn up in French, English and Russian, are highly valued by their owners. As might be expected, most of his letters concern performances of his famous works.

Deems Taylor

America's great native composer Jacob Gershvin, better known as George Gershwin, was born in Brooklyn to Russian-Jewish parents. His father, who accompanied George to Hollywood in the 1930s, spoke English with a thick accent and was very proud of his son's growing fame.

Stopped by a traffic cop for speeding, the elder Gershvin said, "I am Joige Goishvin's father."

The cop, obviously impressed, put away his ticket book. "Oh, in that case, you can go! But take it easy on the speeding. And give my regards to the judge."

Gershwin's letters, those he deigned to write, are full of zest, invariably revealing his enthusiasm for life and work. Before me as I write lie twenty-five intimate letters of Gershwin to his close friend George Pallay. George, whom I have known for many years, threatens to destroy all or part of them. "If you do that," I told him, "I will pray nightly that you sizzle in Hades for twenty thousand eons."

All good wishes
George Gershwin
Rhapsody in Blue
May 17, 1926.

George Gershwin. Musical excerpt from *Rhapsody in Blue*
signed

Come di lontano. from op.31. II

May 28. 1895.
Boston Mass.

Edward MacDowell. Musical excerpt signed

Jerome Kern. Handwritten musical manuscript, an excerpt from "I've Told Ev'ry Little Star" signed

Harold Arlen

Richard Rodgers and Oscar Hammerstein II

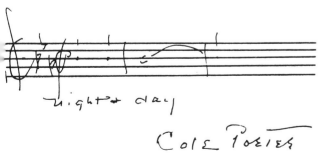

Cole Porter. Musical excerpt signed from "Night and Day"

I recall an early letter, penned during the First World War, in which Gershwin told of his secret passion for Nora Bayes, sweetheart of the American troops.

Most of Gershwin's manuscripts have been gobbled up by that voracious institution, the Library of Congress, but occasionally souvenir excerpts from his famous compositions appear on the market. Such fragments come high and I foresee the day when a thousand-dollar bill will not buy even a single musical note in Gershwin's hand.

The letters and manuscripts of Stephen Collins Foster, a steel-city Northerner who wrote great Southern songs about places he had never visited and folks he had never met, are awesomely elusive. The few letters I have encountered from his pen, set forth in an ebullient script, discuss his famous songs and the pittance he got for them. For "Old Folks at Home," one of the best sellers of all time, he received only five hundred dollars. Foster died in poverty in a cheap New York rooming house.

Jerome Kern, dean of show-music composers at his death in 1945, was a good-natured, pleasant man, unaffected by fame, who invested his surplus talents in collecting rare books and autographs. In 1928 he sold most of his great collection at auction, grossing a cool million. Later Kern said, "I never made as much out of music as I did out of books and autographs. My friends all thought I was crazy for putting hard cash into old volumes and manuscripts. I proved they were wrong, but when I got paid by the auction house, I decided I would do the 'sensible' thing. I put every cent into the stock market. Inside of a year I was broke."

Most composers wrote interesting letters. I once acquired a collection of Cole Porter notes about buying some paintings by Grandma Moses, then unknown. Porter discovered her genius long before the art experts. The average price he paid for several dozen original paintings was only thirty-five dollars each.

Stephen Collins Foster. Handwritten manuscript, signed at top, of "Maggie By My Side"

George Gershwin. First page of original manuscript of "By Strauss," written and signed by Gershwin

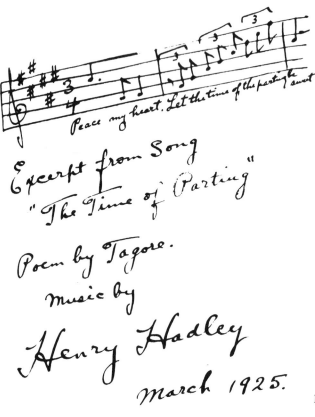

Henry Hadley. Musical quotation signed

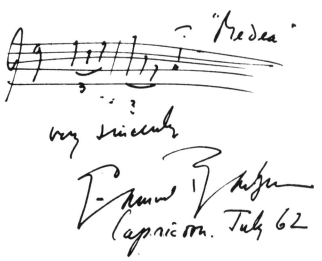

Samuel Barber. Handwritten musical quotation signed from *Medea*

Stephen Collins Foster. Handwritten music signed of "For Thee, Love, For Thee." Courtesy of The Foster Hall Collection, University of Pittsburgh, Pittsburgh, Pennsylvania

Kurt Weill

Louis Jones Very. Musical excerpt signed from *The Emperor Jones*

Count Basie

Hector Villa-Lobos

Meredith Willson. Musical quotation signed

Sigmund Romberg. Handwritten excerpt signed from "When I Grow Too Old to Dream"

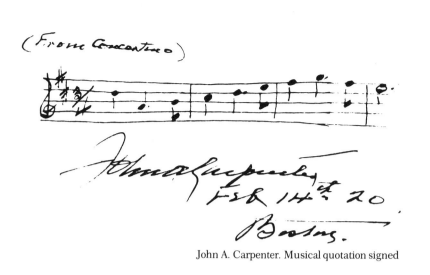

(From Concertino)

John A. Carpenter. Musical quotation signed

Carrie Jacobs Bond

Scott Joplin

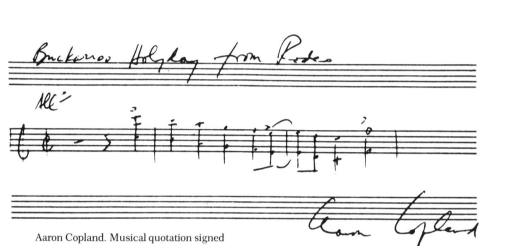

Aaron Copland. Musical quotation signed

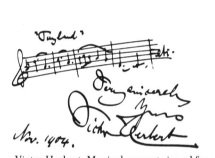

Victor Herbert. Musical excerpt signed from
Babes in Toyland

May 22. 1912

I know a little garden path

Arthur Foote. Musical quotation signed

Erich Wolfgang Korngold. Musical excerpt signed

October 29,1954
Date

George Antheil. Musical quotation signed

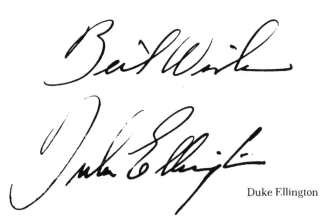

Duke Ellington

Rudolf Friml. Handwritten quotation signed from an early composition, 1908

W. C. Handy. Signed when young

Louis Armstrong

W. C. Handy. Signed after his blindness

Rudolph Ganz

Sigmund Romberg. Handwritten musical excerpt signed from "One Alone"

Louis M. Gottschalk. Musical quotation signed

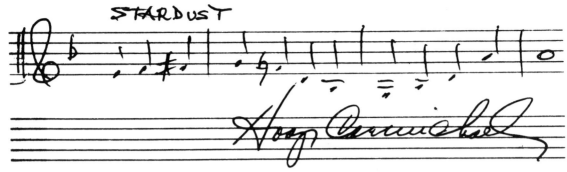

Hoagy Carmichael. Musical quotation signed from "Stardust"

Charles Wakefield Cadman. Musical excerpt signed

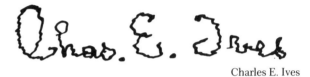

Charles E. Ives

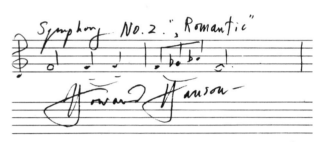

Howard Hanson. Musical quotation signed

Leroy Anderson

LeRoy Anderson

Percy Grainger

To-night, to-night . . . .

Happy Golden Wedding —

Leonard Bernstein. Musical quotation signed
from "Tonight, Tonight"

Time is always too short for the artist
— but art is a heart-rending struggle
and human endurance has its limits.
Only a pedant can devote all of
his life to his craft. An artist
fights against his work, like
Tobias with the angel.

(from my note-book)

Gian Carlo Menotti. Handwritten quotation signed

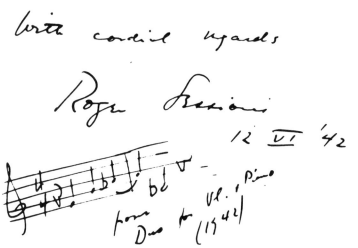

Roger Sessions. Musical excerpt signed

W. C. Handy. Musical excerpt signed

Ernest Bloch. Musical quotation signed

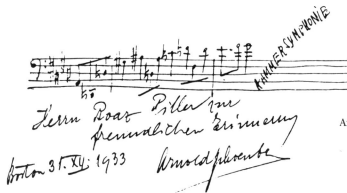

Arnold Schoenberg. Musical excerpt signed

Duke Ellington. Musical excerpt signed. Whenever Ellington signed his name, his writing frequently skipped over the paper, giving an appearance of scuffing or fading to his signature.

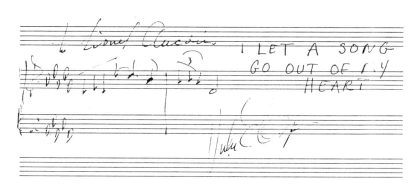

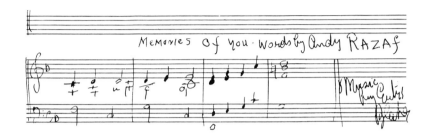

Eubie Blake. Musical excerpt signed

Leroy Anderson. Musical excerpt signed

Kurt Weill. Musical excerpt signed

18 AUTHORS IN FROCK COATS

(1790) The house was built according to a plan of his own. If furnished agreeably to his peculiar system. It was not deficient in splendour but was studiously commodious & cheap. His ideas of building & accommodation were derived from accurate observation & diligent enquiry. They were few more conversant with this branch of knowledge than medway. His mind was incessantly inquisitive, & pregnant with deductions & inferences.

C. B. Brown

Charles Brockden Brown. Handwritten manuscript signed

James Fenimore Cooper. Complimentary close of a handwritten letter in French

June 11. 1740

Jonathan Edwards —

Jonathan Edwards (1740)

"Pshaw!" said the thirty-year-old James Fenimore Cooper, ex-midshipman, as he put down an English romance he had just read to his wife. "I can write a better novel than that."

Cooper couldn't and didn't.

His first novel, *Precaution*, reveals a literary style with so many deficiencies that only Mark Twain has had the stamina to catalogue them. Cooper kept on turning out bad novels and won worldwide acclaim for his inept tales of frontier and naval life.

Whatever his faults as a writer, Cooper must be credited with the invention of the cigar-store Indian. It is a pity he utilized this invention for the red men in his books.

Cooper carried on a huge correspondence, much of it in French. Except when he is involved in a peppery exchange, his letters are almost as lifeless as his novels. Fortunately for philographers, the feisty author was forever suing or being sued, insulting or being insulted.

There were several important American authors before Cooper. One of the finest minds in the eighteenth century belonged to the Reverend Jonathan Edwards, author of a classic treatise on freedom of the will. In an age when churches were unheated during the bitter-cold New England winters, Edwards kept his congregation warm by his blazing threats on behalf of an angry deity. Edwards's letters are hard to come by, but those I have read well repaid the difficulty of deciphering his antiquated script.

The letters of Charles Brockden Brown, written in a morbid, introspective tone, are very similar to his Gothic novels. In

From Uncle Tom's Cabin
Chapt 38

When we can love a
pray-one - ale - through
all the bullets past &
the victory; come - Glory
be to God!
H E B Stowe
49 Forest St Hartford

Harriet Beecher Stowe. Handwritten quotation signed from *Uncle Tom's Cabin*

Faithfully yours
Joel Chandler Harris

Joel Chandler Harris

C. B. Brown

Charles Brockden Brown

Thomas Paine.

Thomas Paine, poet; later changed his name to Robert Treat Paine to avoid confusion with the deist pamphleteer of the Revolution, whom he despised

Horace Mann.

Horace Mann

"The human race is divided into two classes — one goes ahead & does something — the other sits still & wonders why it was not done the other way —"

Wendell Phillips

Wendell Phillips. Handwritten quotation signed

F. Parkman Jr.

Francis Parkman

J. Henson

Josiah Hanson, the original of Stowe's character Uncle Tom

twenty-five years I have handled but six of his epistles, all full of self-searching at the ethereal level. "I am a man. Am in full possession of my faculties and organs . . . Glory is my idol. The road to her temple passes through the field of law, and eloquence is the guide which conducts the pilgrim to it. No one idolizes knowledge more than I." And, in the same letter to his friend William Wood Wilkins: "The rays of ambition are extinct to me, but the darkness of my fate is somewhat illumined by the reflection of them from another."

Both Nathaniel Hawthorne and Henry David Thoreau poured out fascinating letters by the score, but grasping librarians have gulped them all down and it is hard now to find even a thank you note from their mighty pens. Washington Irving's letters are, however, gratifyingly plentiful. They are the jocular products of an urbane traveler. Quite often, too, scribbled fragments from his books appear for sale. They may now be had for a few hundred dollars a leaf, but I have no doubt that someday the last of them will be wafted into the New York Public Library, already the great repository of Irving's manuscripts.

In the mid 1800s there was a group of agitators in the North known as abolitionists, headed by William Lloyd Garrison, Wendell Phillips, Charles Sumner and other descendants of the Pilgrims, who had first legalized slavery in America. The letters of these malcontents, who must in some measure take the blame for starting the Civil War, are abundant and quite interesting. One of the most prolific writers of the period was the half-batty Harriet Beecher Stowe, whose *Uncle Tom's Cabin* was a rabble-rousing fictional attack on slavery. Mrs. Stowe had never visited the South. Her letters, less melodramatic than her books, are mainly soporific diatribes on the-will-of-the-Lord-be-done-amen. Mark Twain knew her in later years in Hartford, when her lunacy was harmless: "She would slip up behind a person who was deep in dreams and musings and fetch a war whoop that would jump that person out of his clothes."

Take a look at the famous photograph of Henry James, sedate and self-satisfied in his tall silk hat. Pretentious and

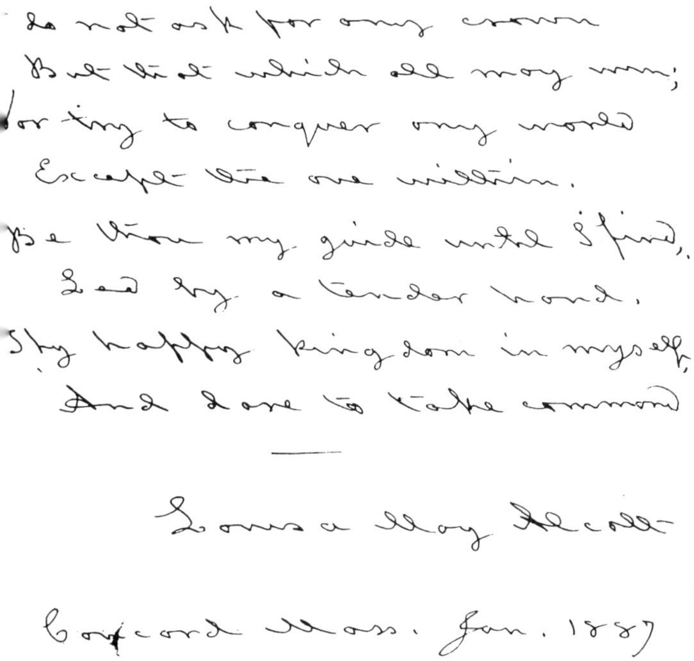
I do not ask for any crown
But that which all may win;
Nor try to conquer any world
Except the one within.
Be thou my guide until I find,
Led by a tender hand,
Thy happy kingdom in myself,
And dare to take command.

Louisa May Alcott
Concord Mass. Jan. 1887

Louisa May Alcott. Handwritten poem signed

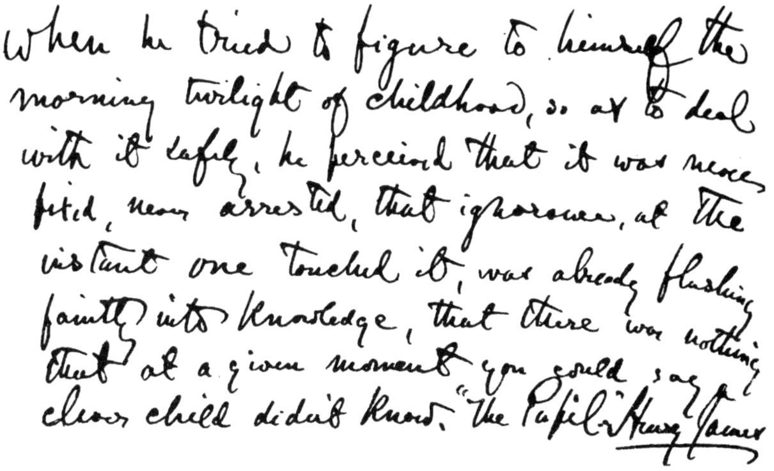
When he tried to figure to himself the morning twilight of childhood, so as to deal with it safely, he perceived that it was never fixed, never arrested, that ignorance, at the instant one touched it, was already flushing faintly into knowledge, that there was nothing that at a given moment you could say a clever child didn't know. "The Pupil" Henry James

Henry James. Handwritten quotation signed from his story "The Pupil"

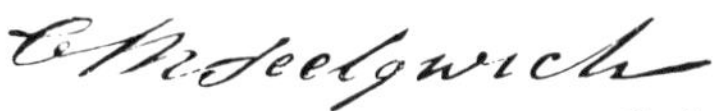
C. M. Sedgwick

Catherine Maria Sedgwick

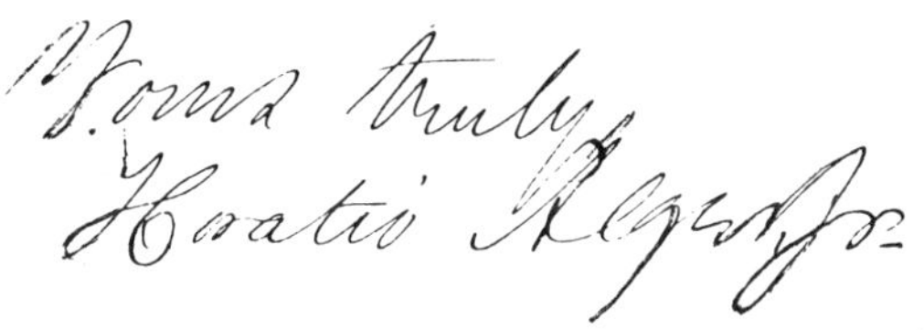
Yours truly,
Horatio Alger Jr.

Horatio Alger, Jr.

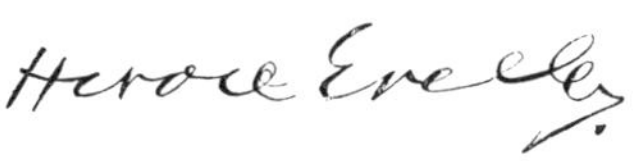
Horace Greeley

Horace Greeley

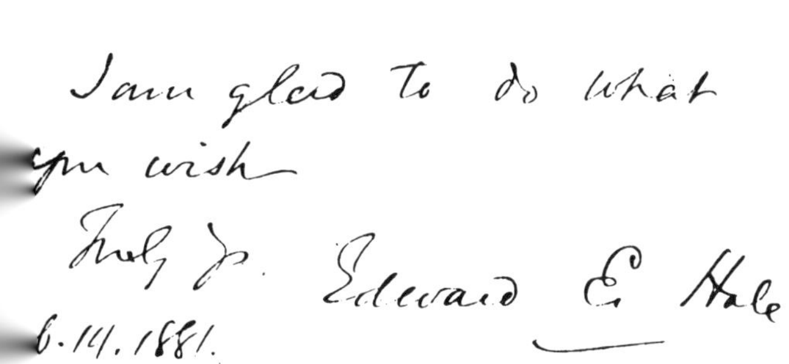
I am glad to do what
you wish
Truly Yrs. Edward E. Hale
6.14.1881.

Edward Everett Hale. Handwritten note signed

venomously dull, like his letters. Of the dozens of James's notes which have passed through my hands, I don't recall a single one that was interesting. James has another literary distinction. He is the only author I know of who could write a six-page letter declining or accepting an invitation.

One of the most popular authors of the nineteenth century was Horatio Alger, Jr., a minister eloped from his flock in Brewster, Massachusetts, to the Bowery in New York. Alger's writing, despite his Harvard education, is ungrammatical. His characters are stereotyped, his plots contrived and repetitive. So who reads him? I do, for one. In my personal library are more than thirty of his books, and I have read them all at least twice and some of them three or four times. I find Alger's tales nostalgic and engrossing. I suppose the bottom line is that I have no literary taste, and I am willing to concede this if I can be left alone to curl up with an Alger tale.

Alger's letters are scarce. Despite the large correspondence he carried on with boys who loved his books, his notes were apparently pitched out by the recipients.

Most of the nineteenth-century writers yielded gracefully to autograph seekers, whom Horace Greeley called "the mosquitoes of literature." Louisa May Alcott kept for a while a record of applicants and allowed only one signature to a customer. Some authors had stock replies. The Reverend Edward Everett Hale, author of *The Man Without a Country*, invariably obliged with: "I am glad to do what you wish." He wrote out this provocative sentence thousands of times. I once had in my files over half a dozen, and was inspired to compose a different imaginary letter to Hale for each such sentence. The first letter read: "Dear Dr. Hale, I am spinster of 42, still a virgin. I pant to sacrifice my charms before the altar of your lust. Can we meet secretly?" Other spurious letters in the series, which I mounted in an album with a portrait of the antediluvian author, a bogus sketch of his "secret life," and his acquiescent replies, involved him in various unsavory schemes, including the kidnapping of a bishop and a murder plot.

Dear Sir,

Mrs Cooper and I desire to make our apologies for not returning your visit. Paul was taken with the cholera (not asiatic) the day after you and Mrs Allison were here, and Mrs Cooper has not left the house before to-day. The boy is now better, and we sail to-morrow. We both beg to wish you well, and a return some day to the land of our common ancestors. You are the only person in this hemisphere who, to my knowledge, has my blood in his veins, and I would very gladly whet this blood with you, but that is now out of the question.

I saw to-day a letter in the Times on the subject of the Slave Trade, signed by Joseph Cooper. The writer was a quaker. Does not this look very like our clan? I would go and see this person, if I had time, for I think it more than probable he would prove to be one of us — not an American, but an Englishman of our stock. The Coopers left England, as you probably know, in 1679 —

Adieu my dear Sir — God bless you and yours.

J. Fenimore Cooper

S. Allison Esqr.

James Fenimore Cooper. Handwritten letter signed on personal matters

Mathew Carey. Publisher and editor

Mark Hopkins. Variant signature

Royall Tyler

Concord March 2d 1840.

Friend Wheeler,

As Mr. Emerson will probably go to Providence after returning from New York, at least one week more than was expected will intervene before he will lecture here — nevertheless we venture to propose to you the eleventh inst. — which may not after all be earlier than you had expected — and if that evening suits will not expect any answer.

I shall be happy to see you, and any of your friends, should they accompany you, at our house.

Yrs. &c
Henry D. Thoreau

St-ge Jan. 29. 55

Rev. & dear Sir,

I am [...] Joulease Put by your Journey hither, I wanted to see you very much. & to have you bring the Books. I must, if Providence allows, be at Westfield the week after the 20 of April to meet my sister, there from distant parts according to appointment. I would not fail of seeing you before that time by any means.

I am fully of your mind about mr. McGregor. I wonder I never thought of him before — I have been a sent along a number of letters, for you which have come to my hand, one that came from Boston I guess has a piece of Gold in it. —

Kind Respects to mrs. B—y
I am Sir
your most affectionately
J. Edwards

Jonathan Edwards. Handwritten letter signed (1755)

Helen Hunt Jackson

Henry David Thoreau. Handwritten letter signed about Emerson's lecture tour

Your Mt Hble Servant
Thomas Paine

Hon.ᵇˡᵉ Robt Morris Esquire

Thomas Paine, Revolutionary author; wrote *Common Sense*

Lafcadio Hearn   Lafcadio Hearn

*he was a hero
and a martyr; and so the civilized
world regards him. That you
should have had a hand in his
capture and death, however true
to your sense of duty at that time,
is now, I trust, a matter of deep
regret on your part, seeing that
while he remembered those in
bonds as bound with them, you
took sides with their cruel op-
pressors.
Yours for the reign of
universal freedom and peace
Wm. Lloyd Garrison.*

William Lloyd Garrison. Conclusion of a handwritten letter signed, giving his opinion of abolitionist John Brown. ". . . a hero and a martyr."

Yrs truly
Henry Adams
Henry Adams

L. Maria Child.
Lydia Maria Child

Richᵈ H. Dana Jr
Richard Henry Dana, Jr.

Lenox. April 7th. 1851

Dear Fields,

*I have received and skimmed
through the Seven Gables; and I heartily
pray Heaven the public may like the
book a great deal better than I do—
else we make a poor business of it.
But I am in the cold fit now, and
should not see its merit, if it had
any.*

*Will you send a copy, with
my regards, to H. T. Tuckerman? And
I wish Miss E. P. Peabody to have one.
Charge these to me.*

*I want a certificate of deposit,
negotiable hereabouts, for a hundred dollars. If payable at the Stock-
bridge Bank, it will be convenient
enough.*

*It is rather remarkable that I had
both your ideas — viz. a collection
of the remaining tales, and a book of
stories for children — already in my
mind. I have been, within a day or
two, to brood seriously on the latter
project, and hope to bring it to pass in
due season. It should not be exclusively
fairy tales, but intermixed with stories of
real life, and classic myths modernized
and made funny, and all sorts of ton-
foolery — The Child's Budget of Miscel-
laneous Nonsense —*

Truly yours
Nath. Hawthorne.

Nathaniel Hawthorne. Handwritten letter signed about *The House of the Seven Gables* (1851): "I heartily pray Heaven the public may like this book a great deal better than I do—else we make a poor business of it."

*A poem without words—
The prattle of a babe*

R. G. Ingersoll

Nov. 26. 92

Robert G. Ingersoll. Handwritten statement signed

the day you are called upon to serve the cause according to your vow.'

'Oh, of course I have thought of that,' Hyacinth

'And would it be indiscreet to ask what you have thought?'

'Ah, so many things, Princess! It would take me a long time to say.'

'I have never talked to you this, because it seemed to me indelicate and the whole thing too much a secret of your own breast for even so intimate a friend as I have been to have a right to meddle with it. But I've wondered much seeing that you cared less and less for the people how you reconcile your change of heart with your engagement. I pity you, my poor friend,' went on with a heavenly sweetness, 'for I can imagine nothing more terrible than to find yourself face to face with and to feel at the same time the spirit dead within you.'

'Terrible, terrible, most terrible

'But I pray God it may never be your fate!' The Princess she added; 'I see you feel it. Heaven help us all!

'Why shouldn't I tell you all?' A short time ago I had a visit from Mr. Vetch.'

'It was kind of you to see him,' Hyacinth

'He was delightful, I assure you. But do you know what he came for? To beg me on his knees to snatch you away.'

'To snatch me away?'

'From the danger that hangs over you.

'Oh yes, he has talked to me about it,' 'He has picked up the idea, but knows nothing what And how did he expect that you be able to snatch me?'

'He left that to me; he had only a general

Henry James. Corrected page of proofs of his novel *The Princess Casamassima*. With the high printing costs of today, no author would dare make so many changes at the page-proof stage of a book.

Washington Irving. Handwritten letter signed

Noah Webster

Mercy Warren

Frank R. Stockton

William H. Prescott. Handwritten excerpt signed from a personal letter

[Handwritten letter, Mordecai M. Noah, dated New York 25 Augt 1825]

Mordecai M. Noah. Handwritten letter signed

[Signature] Ann Stephens

[Signature] Stephen Crane

[Handwritten letter on Doubleday & McClure Co. letterhead, New York, Nov. 27/99, addressed "My Dear Mr. Richards," signed Frank Norris]

DOUBLEDAY
& McCLURE CO.

PUBLISHERS

141-155 EAST 25TH ST.
NEW YORK

Frank Norris. Handwritten letter signed, penned when he was an editor at Doubleday & McClure Co.

[Signature] Parson Mason L. Weems

[Handwritten note] My dear Sir. I never send my autograph in answer to letters, Henry Ward Beecher Jan 14, 1870

Henry Ward Beecher. A refusal to send his autograph, boldly signed

[Handwritten note signed] Wm Cobbett

William Cobbett, known as "Peter Porcupine"; lived and wrote in America for many years

Hartwood, Sul Co., N. Y.

Messrs Copeland and Day:—

. Dear sirs   We disagree
on a multitude of points In
the first place I should · absolutely refuse to have my
poems printed without many
of those which you . just as
absolutely mark "No". It
seems to me that you cut
all the ethical sense out of
the book. All the anarchy,
perhaps. It is the anarchy
which I particularly insist
upon. From the poems which
you keep you could. produce

Stephen Crane. First page of a handwritten letter to his
publishers about proposed cuts in his book of poems, possibly
The Black Riders: "It is the anarchy which I particularly
insist upon."

observe that in France,
in England, in America,
the same things are being
said, or the same sense is
implied, if not quite
articulated. and I often
feel that the appearance
of an enthusiastic moral
Genius, a new Zeno or
Buddh, thinking & acting
with simplicity, would
crystallize the chaos, &
begin the new world. But
this is for the Beginning not
the end of a note. Yours in
the best hope & R.W. Emerson

Ralph Waldo Emerson. Handwritten statement signed, from
a letter: "I often feel that the appearance of an enthusiastic
moral genius, a new Zeno or Buddha, thinking and acting
with simplicity, would crystallize the chaos, & begin the new
world."

William H. McGuffey, college professor and editor. His
eclectic readers, which sold over 120 million copies, had a
disastrous effect on literary taste in America.

George Washington Cable

Edward Bellamy

William E. Channing, Sr.

Geo. W. Peck
Author of "Peck's Bad Boy"

George W. Peck

W. E. Channing
Concord, Mass (1850)

William E. Channing, Jr.

Edward Everett

Edward Everett

Mary Mapes Dodge

Mary Mapes Dodge

Thomas Bailey Aldrich.

Thomas Bailey Aldrich

George Bancroft

George Bancroft

Wm Dunlap

William Dunlap

Dear Hapgood

I have to thank you for the fine puff of my "Varieties" in your last number. You're a noble man; and God grant that we may both become paupers ere we die, to prove the sincerity of our aspiration to that status!

Yours ever fondly,

Wm James

William James. Handwritten letter signed: "God grant that we may both become paupers ere we die, to prove the sincerity of our aspiration to that status!"

This covering falls down — for it has no lining — like an extinguisher over Rip's head. To prevent the recurrence of this accident, he has tied it up with a hat-band of twine. —

A leaf from Swallow Barn.
John P. Kennedy
Feby 18. 1864

John Pendleton Kennedy. Handwritten quotation signed from his famous novel, _Swallow Barn_

Mark Hopkins

Mark Hopkins

Henry George

Henry George

from your affectionate Fathers
Charles Bulfinch

Charles Bulfinch, writer on architecture

J K Paulding

James K. Paulding

THE LAST MEN OF
THE STONE AGE **19**

Long before the first English settlers landed at Jamestown and Plymouth Rock, the Indians had learned to draw pictographs on birch bark with reed pens dipped in berry juice. The celebrated Ojibway chief George Copway (Kah-ge-ga-gah-bowh), friend of Longfellow and prototype of Hiawatha, could write in English as well as pictographs. He explained how the old Ojibways indited their invitations to come and worship in the spring:

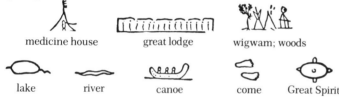

medicine house   great lodge   wigwam; woods

lake   river   canoe   come   Great Spirit

Copway thus translated these provocative symbols:

Hark to the words of the Sa-ge-mah.

The Great Medicine Lodge will be ready soon.

Ye who live in the woods and near the Lakes and by streams of water, come with your canoes or by land to the worship of the Great Spirit.

Not unlike pictographs are the totems of the early Indian chiefs. Usually the totem signature represented the animal clan to which the writer belonged. Colonial and Revolutionary treaties often display a marvelous variety of these fascinating signs manual. Most chieftains handled a pen with difficulty. The quill must have squeaked and sputtered as, laboriously, the Indians drew their totems. Quite a few of the old parchment treaties, once creamy white but now yellowed with age, are safely tucked away in our nation's archives.

A few Indian treaties have come my way. I once showed a handsome example to a friend who is a distinguished historian of Indian affairs.

"Attractive, isn't it?" I said, as the parchment crackled romantically in my hands.

"Yes," he answered slowly, with a tincture of bitterness in his voice, "but I never look upon one of these old deeds without

Samson Occom. Conclusion of a letter in Occom's hand, signed by him and two Indian associates, David Fowler and Peter Cohquoppect

James Printer

Joseph Brant

John Brant, Mohawk chief; son of Joseph Brant

wondering what sort of a swindle the white man was putting over on the Indians."

So far as I can discover, the first Indian to sign his name in the white man's fashion was James Printer, a Natick Indian who helped set type for the famous Eliot Indian Bible in 1663. The last Natick died almost a century and a half ago, his once great race wiped out by the white man's civilization, but my friend Dr. Frank Siebert, a great linguist and Indian expert, once amazed me with his fluent sight reading and translation of this long dead Indian tongue.

Frank Siebert is a pathologist, with a mind as clean and sharp as a scalpel. I had always thought of him as tough and unemotional. Many times we had sat up all night until dawn talking about Indians. One night as we chatted in my dimly lit living room, he told my wife, Diane, and me about a venerable Penobscot Indian who had helped him in his studies of the Penobscot language. The old man had been maltreated by his white neighbors and finally thrown out of his shack to starve. As the doctor finished his story, his words grew halting and broken and in the half light Diane and I saw tears running down his cheeks.

By the middle of the eighteenth century a few red men were reluctantly taking the white man's road and an American minister and educator, Eleazer Wheelock, opened his famous Indian Charity School at Lebanon, Connecticut. Two of his prize pupils were the Mohegan Samson Occom and Joseph Brant (Thayendanega).

Under the sponsorship of Wheelock, Occom traveled to England to preach and collect contributions to found a college for Indians. Occom won the patronage of Lord Dartmouth and raised twelve thousand pounds. The sight of so much wealth dazzled the Right Reverend Doctor Wheelock, so he ruthlessly cut Occom out of his plans and used the money to establish Dartmouth, a college primarily for whites, with himself as founder and president. The broken-hearted Indian turned to liquor for solace.

More fortunate was Joseph Brant, the Mohawk war chief, who espoused the British side during the Revolutionary War

Dear Sir I am your faithful
friend and most Obedient
& Humble servt.

Jos. Brant

Joseph Brant. Handwritten note signed

John Ross

and with a colonel's brevet led savage raids on American settlements. Before and after the war he visited London, where he was eagerly cultivated by Boswell, had his portrait painted by Romney and was feted by the Prince of Wales. I once owned an original treaty signed by Brant, dated just after the Revolution, in which the Mohawk leader ceded almost the entire state of New York to the victorious Americans.

Perhaps the most interesting educated Indians of the nineteenth century were John Ross, the Cherokee leader who fought valiantly all his life to protect the rights of his people, and Ely S. Parker, chief sachem of the Iroquois Nation and intimate friend and aide-de-camp of General U. S. Grant. When Lee surrendered to Grant at Appomattox Court House, it was Parker who wrote down the surrender terms at Grant's dictation.

The Five Civilized Tribes turned out a whole host of remarkable men—John Ridge, Elias Boudinot and Stand Watie, for instance—but the greatest genius of them all was an illiterate half-breed named Sequoyah (George Guess), who, working from a battered old spelling book in English, a language of which he spoke only a few words, devised a Cherokee alphabet (actually a syllabary), a feat which had defied the skill of missionaries for more than a century. By copying the English alphabet, turning some letters upside down and others sideways and creating some letters of his own, Sequoyah produced a letter for each of the eighty-five syllables in the Cherokee tongue. With Sequoyah's syllabary, an intelligent Indian could learn to read and write his native language in less than a week! If English were adaptable to a syllabary, a typical sentence, "I see you are a busy bee," would be written "I C U R A BZ B."

The most controversial Indian of the last century was the Reverend Eleazer Williams, a mixed blood who claimed to be the "lost dauphin," true heir to the throne of France. Williams flogged himself with bramble bushes and rubbed his wounds with tartar emetic to produce scars similar to those left by chains. Asserting that the scars were caused by a beating at the hands of a ruthless French jailer, he put forth his claim to the

E. S. Parker
Col & aid.

Ely S. Parker. Photograph signed as colonel and aide-de-camp to U. S. Grant

Stand Watie
Chief of the Cherokee Nation

Stand Watie

Chief Joseph, ✗ His mark

Washington D.C.
Feb. 1903

Andrew Whitman,
Interpreter

Chief Joseph. His X-mark signature

Eleazer Williams

Eleazer Williams

Chief Joseph. Signature copied by him from his name written by a white man. Notice that he had no idea of how the letters of his name were formed.

Ouray

Ouray

Plenty Coups

Plenty Coups

Sitting Bull

Sitting Bull

GERONIMO

Geronimo

French throne and found many supporters until it was proved that he was a pathological liar. His letters usually concern missionary affairs.

Red Cloud, the famous Sioux leader, signed with an X, as did Chief Joseph, except on a few occasions when he consented to copy his signature written out for him by a white man. His copies are quaintly done, with crudely formed letters starting and ending in unexpected places, for the great chief had no knowledge of what the letters meant or how to form them. The retreat of Chief Joseph after he was driven from his Oregon home is one of the greatest military feats of all time. With fewer than three hundred warriors and encumbered by women and children, Chief Joseph outmaneuvered and outfought the troops of three American armies sent against him. When he surrendered at last, he held his gun high and said: "Hear me, my chiefs, I am tired. My heart is sad and sick. From where the sun now stands I will fight no more forever."

Ouray, chief of the Utes, was unusually well educated for a Western Indian. He spoke Spanish and English and was able to pen his name in a bold, childlike script.

Sitting Bull and Plenty Coups, the Crow chief, learned to sign their names late in life. Sitting Bull's signature, a laboriously drawn scrawl, took him over a minute to write. His early pictographic signature showing an immovable (sitting) buffalo bull is artfully sketched. While traveling with Buffalo Bill's circus in the 1880s he signed his name upon payment of a one-dollar fee. To white men who called him a thieving savage, he replied: "When I was a boy the Sioux owned the world. The sun rose and set on their lands. They sent ten thousand horsemen to battle. Where are the warriors today? Who slew them? Where are our lands? Who owns them?"

The penciled signatures of Geronimo, written during the World's Fair at St. Louis, are quaint relics of a great warrior whose small band of Apache braves held a whole American army at bay for several years. Geronimo drew his signature sideways, starting at the top G and coming down to the terminal O, so that the completed effort, requiring several minutes to print, looked like a fancy totem pole until turned to

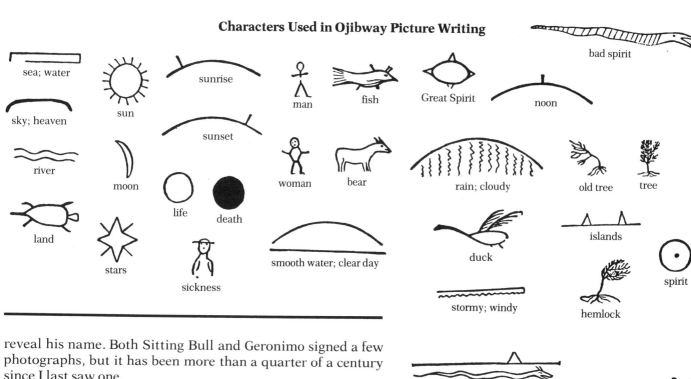

Colonial Indian treaty, 1638, signed by Chief Wehanownowit with his totem signature

Characters Used in Ojibway Picture Writing

sea; water	sunrise	bad spirit
sky; heaven	sun	man fish Great Spirit noon
river	sunset moon	woman bear rain; cloudy old tree tree
land	life death	
stars sickness	smooth water; clear day	duck islands
	stormy; windy	hemlock spirit

reveal his name. Both Sitting Bull and Geronimo signed a few photographs, but it has been more than a quarter of a century since I last saw one.

Like the noble savage himself, the few old Indian documents and signatures that turn up from time to time are gradually vanishing. More and more of them disappear into library vaults and it will not be long before these great relics of America's past are unobtainable at any price.

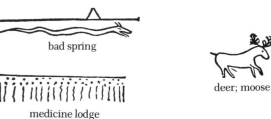

bad spring

medicine lodge

deer; moose

war · woods · bad

bad medicine · worship

night

spirits above

animals under ground

fire

dream

wounded water god

scalps; number · young warrior · great

fight man; bad spirit · mountains · spirits under water · cold; snow · sea monster eat man

ran · walked · hand; did so · bear killed · see · speak · stand

Colonial Indian treaty, July 13, 1713, signed with totems by eight Indian chiefs of the Penobscot, St. Johns and Kennebec tribes, by which the Indians ask pardon for "all acts of Hostility towards all the Subjects of Great Britain" and "confess our hearty and sincere Obedience unto the Crown of Great Britain." The signatures of the white men were affixed by an amanuensis, but the chiefs personally signed their signums or totems. Note that the phonetic spelling of the Indian names varies greatly in the same document.

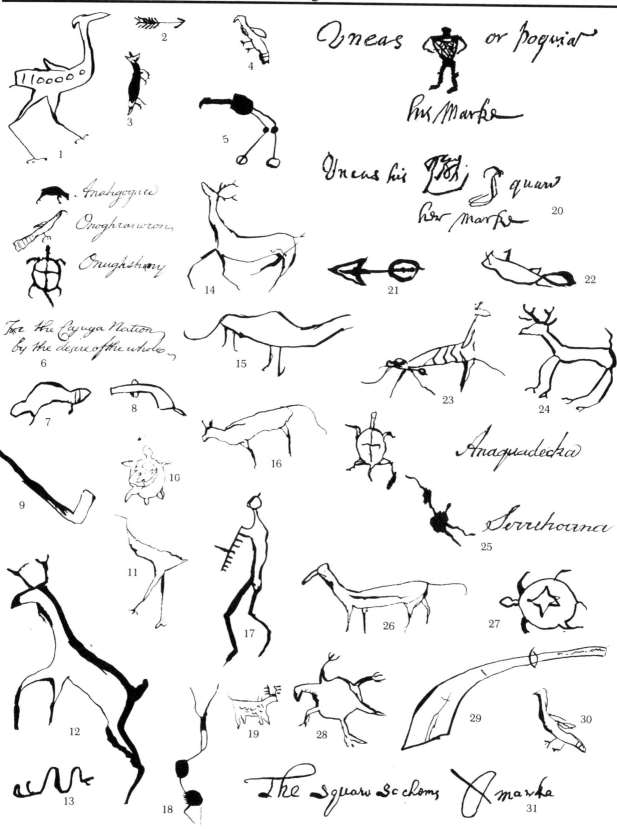

Anahgoyue
Onoghranuron
Onughshuny

For the Cayuga Nation
by the desire of the whole

Uneas or Poquia
his Marke

Uneas his Squaw
her Marke

Anaquadecka

Serrihouna

The Squaw Scchong marke

1. Tahondo of Cheoquogy (1768)
2. Whengohatong or "The Volunteer" (1785)
3. Canageh (1754)
4. Anyhar Ungquas (1754)
5. Sagehsadon or Fegassygta (1758)
6. Three Cayuga chiefs (18th century)
7. Canechwadecron, Onondaga tribe (1749)
8. Taydaya, Cayuga tribe (1768)
9. Tacknecderus, Shamokin tribe (1749)
10. Tawarah or "The Sweet House" (1785)
11. Tawis Tawis, Oneida tribe (1749)
12. Ta Kachquentas, Cayuga tribe (1749)
13. Saliskagach, Oneida (1736)
14. Agash Tass, Seneca (1749)
15. Ayackcagee or Tagachkahotoo, Seneca (1736)
16. Qualpagh ach, Delaware (1749)
17. Tahaskwanguoras, Oneida (1736)
18. Caruchcanachqui, Seneca (1749)
19. Aclquantugality (1754)
20. Uncas, great Mohegan chief, and his squaw
21. Tagunhunty, Onondaga tribe (1736)
22. Robert White, chief of Nanticekes (1758)
23. Sagughsonyont or ThomaKing (1758)
24. Canasatego, Onondaga tribe (1749)
25. Anaquadecka and Serrehouna (18th century)
26. Peter Ontachsux, Mohawk (1749)
27. Kanickhungo, Seneca (1736)
28. Cayianockea, Seneca (1749)
29. Tokahayoa, Cayuga chief (1758)
30. Hawycula (1754)
31. Wife of chief sachem of Powtuckets

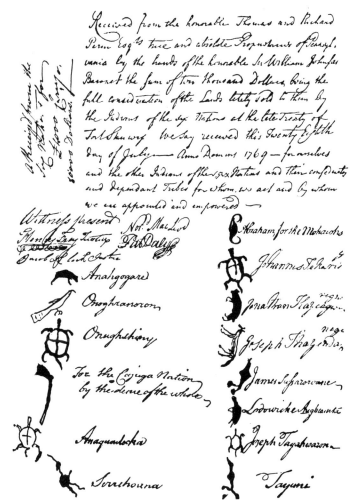

Indian treaty with Thomas and Richard Penn, signed with totems by fourteen chiefs of the Iroquois (Six Nations), 1769

Pontiac (called Pondiack by his contemporaries)

Red Jacket, Seneca chief

G. H. M. Johnson, chief of the Six Nations. The Z mark indicates that he is the "right arm" of the nations.

King Philip

Chief Two Guns White Calf. Pictographic signature

Oo-no-leh (Cherokee friend of Sequoyah). Handwritten letter signed in Cherokee. After the removal of the Cherokees to Oklahoma, Sequoyah, inventor of the Cherokee alphabet, vanished into the Southwest and Oo-no-leh went in search of him. In this historic letter, preserved in the National Archives, Oo-no-leh reports that Sequoyah had died in Mexico. "I met with Standing Rock who attended Sequoyah during his last illness and witnessed his death and burial. . . ."

Sitting Bull. Drawing of his capture of an enemy horse, signed with his pictographic signature of a seated (immovable) buffalo bull

Nunda Livingston County N.Y.
May 30th 1849

Hon H. R. Schoolcraft.

Dear Sir,

Being desirous of obtaining all the information possible in regard to Indian Affairs, and of the movements and intentions of the Government respecting the Indians under their jurisdiction, I have to request, if within your power, to be furnished with such public documents as relate to them, many copies of which I have no doubt can be well spared. The Senecas at present are doing very well. The Tonawandas still remain in possession of their homes, and I hope & trust that they will be allowed to do as long as they choose. I am at present engaged as an Engineer upon the Genesee Valley Canal, and shall probably remain here for some time.

I am Respectfully Yours
Ely S. Parker

Ely S. Parker. Handwritten letter signed on Indian affairs

H. R. Schoolcraft Esq.
Washington City
D. C.

Rossville, Cherokee Nation,
July. 13th 1822.

Mr. D. Brown.
 Dear Sir,

Yours, of the 10th of June last, came to hand a few days since, It gives me pleasure to hear that you good health, as well as those of your Cherokee friends there; but I feel sorry to hear that Mr. Jo. Ridge. has not recovered from the disease with which he has been so long afflicted — but as it cannot be efficacious for man to say unto him, "take up thy bed & walk", therefore his situation can only be confided to the will of Him, who hath the healing power.

The pamflet, containing the letter of Mr. Lewis, to a member of Congress, on Indian Civilization, which the Rev.d Mr. Westbrook had the goodness to send me, has been received, — For which you will please to return to him my sincere thanks. — To reflect seriously on the condition of the Indian Tribes, inhabiting the continent of America, and to review the miserable fate which has befallen & crept into oblivion the numerous Tribes

John Ross. Handwritten letter on Indian matters, penned in his attractive, ornate script

My kindness wishes to you from your Friend Two Guns White Calf.

Chief Two Guns White Calf. Conclusion of a handwritten letter

GIANTS IN
20 # BOOKLAND

An angry midday sun burned the deck of the steamship *Orizaba* on its way to Key West, April 27, 1932, as a young poet, Hart Crane, lurched to the stern of the vessel, quietly took off his coat and vaulted over the rail. The dark sea, long in his poetry and in his blood, reached up and embraced him,

> Where icy and bright dungeons lift
> Of swimmers their lost morning eyes,
> And ocean rivers, churning, shift
> Green borders under stranger skies . . .

Exactly a year later, a freshman at U.C.L.A., I was in the library, browsing through a heap of new poetry books, most of them of the George Dillon variety of puling, adolescent verse, when I came upon Crane's *The Bridge*. To this day I recall exactly where I was standing when I opened the book. I remember the chill of wonder and excitement that swept over me as I leaned against the stacks and read the entire epic, a Magellanesque voyage into the realm of rarefied imagination.

I hurried to tell a few of my English professors that I had unearthed the greatest poet since Whitman. None had ever heard of Hart Crane and only one, Professor Franklin P. Rolfe, was enthusiastic enough to suggest that I prepare a term paper on my discovery.

Much has been written of Crane's seamy life, his errant homosexuality and his alcoholism. Some years ago I was visited in my office by a man who announced that he was from Cleveland (Crane's hometown) and was interested in poetry. The discussion fell upon Hart Crane.

"He and I were both members of the Cleveland poetry club," he told me. "Naturally I knew him well."

"What was he like?" I asked.

"Surly and unpleasant, when sober. But when drunk, which was most of the time, he was overbearing and insolent, ready to brawl over anything. He was forever getting picked up by the cops for assaulting boys in public latrines."

I said, "You should be grateful you had the chance to know personally the greatest poet of this century."

My visitor snorted. "Greatest poet! Why, Crane was a lousy

Very truly yours,

Hart Crane

Hart Crane

Do your duty to-day & repent to-morrow.

Truly yours,

Mark Twain

Mark Twain. Handwritten epigram signed

The Spectacles.
By Edgar Allan Poe.

Some persons ridicule the idea of "love at first sight"; but those who think clearly, not less than those who feel deeply, have always advocated its existence. Modern discoveries, indeed, in what may be termed ethical magnetism, or magnetæsthetics, render it probable that the most natural, and, consequently, the most real and the most intense of the human affections, are those which arise in the heart as if by electric sympathy — in a word, that the brightest and most enduring of the psychal fetters are those which are riveted at a glance. The confession I am about to make, will add another to the already numerous instances of the truth of this position.

It is necessary that I be somewhat minute. I am still a young man — not yet twenty-two. My name, at present, is a very usual and rather plebeian one — Simpson. "I say at present"; for it is only lately that I have been so called — having legislatively adopted this surname, within the last year, in order to receive an inheritance left me by a distant male relative — Adolphus Simpson, Esquire. The bequest was conditioned upon my taking the name of the testator; — the family, not the Christian name. My Christian or baptismal names are Napoleon Buonaparte. I am now Napoleon Buonaparte Simpson. I as-

Edgar Allan Poe. First page of an original manuscript, with his signature meticulously printed at the top

writer. There were a lot of guys in the poetry society who could write circles around Crane. Sam Loveman, for instance.

"Take it from me," he concluded, obviously refraining with difficulty from mentioning his own superiority to Crane. "Hart's reputation won't last. He'll be forgotten in a few years."

A few months later I was in Cleveland, visiting some friends, and Winsor French, a columnist for the *Cleveland Plain Dealer*, asked to interview me for a series of profile articles. He was an elderly man, crippled by arthritis and confined to a wheelchair. I met with him in his high-rise apartment and we downed half a dozen drinks while he chatted with my wife, Diane, and me.

I asked, "Did you ever meet America's greatest poet?"

"Yes," he said. "I was a member of the poetry society."

"I hear he was quite a spoiler. Always drunk and disorderly."

"That's utterly false. He drank, of course, but rarely excessively. His conversation was delightful, full of beauty and as rich in metaphor as his poems. I used to stroll with him through the streets at night and we would talk for hours and hours. He was one of the sweetest, kindest men I ever met—always considerate of others."

"How well did you know him?" I asked.

French, by now quite drunk, raised himself with difficulty in his wheelchair and placed his bony hand in mine.

"How well did I know him! Why, dearie, I was his lover!"

French told me about a cache of Crane's letters "somewhere in one of my trunks, packed away."

I urged him to write a memoir of Crane.

Not long after my visit, French died suddenly. I presume his nurse threw out Crane's letters. Nurses and heirs are addicted to the destruction of historic and literary papers.

Crane's close friend Samuel Loveman teased me for years with a collection of Hart Crane's letters which I longed to own. He finally sold them to a library. Loveman acquired from Crane's mother all the unused bookplates of the poet, and books bearing Crane's ownership plate turn up frequently.

Along here just suits me. I'd like to stay on this soil and glistening water forever. No wonder that Cezanne painted as he did. You see his light and color everywhere here. I'll probably see you in the fall. All best. — Hart Crane

Hart Crane. Handwritten note signed about his visit to Marseilles and vicinity. "No wonder that Cezanne painted as he did. You see his light and color everywhere here."

Women sit or move to & fro, some old,
some young,
The young are beautiful, but the old are
more beautiful than the young.
Leaves of Grass — page 217

Walt Whitman
Jan. 13 1891

Walt Whitman. Handwritten lines from _Leaves of Grass_
signed

"133 Dean St Brooklyn New York "
Brooklyn Aug 9th/55

Dear Sir

I am about having the remains
of my beloved son (E A Poe) brought to
Greenwood, My Literary friends assure me
when he is placed there there will be an
exertion made to have a handsome
monument to his memory erected immediately. I have obtained the ground and
am now making arrangements to have
the body removed, This has taken all my
ready means, will you loan me $5 or
$10, until the first week in October, when
I will be again in receipt of money and
will return it to you most gratefully. I
cannot ask my friends here, as they will so
soon be called upon to contribute, to this
great wish of my heart. please reply as
early as possible. Your friend
Maria Clemm,

Maria Clemm, mother-in-law of Poe. About arrangements for
a monument to Poe

Emulate the crayfish if one is offered to you. The chances are
Crane never saw it.

The letters of Crane, usually typed, are among the most
illuminating of any American poet. Frequently he discusses the
genesis of his poems and comments on the creative process.
Even his short notes are piquant and appealing. Not more than
a dozen letters have come my way during my long, sentimental
quest.

The manuscripts of Crane's predecessor and mentor, Walt
Whitman, are abundant by comparison. In his own day,
Whitman was scowled at for his homosexuality. It is said that
the mothers in Camden, New Jersey, when the great gray poet
lived there, called their young sons off the street whenever they
caught sight of Walt, who used to carry a basket and peddle
signed copies of his books from door to door. Those who bought
the wares of this eccentric peddler have reason to rejoice.
Whitman's letters and inscribed books, bearing that bold black
script and sprawling signature, command handsome prices on
today's market.

Emerson called Edgar Allan Poe "the jingle man" and there
is much truth in this appellation. Poe's verses are artificial and
forced. I once analyzed "Annabel Lee" for a Poe buff, pointing
out a few of its defects, including the abundant clichés, like
"many and many a year ago" and "loved with a love that was
more than love" and so on. As a poet, Poe never rose much
above the level of his contemporary N. P. Willis. But his short
stories are full of vigor and power and originality. I suggest
that all lovers of detective fiction, a genre originated by Poe,
get together once a year and drink a cask of Amontillado to the
memory of this great story writer.

Poe's letters are very scarce. His fastidious script is a
delight to read and I doubt if he ever wrote a dull letter. A few
years ago I owned a note of Poe in which he revealed that he
had received only twenty dollars for his famous tale "The
Black Cat." The original manuscript of this story, should it

Zelda Fitzgerald. Declining to send her autograph because "The warden is very particular about letting forged signatures be sent in the mail from here"

'O the bleeding drops of red!'

O CAPTAIN! MY CAPTAIN!

BY WALT WHITMAN.

Walt Whitman. Corrected proofs of his celebrated poem on Lincoln "O Captain! My Captain!"

---

come to light, would today be worth at least fifty thousand dollars.

Speaking of underpaid geniuses reminds me of a story told me by my friend Barney Ruder, a well-known book and manuscript dealer in the twenties and thirties.

"Eugene O'Neill was a rising star in the theatrical world," said Barney, "widely acclaimed as America's greatest dramatist, and I got the idea that perhaps his manuscripts might sell. The vice president of Liveright, O'Neill's publisher, consigned to me the corrected proofs of *Strange Interlude*. Within a day or two I sold those proofs for thirty-five hundred dollars. Other consignments followed. Suddenly somebody at Liveright discovered that the sales were improper, as the proofs really belonged to O'Neill. I agreed to turn over my share of the profits to the dramatist. I met him at his hotel and gave him a check—a big check."

Ruder paused. "O'Neill was amazed at the size of the check. It was more money than he had ever got from any of his plays. His first act, I heard later, was to buy something he'd always wanted and could never afford—half a dozen monogrammed, custom-made silk shirts!"

O'Neill's letters today are eagerly sought. Most of them reflect his keen interest in the theater. His intimate letters are signed "Gene," and those penned in his last years bear a tremulous replica of his beautiful early signature, evidence of the alcoholism and Parkinson's disease which disabled and finally destroyed him.

Two giants of the modern era—Ernest Hemingway and F. Scott Fitzgerald—were both titans of the pen, pouring out fascinating letters by the score. Hemingway was one of the most prolific letter writers of his generation. An acknowledged master of the four-letter word, he put a right uppercut in every letter, even those to total strangers. Most of his epistles are about bullfighting or big-game hunting or fishing. I recall a letter in which he couched in scatological terms his opinion of Faulkner:

. . . I think he is a no good son of a bitch myself. But some of the Southern stuff is good and some of the negro stuff is very good. . . . His last book A Fable isnt pure shit. It is impure diluted shit and there

"Well, Spring isn't everything, is it, Essie? There's a lot to be said for Autumn. That's got beauty, too. And Winter—if you're together."
(*Ah, Wilderness!*)
Eugene O'Neill
Jan. 1941

Eugene O'Neill. Handwritten quotation signed from *Ah, Wilderness!*

Ernest Hemingway.

Ernest Hemingway. Early signature, 1921

On Sat mama and I went cross
the ford at the river It is very
much higher.
I got six clams in the river
and some weat six feet tall
your loving son
Ernest m Hemingway

Ernest Hemingway. Handwritten note to his father, 1908,
age 10

Paris, 1926

Dear Miss Emerson, I
absolutely refuse to give
you my autograph
Obstinately
F. Scott Fitzgerald

F. Scott Fitzgerald. Handwritten note signed, refusing "to
give you my autograph"

Dear Miss Long:
I'm sorry to have to refuse
your request but I have gone to
Zion City for the horse races and
won't be back until next June
Sincerely
Scott Fitzgerald

F. Scott Fitzgerald. Handwritten note signed, refusing to
send his autograph as he has "gone to Zion City for the horse
races"

"When many strikes on an
Anvil they must strike
by measure."

Herman Melville

Herman Melville. Handwritten quotation signed

isnt a shit tester at Ichang where they ship the night soil from Chungking to but would fault it.

Even during his lifetime, Hemingway's letters and first
editions were wildly sought and fetched hefty prices. Papa's
close friend the humorist Robert Benchley had the good
fortune to pick up for a few cents from a mentally retarded
bookman a slim rarity by Hemingway, published in Paris when
Ernie was only twenty-four. Benchley knew that an inscription
by Hemingway would add enormously to the book's value.

Handing the rarity to Hemingway, Benchley said, "I wonder if you'd mind inscribing this for me?"

"I'd be delighted to, Bob," said Papa, who correctly divined
the commercial motive behind Benchley's request. Whereupon
Hemingway wrote a full-page inscription so crammed with
obscenities and four-letter words that Benchley later observed,
"He forever rendered the book unsalable!"

F. Scott Fitzgerald, who was envious of Hemingway's
literary skill (or was it vice versa?), wrote some of the funniest
letters of any author of our time. He was forever adventuring
upon a drinking spree or recovering from a long hangover. His
replies to autograph seekers are hilarious. Sometimes he
would pose as a convict, appending a prison number under his
signature.

Herman Melville, the mariner and mystic, is regarded by
many critics as one of America's greatest prose writers, yet his
novel *Moby Dick* was not appreciated until thirty years after
his death in 1891. Melville's letters are seldom encountered
and perhaps it is just as well, for he was not an interesting
letter writer and confined his poetic paroxysms to his novels.

Mark Twain was the most delightful of correspondents,
certainly among the world's greatest letter writers. The humor
and wisdom that were his trademarks never failed him. Once
he dispatched to the editor of *The New York Times* an irate
letter that complained about the "govment" in prose
punctuated with five goddams. This he signed with the name of
his friend William Dean Howells, sending a copy to Howells
with the note: "I sent this complaint with your name signed
because it would have more weight."

Santa Claus
comes with
a smile and
a tear.
Santa Claus
has been robbed.
not of Burglars
but Angels.
The Children
will pray for
Santa Claus?

Emily Dickinson. Handwritten poem (unsigned)

Diadems - drop -
And Doges - surrender
Soundless as dots,
On a Disc of Snow

E. Dickinson

Emily Dickinson. Handwritten stanza signed

Whenever Mark Twain was asked for a sentiment, he complied; and his collected sentiments would make Marcus Aurelius blush. In a book inscribed for a young lady he wrote: "Clothes make the man, but they do not help the woman."

I never think of Emily Dickinson without being reminded of Wordsworth's Lucy:

-    A violet by a mossy stone
     Half hidden from the eye,
     Fair as a star, when only one
     Is shining in the sky.

In my mind there is not the slightest doubt that Emily Dickinson is the greatest woman poet who ever lived, certainly superior to Sappho and Elizabeth Barrett Browning. In the variety and brilliance of her imagery she suggests Shakespeare and Keats, without in any way imitating them. At a time when critics were acclaiming hack versifiers like Hannah F. Gould, Lydia H. Sigourney and Helen Hunt Jackson, not one of whom ever wrote a line of real poetry, Emily was quietly turning out in her beautiful cursive script some of the greatest lyrics in English.

The letters of Emily Dickinson are wrought of the purest poetry. It is hard to tell where the poetry stops and the letters begin. I can think of no greater treasure than a letter by Emily Dickinson. Almost always she wrote in pencil and signed simply "Emily," yet such unpretentious notes sometimes change hands for thousands of dollars.

The time is not far distant when even the fortune of an Arab potentate will not buy a letter or manuscript of this great poet.

That Bells should
ring, till all
should know
A soul had
gone to Heaven
Would seem
to me the more
the way
A good news
should be given.

Emily

Emily Dickinson. Handwritten poem signed "Emily"

RAND, AVERY & CO., PRINTERS.

Boston Sept. 24 [1]

Dear friend

Yours rec'd — I am now back here finishing up — only staid a few days in Concord, but they were mark'd days. Sunday, Emerson & his wife, son Edward & wife &c. gave me a dinner — two hours — every thing just right every way — a dozen people there (the family & relatives) — for my "part" I thought the old man in his serenity and alert quietude & withdrawnness & more eloquent grand, appropriate & impressive than ever — more indeed than could be described — Isn't it comforting that I have had — in the sunset as it were — so many significant affectionate hours with him under such quiet beautiful appropriate circumstances?

The book is done & will be in the market in a month or so — all about it has proceeded satisfactorily & I have had my own way in every thing — the old name "Leaves of Grass" is retained — it will be a $2 book — — I shall probably go on to New York in about a week — shall stay at Johnston's (address me there Mott avenue & 149th street N Y City) about a week or ten days — Besides this general death-gloom of the nation — have you heard of the sudden & dreadful death of our young friend Beatrice Gilchrist in performing some chemical experiment with ether? Joaquin Miller is here — is with me every day — Longfellow has been to see me — I have met O W Holmes, & old Mr James. With love Walt Whitman

Walt Whitman. Handwritten letter signed to John Burroughs, 1881. "Emerson . . . gave me a dinner . . . Joaquin Miller is here—is with me every day—Longfellow has been to see me—I have met O. W. Holmes . . ."

I have the honor of sending you, herewith, at your desire, the Prospectus of the "Penn Magazine," and should be grateful for any interest you would exert in its behalf.

With high respect.
Yr Ob. St.
Edgar A Poe

Edgar Allan Poe. Conclusion of a handwritten letter signed about the *Penn Magazine*

FINCA VIGIA, SAN FRANCISCO DE PAULA, CUBA
24/7/56

Dear Mr. Rider:

Thank you very much for your letter. The most readable of Faulkner is Sanctuary and Pylon. I think he is a no good son of a bitch myself. But some of the Southern stuff is good and some of the Negro stuff is very good. Also a short story called The Bear is worth reading. His last book A Fable isn't pure shit. It is impure diluted shit and there isn't a shit tester in the at Ichang where they ship the night soil from chungking to but would found it.

We used to smoke sailfish roe in the smokehouse here on the Finca and before that at K.W. It is very good.

Good luck to you and don't send any more airplanes.

Best always,
Ernest Hemingway

Ernest Hemingway. Handwritten letter signed

July, 1933

Don't expect me
I've gone fancy
I'm all set
With Bryan Dancy.
Scotty's
Michael's Berries
Back at midnight
Out with Fanny
F. Scott Fitz

F. Scott Fitzgerald. Handwritten verses signed, obviously penned while drunk

Dear Tim Jo:

This is a late reply to your letter — and a still later one to a former letter which I kept postponing to answer and finally never did! — but — well — you know how it is. Laziness is the only available excuse, I guess! And then I rather expected I'd meet you around the theatre sometime or other. Why is it you never come around? Or do you? I'm so little there myself that I might well have missed you. But I would like to have a talk with you sometime and hear how your work is coming along, etc.

Yes, I know Duncan Macdougal — used to know him quite well. As I remember, he wrote my agent about "A. C." in Australia and there was some hitch as the rights were already under option or something. Whether they still are, I don't know. I'd ask the people at the American Play Co. when I next get to town.

With all best wishes!
Eugene O'Neill

Eugene O'Neill. Handwritten letter signed about the rights to "A. C." (Anna Christie).

Pittsfield Nov. 16th 1857

Dear Sir — As my arrangement are about maturing, it is necessary for me to know of my positive engagement. And would therefore like to fix upon the time for lecturing in your part of the country, at one place or more, as you may have already arranged, or as may be hereafter arranged. —

I am engaged at Detroit on the 12th Jan. and would like to go on to you as speedily as may be from there. Would 15th or 16th Jan. at Rockford answer? Or as you know the routes &c better than I, perhaps you could name the earliest day after the 12th which would best accommodate me. Please write at once, addressing me at Boston, Mass. care of Chief Justice Shaw. Yours &c

H Melville

Herman Melville. Handwritten letter signed about a lecture tour

Act. 1.
=
Scene 1.
=
A village cottage, with back door looking into garden. A closet & the ordinary furniture. Old lady of 50, cheaply & neatly dressed. Wears spectacles — knitting.
=
Aunt Winny. (The old lady) — Tom!
[no answer.] Tom! [no answer.] What's gone with that boy, I wonder? You

Mark Twain. First page of the original manuscript of *Tom Sawyer*, originally conceived as a play with "Aunt Winny" instead of "Aunt Polly"

Aunt Betsey — the wickedness of this world — but I haven't time to moralize this morning.

Good-bye.

Sam. Clemens

P.S. — All send their love.

Mark Twain. Conclusion of a youthful letter, about 1850 (age 15), signed "Sam Clemens"

powers under control; consequently, also, I am writing in my work-a-day hand, with my every-day pen. — Otherwise this handsome page would have tricked me into doing my very carefulest & nicest — with a brand-new pen — Thus:

With great Respect I remain Yours Very Truly, Samuel L. Clemens, Mark Twain

— instead of dashing the thing off in my loose & reckless every-day style —Thus:

Truly Yours S L. Clemens Mark Twain.

Hartford, June 11, 1887.

Mark Twain. Second page of a handwritten note, signed several times, displaying his handwriting on good behavior as well as his regular "loose & reckless every-day style"

MUSKET-AND-SABER
HISTORIANS **21**

"I have observed," wrote Bernal Díaz in his *Conquest of New Spain*, "that before beginning to write their histories the most famous chroniclers compose a prologue in exalted language, in order to give lustre and repute to their narrative. . . . But I, being no scholar, dare not attempt any such preface. . . .

"I am now an old man, over eighty-four years of age, and have lost both sight and hearing. . . . I have gained no wealth to leave to my children and descendants, except this true story."

With these words begins the incredible tale of how Hernán Cortés, with only about five hundred men, conquered and enslaved the land of Montezuma and seized the great treasure of the Aztecs. Bernal Díaz, who fought with Cortés in many battles where the Indian arrows were so thick they blotted out the sun, came home with many wounds and no riches. But his simple and direct story of one of the most exciting adventures and daring military feats in history has all the power and beauty of Thucydides.

Letters and documents bearing Díaz's ornamental signature turn up occasionally and they are worth many times their weight in doubloons.

Cortés himself penned five long letters, models of historic elegance, to the Emperor Charles V, recounting his exploits in the conquest of New Spain. If you can find the original manuscripts of these famous letters, you will possess a greater treasure than a frigateload of the golden artifacts the conquistadors took out of Mexico.

Many of the early Spanish historians like Bernal Díaz del Castillo and Cortés wrote their histories with Toledo blades before they picked up their quills. Doubtless they sent out many letters about their adventures, but such dramatic fragments of history have long ago fallen prey to worms and mold.

The first letter ever written from America was hastily scrawled by Columbus on board a pitching *Santa Maria* during a terrible storm which threatened to capsize the little ship in its homeward voyage. The letter was sealed in a cask and pitched into the sea by Columbus himself in the hope that should his vessel founder, his record of discovery would reach friendly lands.

Bernal Díaz del Castillo

Hernán Cortés

Christopher Columbus

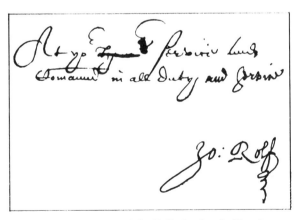

Of plimoth plantation

And first of ÿ occasion, and jndusments ther vnto; the which
that ÿ may truly vnfould, ÿ must begine at ÿ very roote & rise
of ÿ same · The which ÿ shall endeuor to manefest in a plaine
stile; with singuler regard vnto ÿ simple trueth in all things,
at least as ~~farr~~ near as my slender judgmente can attaine
the same

1. Chapter

It is well knowne vnto ÿ godly, and judicious; how euer since ÿ
first breaking out of ÿ lighte of ÿ gospell, in our Honourable nation of England (which was ÿ first of nations, whom ÿ Lord adorned ther with, after ÿ grosse darknes of popery which had couer-
ed, & ouerspred ÿ christian world) what warrs, & oppositions euer
since, satan hath raised, maintained, and continued against the

William Bradford. Handwritten beginning of Bradford's *History of Plimoth Plantation*

Bartolomé de Las Casas, historian of the Indies

Captain John Smith

John Rolfe, husband of Pocahontas

This historic letter of the admiral has never come to light and I like to think that somewhere in the Azores, lodged high between ocean-girt rocks and bearded with seaweed, lies the old cask containing his dramatic message. What would Columbus's great letter be worth? If I owned it, ten million dollars would not beguile it from me.

The early narratives of Spanish explorers, often filled with tales of brutal cruelties inflicted on the Indians, are certainly matched by the English chroniclers of the New World.

Most redoubtable champion of early liars and author of *The Generall Historie of Virginia*, Captain John Smith doubtless dispatched many a missive extolling the virtues of the Jamestown colony, but the heedless recipients evidently read them with relish and used them to start their fires. Whenever anything from Smith's pen appears on the market it fetches a resounding price.

Among the more delectable of Smith's inventions is the famous story of how Pocahontas saved his life at the risk of her own. What a prize would be a letter recounting Smith's tale!

By comparison with the Spanish historians and John Smith, the New England chroniclers seem like postal profligates. The Pilgrim fathers were aware of the importance of their mission and documented it with a profusion of histories. William Bradford's *History of Plimoth Plantation*, indited in his artistic and very legible script, is a pious record of misconduct, for the Pilgrims treated the Indians almost as badly as did the Spaniards.

Inspired by religious fanaticism, the Pilgrims landed at Plymouth to establish a colony where only *their* beliefs would be tolerated. Dissenters were clapped into the stocks, imprisoned, whipped or, like Roger Williams, driven out. But religious intolerance was not the Pilgrims' only contribution to America. They were the first to legalize slavery in the New World, and their descendants, more than a century later, were among the first to abolish black slavery when they discovered they could bring indentured servants (actually slaves) from

John Alden

Myles Standish

Luys Hernandez Biedma, historian of De Soto

John Winthrop

Dear Sir
I wish the Ladys all the happiness in the world: but not enough to make 'em take root in Ireland.

Your most faithfull Servt
W Byrd.

William Byrd II (of Westover). Conclusion of a handwritten letter signed

Ireland and the Continent—pretty girls and strong boys—without making the heavy investment necessary to buy slaves from Africa. And while this white slavery flourished in New England, descendants of the Pilgrims were organizing anti-slavery associations to fight black slavery in the South!

The New Englanders' treatment of the Indians was brutal and immoral. After a fierce war, the people of Massachusetts Bay finally cornered and slew the last of the great Indian leaders, King Philip. They utterly wiped out his tribe. They slaughtered the old men and women, sold the young boys into slavery and kept the girls as servants or concubines. As for Philip, they cut off his head and flaunted it on a pike as a warning to other copper-colored heathen.

The documents of the Massachusetts Bay historians who set down these malefactions are very scarce but for the most part obtainable, especially when affixed to legal papers. Autographs of some of the more humane historians, like Daniel Gookin and Thomas Mayhew, occasionally come to light and excite great interest among philographers.

I can never hold in my hands any paper bearing the signature of John Eliot, the "Apostle to the Indians," who translated the Bible into Natick, without a feeling akin to reverence. By his understanding and sympathy toward the First Americans, Eliot offset much of the mischief done by the Pilgrim fathers and their descendants.

It is refreshing to turn to the later Virginia historians Robert Beverly and William Byrd II of Westover. Byrd's _History of the Dividing Line_ is an amusing narrative, full of adventures related in a clear, pleasant style. For anyone who may be interested, I pass along Byrd's prescription for impotence: Eat lots of bear meat.

John Williams, author of _The Redeemed Captive_

Nathaniel Morton, author of _New Englands Memoriall_

William Hubbard, chronicler of the Indian wars

Daniel Gookin

These two young men Tho: Foster & Sam: Gary have approved themselves both by theire confession of Christ, & conversation in christ, to be Godly & are received to the full comunion of the church.

John Eliot.

John Eliot. Handwritten document signed, admitting two men into the church

Father Sahagun, Mexican historian

Father Torobio Motolinia, New World historian

Gonzales Fernandez Oviedo, chronicler of the Indies

Christopher Columbus. Handwritten letter signed

I presume not to add a Word as to our Mat
ters, nor not to urge to you Remembrance
yr Maxime of Queen Experience [Secun
da Cogitationes Meliores] only to pray
you to remember yt all Lands & all Nations
are but a Drop of a Bucket in ye
Eyes of ye King of Kings & Lord of
Lords whom I humbly beseech to ad
orne yor heads with yt heavenly Crowne
at yor parting from us [Beati Pacifici]
So prays yor most unworthy Svant
Roger Williams

Roger Williams. Handwritten letter signed

ENTERTAINERS
22 PLUS

Edwin Forrest

Edwin Booth. Conclusion of a handwritten letter signed

Harry Houdini. Original profile silhouette, with signature

Not long before John Barrymore died, he starred on Broadway in a farce called *My Dear Children*. Although the amnesic actor blew many of his lines, he was a brilliant improvisator, who zealously mocked his own flamboyance. From the first row of the balcony I watched him cavort, awed by his mastery of the stage. At one point he totally forgot his lines and uttered what I thought was a delectable *bon mot*. I roared with laughter, but the rest of the house was silent.

Barrymore paused, held up his hand for the onstage cast to freeze and advanced to the apron of the stage. Looking directly at me, he bowed and said, "Thank you, my friend."

Of letters by theatrical figures, Barrymore's are among those most sought after. He wrote seldom, but his few notes were usually comic and incisive.

The great stars of the footlights have always evoked the interest of historians. Starting with Edwin Forrest and Junius Brutus Booth, their letters are quite readily available and eminently readable. I once owned a collection of more than fifty of Edwin Booth's letters to a close friend who constantly nagged him for hitting the bottle. In one letter Booth wrote: "Your note urging me to stop drinking has so upset and depressed me that I have downed a whole pint of whisky while reading and re-reading it."

The great showman Harry Houdini, who wrote out his motto—"Secure knots secure not Houdini"—hundreds of times for admirers, was himself a philographer. He owned a large collection of the letters of Robert Houdin, a French magician from whom he took his name and whom he later unmasked as an impostor. Many of Houdini's most interesting notes are about his exposure of crooked mediums. There was no trick the mediums could perform that Houdini could not pull off better. Once he snapped a photograph, surrounded by clouds of ectoplasm, of a young man who was killed in the Boer War and of whom no photograph was known to exist. This feat so awed his friend Sir Arthur Conan Doyle, a believer in spiritualism, that Doyle proclaimed Houdini a "natural medium." Houdini then explained: "My assistant got the picture from a group photograph in a rare regimental history at the British

Jenny Lind (Goldschmidt). Conclusion of a handwritten letter in French, signed with her married name

Julia Marlowe

Laurence Barrett

Museum. I had the photograph blown up and surrounded by filmy clouds. Thus I was fully prepared when the boy's mother asked me to photograph him in spirit land."

The master of humbug, Phineas T. Barnum, has always held the interest of collectors. His letters, penned in a rapid and sloppy script, are readily obtainable. Most of them are about circus or museum matters. Of a rival white elephant he wrote:

The opposition "White Elephant" which I proved was a common small elephant painted white in Liverpool died the other day according to its owner's declaration but it was "dyed" already, and its only death consisted in rubbing off the white paint and restoring it to its original color! My elephant stands the test with all intelligent people. But "the masses," whom a writer called "them asses" believe in nothing short of a snow white elephant all over, and therefore don't think much of mine.

Letters of Barnum about his famous midget, Tom Thumb, or his enormous elephant, Jumbo, are especially sought by circus historians. Barnum's greatest triumph came when he hired Jenny Lind, the "Swedish nightingale," for an American tour. A huge and enthusiastic crowd, all shills hired by Barnum, met her at the boat and showered her with bouquets. The resultant publicity made her tour a phenomenal success.

Jenny Lind wrote many letters, a few in English but most of them in German. She described her activities with enthusiasm and her epistles brim with Old World charm.

Recently there has been a great interest in opera stars. Caruso, who once was arrested for pinching a lady's fanny in Central Park, was as much an American as an Italian, for it was in this country that he scored his biggest hits. A skilled caricaturist, Caruso made hundreds—nay, thousands—of sketches of himself and other opera stars. I can think of no more exciting or picturesque souvenir than such a relic of the great tenor. Most letters of other opera stars are still modestly priced, but the value climbs almost daily.

Among virtuosos and conductors, Arturo Toscanini is preeminent with collectors. Despite the fact that he wrote thousands of letters and signed tens of thousands of photographs, the demand is so lively that the cupboards of every autograph dealer are always bare of his artistic scrawl. Toscanini liked flashy ink and often signed in resplendent red or green.

Barnum's dwarfs: Charles S. Stratton ("Tom Thumb"), Lavinia Stratton (his wife), Minnie Warren and G. Will Nutt (Commodore Nutt)

Enrico Caruso. Self-portrait signed

Charlotte Cushman

James H. Hackett

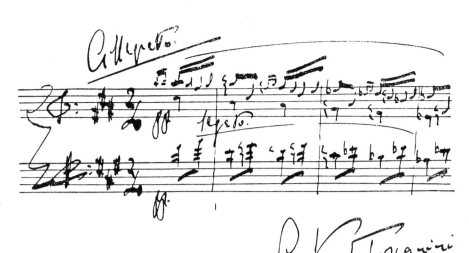

Arturo Toscanini. Handwritten music signed

Dear Clara –

Thanks a thousand times for you letter – and your damnably incisive memory!! The first chance I get – I will go out with Bruce – It was grand seeing you I hope as soon as things slow down a bit – we can all get together with Andy Martin and relax!! – all the best.

Jack –

John Barrymore. Handwritten letter signed "Jack," to a woman about her "damnably incisive memory!!"

John Barrymore

Ethel Barrymore

Lionel Barrymore

William Gillette

Helena Modjeska

Fanny Kemble

G. Harrison, Esq.
        Dear Sir,
                I do not think it
at all possible for me to play with you at
Troy after the 20th Sept. I appear for
a few nights this week at Albany — if you
could open the next week, I might arrange
to play with you — but I have to visit
Portland, and then appear at Niblo's on
the 3rd October.

                Yours, very truly,
                        WE Burton

Glen Cove, L.I.
    Sep. 4, 1856,

William E. Burton. Handwritten letter signed about his theatrical engagements

Lillian Russell

Lillian Russell

Mary Martin

Mary Martin

Lester Wallack

Lester Wallack

Laura Keene

Laura Keene, star of *Our American Cousin* on April 14, 1865, the night Lincoln was shot in Ford's Theatre

Best wishes (and please don't call me "Sir"!!!)

Cornelia Otis Skinner

Cornelia Otis Skinner. Handwritten note signed: "Please don't call me 'Sir'!!!"

Lola Montez

Lola Montez

John Drew

John Drew

Shirley Booth

Shirley Booth

Helen Hayes

Helen Hayes

P. T. Barnum. Signed photograph

Howard Thurston

Howard Thurston, magician

Katharine Cornell

Katharine Cornell

Baltimore Museum
Admit Two

Chang Eng

Chang and Eng. The original Siamese twins, born in Siam but became naturalized American citizens. Museum pass signed

Marie
Emilie
Cécile
Annette
Yvonne Dionne

The Dionne quintuplets

RECORD

Jumped High Bridge, July 18, '86—110 ft.
" Brooklyn Bridge July 23, '86—140 ft.
" Covington Bridge, May 7, '87—110 ft.
" Pittsburg, Bridge. July 4, '87—100 ft.
Swam from Albany to New York, 150 miles, in 6 days, 1 hr., June 16 to 20, 1888.
Jumped Poughkeepsie Bridge, Nov. 9, '88—223 ft
Swam from High Bridge to Battery, 12 miles, in 3 hrs. 60 min., April 20, '89.
Jumped Passaic Falls, May 21, '89—105 ft.
Jumped High Bridge, Cleveland. July 4, '89—160 ft.
Jumped Pawtucket Falls, R. I. Aug. 8'89—60 ft.

STEVE BRODIE,
CHAMPION BRIDGE JUMPER AND SWIMMER OF THE WORLD,
•114 BOWERY,•
New York, Sept 17th 1894

City Editor—Dear Sir—
I have just sent the following offer to Col. Breckenridge & am anxiously awaiting his answer which I hope will be one of acceptance
Yours Sincerely Steve Brodie
Col. Breckenridge

Steve Brodie, famed for jumping off the Brooklyn Bridge, from which originated the expression "take a Brodie." Handwritten letter signed

I make it a very strong point never to give my autograph to anybody

very truly,

Eugen Sandow

Eugen Sandow, circus strong man. Handwritten note signed, refusing to send his autograph

"The more you look, You never see nothing;"

A. Herrmann

A. Herrmann, magician. Handwritten quotation signed

Emma Eames Story — Emma Eames Story

Hazel Scott — Hazel Scott

Lawrence Tibbett — Lawrence Tibbett

Leopold Stokowski — Leopold Stokowski

Lillian Nordica — Lillian Nordica

John McCormack — John McCormack

Best wishes from Grace Moore

Grace Moore. Original profile silhouette signed

Mischa Elman

Eugene Ormandy

Nathan Milstein

Roland Hayes

Van Cliburn

Isaac Stern

Paul Whiteman

Vladimir Horowitz

Josef Hofmann

Leopold Auer

Harry Lauder. Self-portrait signed

Helen Morgan

"Fats" Waller

Paul Robeson

Gene Krupa

Leopold Damrosch

Harry James

Geraldine Farrar

Benny Goodman

Theodore Thomas

Walter Damrosch

Bruno Walter

Anton Seidl

FATAL
23 ENCOUNTERS

Andrew Jackson. Last line from a handwritten letter signed

Marquis de Montcalm. Last two lines and signature from a handwritten letter signed

Major General Pakenham

On September 13, 1759, on the Plains of Abraham near Quebec, General James Wolfe, thirty-two, and the Marquis of Montcalm, forty-seven, clashed in a bloody battle that decided the future of Canada.

The British general, Wolfe, was mortally wounded. Barely conscious, he heard the cry, "They run! They run!"

"Who runs?" he asked, raising his head.

"The enemy, sir."

"Thank God!" said Wolfe. "Now I can die content."

Montcalm was also fatally wounded. His last words were "Don't be troubled for me, my good friends."

Wolfe's stratagem of scaling a dangerous cliff with his entire army to surprise the French on the plains above has always impressed me. I have often thought that the bit of lead that cut him down at thirty-two determined the fate of the future United States, for had Wolfe lived, who can doubt that he would have commanded the British army against Washington? And would Washington have coped successfully with the daring and artful Wolfe?

Autographs of Wolfe and Montcalm are very elusive. Most of Wolfe's letters date from his barracks years in England and Montcalm's are nearly always about pedestrian family affairs. Still, it is exciting to touch and look upon the handwriting of these two heroic young men who lived and died in an age when patriotism was in flower.

The most famous infantry clash in the War of 1812 accomplished little because the war was already over. Unaware that a treaty of peace had been signed at Ghent on December 24, 1814, the British commanding officer near New Orleans, Sir Edward Pakenham, decided he was going to drive the entrenched Americans, commanded by Andrew Jackson, out of New Orleans. Pakenham was brave and smart, but he was also

Marquis de Montcalm. Page from a handwritten letter on military maneuvers

rash. On the morning of January 8, 1815, he sent up the signal rocket to storm the American positions. The wily Jackson was ready. Pakenham was struck by a ball, swayed and pitched forward. His troops, melting under the deadly fire of the Americans, fell back. The British lost two thousand killed or wounded and the Americans eight killed and thirteen wounded. It was a great victory that humbled an arrogant Britain and set Jackson's course for the White House.

In twenty-five years I have seen only one document of Pakenham, but scores of intriguing Jackson letters have passed through my hands. Penned in a virile frontier script in thick, iron-gall ink that often corrodes the pure rag paper, Jackson's letters are always outspoken, sometimes tempestuous. There was nothing of the scholar about "Old Hickory" and his rough expressions still have the bark on, but he certainly ranks as one of the great letter writers among soldiers and Presidents.

On the morning of June 25, 1876, General George A. Custer, in search of the chief encampment of the hostile Sioux and Cheyenne, was told of a large Indian village just discovered by his scouts on the Little Big Horn River in Montana territory.

Statistics show that five white men were killed for every

George A. Custer

Sitting Bull

Sitting Bull

Major Frederick Benteen, second in command to Custer at the battle of the Little Big Horn. By ignoring irrational orders from Custer, Benteen saved his troops from certain destruction. He was, in characteristic army fashion, court-martialed.

Indian in the frontier wars. The Indians were tough fighters, crack shots who rode as if glued to their horses. There was an army maxim that you should not attack Indians unless you outnumber them. The report from Custer's scouts indicated that he was outnumbered at least two to one and possibly the odds against him were even greater.

"We will destroy the fighting power of the Sioux and Cheyenne forever," said Custer to his officers. "A quick, three-pronged surprise attack and it will be all over for them."

As Custer got his troops ready for the surprise assault, one of his Crow scouts, Half-yellow-face, said to Son-of-the-morning-star (Custer): "Do not divide your men. There are too many of the enemy for us, even if we all stay together."

Custer replied, "You do the scouting and I will attend to the fighting."

Half-yellow-face stripped and began painting his face. Custer was familiar with Crow customs and he knew that when an Indian expected to go before the Great Spirit he put special paint on his face.

"Why are you doing all this?" he asked Half-yellow-face.

"Because you and I are going home today, and by a trail that is strange to us both."

It was to be the final confrontation between Custer and his old enemy the fierce medicine man Sitting Bull. When the dust cleared over the battlefield at the Little Big Horn, Custer and his entire immediate command were dead.

Custer's letters about his Indian campaigns are very scarce and elicit enormous prices from collectors. They are among the most revealing of frontier documents. You can almost smell the gunpowder and hear the swish of arrows as you read them.

Andrew Jackson. Sight draft addressed to James Monroe and issued by Jackson at New Orleans to pay his victorious troops

(No.   )

New Orleans Feb: 16th 1815

Exchange for $25000

Ten Days after Sight pay this _my_ SECOND OF EXCHANGE, (First and Third unpaid) to _Joseph Saul Esqr. Cashier of the Bank of Orleans_ or Order, _Twenty five thousand Dollars_ for Value received, which place to Account of _Iv your Obt. Servt._

The Honbl. _James Monroe_
Secretary of War

Andrew Jackson
Major Genl. commdg.
7th Me. District

Alexander Hamilton. Handwritten note signed

Daniel Sickles

Aaron Burr

Alexander Hamilton

Aaron Burr. Signed in old age (1833)

Philip Barton Key

Custer's wife, Elizabeth Bacon, received hundreds of letters from her celebrated husband. Many of them she published and some of them she gave away. But there were others she never let anyone look at. Just before she died, Libbie got the suppressed letters together and built a big bonfire in her backyard. I flinch whenever I think of this unpardonable conflagration.

Alexander Hamilton and Aaron Burr were bitter rivals. As New York lawyers, they faced one another in the courtroom. As opposing politicians, they squabbled over power. As handsome men, they vied for attention from the ladies at every ball. It was almost inevitable that they trade bullets on the field of honor.

They met at Weehawken, New Jersey, on the banks of the Hudson, on the morning of July 11, 1804. Hamilton fired into the air. Burr shot to kill, and Hamilton slumped forward, mortally wounded. Burr was forced to fly by night from New York and spend the rest of his long life as an outcast.

As his old enemy lay dying on the afternoon of the duel, Burr scribbled a note to Dr. David Hosack to ask about Hamilton's condition. Not long ago I appraised this unpublished note at several thousand dollars.

The letters of Burr and Hamilton are strikingly similar. During the Revolution, both served as aides to Washington, though Burr only briefly, and their military letters relate to the same subjects. Romantic indeed are letters in the handwriting of young Colonel Hamilton, signed by George Washington. Hamilton also turned out vast numbers of letters as secretary of the treasury, many containing astute observations on the art of raising money. An economist recently told me: "If Hamilton were alive today, I have no doubt he could balance the national budget."

Hamilton and Burr penned hundreds of legal letters and I recently sold a court document signed by both, a unique souvenir of their lifelong feud.

The bloodiest duel ever fought with pistols took place at Bladensburg, Maryland, on March 22, 1820, when an irate Captain James Barron faced the Tripolitan hero Commodore Stephen Decatur. Barron was incensed by Decatur's criticism of his actions during a naval battle and challenged him to

God Bless you all
James Barron

James Barron

Stephen Decatur

Done in Triplicate at Ghent
the twenty fourth day of December
one thousand eight hundred and
fourteen

Gambier

Henry Goulburn

William Adams

John Quincy Adams

J. A. Bayard

H. Clay

Jon a Russell

Albert Gallatin

Signatures on the treaty of peace signed at Ghent, December 24, 1814, ending the War of 1812. Among the celebrated signers are John Quincy Adams, Henry Clay and Albert Gallatin.

James Shields

Abraham Lincoln

exchange bullets at twenty paces. Both men were expert shots. Decatur's intention was to wound his adversary in the hip. Barron's avowed purpose was to kill the commodore.

At the word "Fire," Barron spun around and fell to the ground, hit in the hip and bleeding badly. After a few moments, he managed to raise himself on one elbow. He took steady aim at Decatur, who stood erect, awaiting the shot. The ball struck Decatur in the belly, the favorite target of duelists, and within a few hours the famous commodore was dead. Barron recovered and spent the rest of his naval life "awaiting orders."

The letters of these two officers do not turn up often. Decatur's letters are usually mere routine naval orders that convey little of the drama of his great career. Barron's are more unusual, for he was short-fused and was forever getting into or out of some difficulty.

There is seldom anything comical about murder. But when Congressman Daniel Sickles discovered what he called "a guilty intimacy" between his wife and Philip Barton Key, United States attorney for the District of Columbia, he set out to avenge himself in an unusual way. On the afternoon of February 27, 1859, he took his pistol and waited in the streets of Washington for his quarry. As soon as he spotted the cuckolder, he began chasing him, firing as he ran. Key dodged from tree to tree and from bush to bush in an effort to elude Sickles's bullets. The frantic pursuit scattered spectators and ended only when Sickles scored a fatal hit.

Sickles was tried for murder. He pleaded the unwritten law and after a twenty-day trial filled with lurid testimony was found not guilty. Sickles later became a distinguished general in the Civil War.

Key's autograph letters are very scarce, but not long ago I acquired and sold his original oath as United States attorney for Columbia. Far more abundant are the papers of his murderer, whose war correspondence reflects the brilliance and excitement of a gallant career. Even Sickles's signature captures the color and boldness of his personality.

Some duelistic encounters never came off. As an Illinois lawyer in 1842, Lincoln was challenged to a duel by the state auditor, James Shields, who was aggrieved over several derogatory letters in the newspaper that were attributed to Lincoln. After some verbal dalliance, Lincoln reluctantly accepted the challenge. He chose broadswords as weapons and when the two met on the field of honor, Shields, a much shorter man, with much shorter arms, wisely agreed to settle the dispute without bloodshed.

is your courage & fidelity w.^h have
involved you in this business — Indeed
I hear on all hands but one sentiment
& one hope exprest — that you may
emerge w.^h as little suffering of mind
as posible — Meanwhile your old Regiment
sends you an assurance of our continued
Confidence & affection.

I am ever My Dear Colonel
Your faithfull & affe. Servant
Jam: Wolfe

James Wolfe. Last page of a handwritten letter signed

Fort Lincoln D.T.
Sunday 5th

My dear Little Girl

George A. Custer. First page of a handwritten letter to his wife, Libbie: ". . . it will all be the same one hundred years hence."

Hermitage
Oct.r 25.th 1842 —

Miss Alice Egerton;
My dear Miss,

Andrew Jackson. Handwritten letter signed to a young lady who had requested a lock of his hair. Sending the lock, Jackson notes: "I shall meet you in the realms of bliss."

George A. Custer. Photograph signed as major general

Alexander Hamilton. Handwritten letter signed supporting John Adams against Thomas Jefferson

Aaron Burr. Last paragraph of a handwritten letter signed

THE TOUGH
AND THE ROUGH 24

Babe Ruth

Babe Ruth

"Not now," snapped Reggie Jackson to the twenty-three-year-old black woman who had asked for his autograph in a theater while the home-run king was watching a movie.

The woman left, but came back later to demand his signature, this time insolently.

"Absolutely not," reiterated the slugger.

Sharp words flew. Soon the two were wrestling in the aisle. The brawl drove most of the audience out of the theater and wound up with the girl suing Reggie and Reggie countersuing for harassment.

A whole scenario for a signature worth about a dollar!

In earlier days, the great sports heroes treated their fans with gallantry. Take Babe Ruth and Lou Gehrig. Long after the other players had showered and left the ball park, Ruth and Gehrig were still on the field signing baseballs. Though they must have signed ten thousand during their careers, such spheroids are nevertheless highly prized and fetch fancy prices whenever they come on the market.

Most sports personalities today are generous with their signatures, but ball park collectors are as pestiferous as gadflies armed with pencils instead of stings. Understandably the heroes of the sports pages are hot-tempered.

Joe DiMaggio once presented Marilyn Monroe, whom he was courting, with a check for ten thousand dollars. It was a very private gift and Marilyn cashed it privately. Joe was furious a month later when his canceled checks came back from the bank minus the "secret" check with Marilyn's endorsement. He called the bank.

"Get that check or there's going to be trouble."

The manager apologized.

"I want the check, not an apology," said Joe.

The word was flashed to the tellers and clerks. "If the check is back by morning, no questions will be asked. Otherwise, someone is going to get fired."

One of the most dramatic souvenirs in the history of baseball was "discovered" in the files the next morning. No Broadway columnist ever got wind of the gift or the theft.

There are some sports—hockey, tennis, basketball and

Best Wishes
Lou Gehrig

Lou Gehrig

Joe Di Maggio

Joe Di Maggio

Abner Doubleday
Bvt. Major General, U. S. A.

Abner Doubleday, originator of baseball

Chas. Gehringer
Baseball Hall of Fame

Charles Gehringer

Hank Aaron Hank Aaron

My best always
Jack Nicklaus

Jack Nicklaus

Muhammad Ali

Muhammad Ali

John L. Sullivan. Handwritten slogan signed: "I never break my word."

Jack Dempsey

Jack Dempsey

Yours Pal
John L. Sullivan

John L. Sullivan. Signature signed late in life

Yours Truly
Jas J Corbett
June 11/92

James J. Corbett

Gene Tunney

Gene Tunney

soccer, for instance—that have not yet tugged at the wallets of philographers. And even the best letters of the superheroes of golf, such as Bobby Jones and Jack Nicklaus, are autographically inexpensive.

The most explosive figures in sports are the heavyweight champs, whose deeds and misdeeds are frequently front-page stuff. John L. Sullivan, the mightiest of the old-timers, always obliged with a corny sentiment and a bold signature when confronted with an autograph album. I once owned a collection of John L.'s letters to an old friend which revealed that the Boston Strong Boy, under his cocky ferocious façade, was a lovable and maudlin man. Jim Corbett, the slick boxer who felled this giant of the ring, prided himself on a florid signature and his letters are models of calligraphic elegance. Just as Corbett and Sullivan were rivals in the arena, so they vied for penmanship honors. The prize, if one were awarded, would have to go to Corbett, who started his career as a bank teller in San Francisco.

Almost every heavyweight who ever wore the championship belt was an unusual or exciting personality. There was the bruising Jack Johnson, who almost never wrote a letter, and the prolific Gene Tunney, a student of Shakespeare, whose fancy footwork in the ring was not unlike the verbal facility in his correspondence. The few letters of Muhammad Ali that have come my way invariably reveal the underlying sincerity and courage of this remarkable man.

The greatest athlete who ever lived, the Sac and Fox Indian Jim Thorpe, wrote many interesting letters, some of which discussed his endless battle with the bottle. Whenever Thorpe entered a bar, which was often, he was hailed with joy, slapped on the back and plied with drinks. Liquor may have elevated his spirits but it did not improve his handwriting. I have seen erratic scrawls which were doubtless inspired by whiskey, for his usual hand was a fine, Palmer-like script.

First day cover signed by seven baseball "greats," including Stan Musial, "Dizzy" Dean, Ted Williams, Lou Boudreau and Bob Feller

Roberto Clemente

Connie Mack

Ty Cobb

Willie Shoemaker

Ty Cobb. Full signature from a contract.

Robert Fitzsimmons

Joe Frazier

Robert T. Jones, Jr.

Jack Johnson

Glenn Cunningham

Joe Louis

Rocky Graziano

Willie Mays

Sugar Ray Robinson

Mickey Mantle

Helen Wills Moody

Harold ("Red") Grange

Bob Mathias

Amos Alonzo Stagg

It has been my experience that tobacco slows up the reflexes of athletes, lowers their morale and does nothing constructive.

Athletes who smoke are the careless type and any advertisement to the effect that smoking cigarettes helps an athlete is a falsehood.

Yours very truly,

K. K. Rockne
Director of Athletics

Knute Rockne. Typed opinions on the effect of smoking on athletes

Grantland Rice

Grantland Rice

Jim Thorpe. Handwritten letter signed to Irving Wallace about a story concerning his life in New York

HEROES OF THE
25 LONE STAR STATE

Senator Sam Houston was a big, powerful man, lithe and sun-browned, with dark hair and fierce eyes, like one of the Indians among whom he once lived. The Cherokees called him "the Raven," but his senatorial colleagues had another name for him—"the great 'I am' Houston."

Houston got this strange moniker because of the way he scrawled "Sam" in his signature. It looked like "I am" and Houston wrote it as large as the sheet under his pen. In the autograph albums of the time, his huge signature fills an entire page. Beneath his name appears a defiant paraph, proclaiming the strength and courage of the writer.

During his long career as a soldier and statesman, the hero of Texas and avenger of the Alamo wrote hundreds of letters. Those on military affairs are by far the most interesting and revealing, for Houston showed even more daring on the battlefield than on the rostrum.

Houston's compatriots are also an intriguing group: the astute presidents of Texas—Mirabeau B. Lamar, David G. Burnet and Anson Jones—and the great colonizers Moses Austin and his brilliant son, Stephen F. Austin, both of whom signed as often in Spanish as in English.

Whoever writes of the history of Texas must perforce tell sad stories of the deaths of patriots. Most famed in the saga of heroic deaths is Colonel David Crockett, an adventurer from Tennessee who joined the beleaguered garrison of Texans at the Alamo in San Antonio and died with one hundred and eighty-two others when Santa Anna stormed the little fort in March 1836.

Crockett's letters are as dramatic and homespun as his buckskin jacket and coonskin cap. He warred perpetually against his political foe, Andrew Jackson—"King Andrew I," as he called him. Crockett's rough script and atrocious spelling add a rugged charm to his lively prose.

In 1834 Crockett helped to prepare an autobiography, a vigorous, almost quixotic recital of his frontier adventures and foray into Congress. From manuscripts that have passed through my hands I have discovered that this celebrated autobiography, an American classic, was ghost-written, prob-

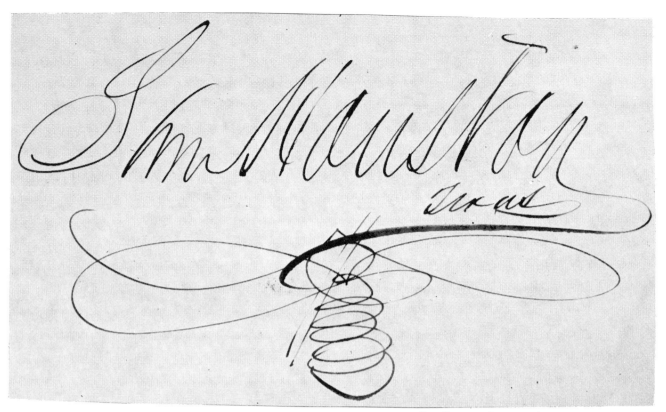

Sam Houston. Signature from an album, actual size

Moses Austin

Stephen F. Austin. Signature in Spanish

John C. Hays, founder of Texas Rangers

From the day that capt.
Kraats interd Texas with
his company he was in
=view, and will be allowed
pay for two months in=
advance.

Sam Houston

City of Houston,
11th may 1835.

Sam Houston. Handwritten note signed

David Crockett. Inscription from his autobiography, penned and signed by Crockett, testifying that "this Book was written by my self and [is] the only genuine history of my life that ever has been written."

ably by Thomas Chilton, although Crockett vehemently claimed the authorship.

When the Mexicans assaulted the Alamo, Santa Anna found Colonel Crockett still alive, wielding his empty musket as a club and surrounded by a circle of dead and dying Mexicans. Crockett was seized and brought before him.

"Shoot him," ordered the Mexican general.

Furious, Crockett sprang at Santa Anna, but before he could touch him, half a dozen Mexican sabers were sheathed in his body.

So popular was Crockett as a folk hero in his own day that had he survived the Alamo, I have no doubt he would have been elected President of the United States.

Ill in his room at the time of the Mexican assault was Colonel James Bowie, co-commander of the Alamo, a tough frontiersman who shares with his brother, Rezin P. Bowie, the distinction of popularizing the heavy, broad-bladed knife that bears their name.

Santa Anna's forces found Bowie slain in the bed from which he was unable to rise. At the door of Bowie's adobe room were two dead Mexicans, victims of the colonel's pistols, and over him lay a third, a bowie knife thrust into his belly.

Bowie's letters are extremely elusive and even routine documents in his rugged script excite great interest whenever they appear on the philographic market.

"How can I get an exciting letter of Colonel William Barret Travis?" is a question often put to me by collectors of Texana. The answer is, "You can't, unless you are uncommonly lucky." The handsome young attorney who was in command of the Alamo on that fateful day in 1836 was only twenty-seven when he died. His few surviving letters are zealously guarded in Texan archives.

But there is this hope. On rare occasions legal documents of Travis surface on philographic waters and my advice is this: "Snap one up, before the few remaining disappear forever into public collections."

James Bowie

William Barret Travis

James Bowie. Two paragraphs from a handwritten letter about his inadequate troops. "Our force is very small . . . It would be a waste of men to put our brave little band against thousands."

The Alamo. Original, unpublished watercolor by Edward Everett, 1847

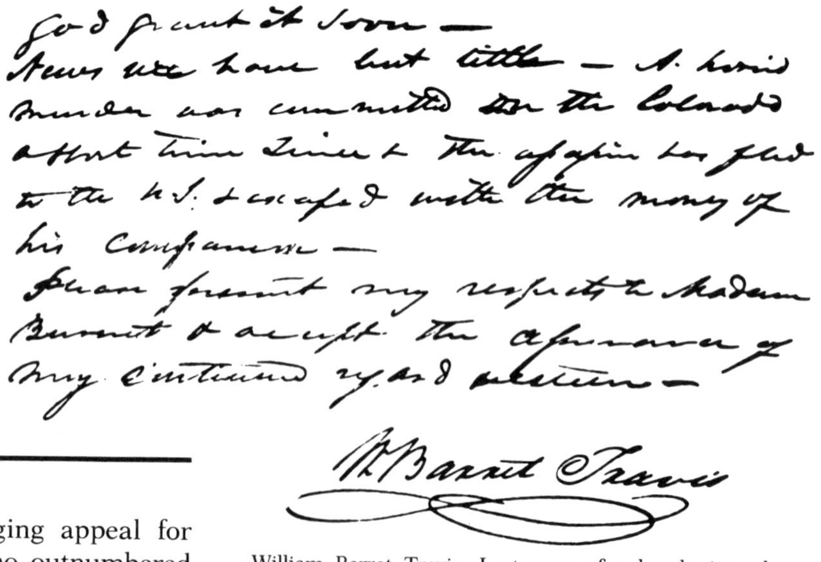

God grant it soon—
News we have but little— A horrid
murder was committed on the Colorado
a short time since & the assassin has fled
to the U.S. & escaped with the money of
his companion—
Please present my respects to Madam
Burnet & accept the assurance of
my continued regard & esteem—

W. Barret Travis

William Barret Travis. Last page of a handwritten letter signed to David G. Burnet

Travis was an eloquent writer. His ringing appeal for reinforcements for the little garrison at the Alamo, outnumbered tenfold by the besieging Mexicans, is one of the greatest letters ever penned. Whoever can read this moving letter without a tug at the heart must be made of stern stuff:

The enemy has demanded a surrender at discretion otherwise the garrison are to be put to the sword if the fort is taken. I have answered the demand with a cannon shot, & our flag still waves proudly from the wall. *I will never surrender or retreat.* . . . I call on you in the name of Liberty, of patriotism & everything dear to the American character to come to our aid. . . . If this call is neglected, I am determined to sustain myself as long as possible & die like a soldier who never forgets what is due to his own honor & that of his country. *Victory or death.*

David G. Burnet and Mirabeau B. Lamar. Original legislative act of the Republic of Texas on the national flag

Stephen F. Austin. Handwritten letter signed, penned during the fight with Mexico

Thomas J. Rusk. Conclusion of a handwritten letter signed

have enemies who would take much pleasure in magnifying the plain Rusticity of my manner into the most unparalleled grossness and indelicacy. I have never enjoyed the advantages which many have abused, but I am proud to hope that your answer will show, it that I have never so far prostituted the humble advantages I do enjoy, as to act the part attributed to me. An early answer is Requested, I am, Sir, most Respectfully Your obt servt

David Crockett

David Crockett. Conclusion of a handwritten letter signed, written to Congressman James Clark after Crockett had visited the White House: "I have enemies who would take much pleasure in magnifying the plain Rusticity of my manner into the most unparalleled grossness and indelicacy. I have never enjoyed the advantages which many have abused. . . ."

Juan N. Almonte, Mexican general under Santa Anna. Last page of a handwritten letter signed

MEN IN BLACK
26 ROBES

Roger B. Taney

Don't picture them draped in black, staid and dignified as saints in niches, for the great men of the Supreme Court were a wild and controversial lot. There was the jovial William Howard Taft, whose mighty girth got wedged in the White House bathtub when he was President. His behind had to be oiled before his aides could extract him. Roger B. Taney, thin and almost mummified, with a face like crinkled parchment, whose Dred Scott decision roused the North to wrath. And Salmon P. Chase, who, as Lincoln's secretary of the treasury, connived so openly to wrest away the presidency that Lincoln made him chief justice just to get rid of him.

Patrick Henry turned down the job as first chief justice, but John Jay, coauthor of *The Federalist*, a series of papers defending the new Constitution, took the post. Jay was a shrewd Yankee from New York. I once had a sheaf of papers written from his farm near Bedford during his long retirement. Indited in his meticulous and very legible hand, they comprised bills and payments and Jay's own drafts of letters demanding money from his debtors. Jay was tight-fisted and miserly. Had he lived in our century, he could have made a fortune as a collection agent.

The mighty personality and intellect of John Marshall dominated the Supreme Court for more than three decades. His clashes with Andrew Jackson were legendary. A fiery apostle of federalism, Marshall confined his inflammatory opinions to court decisions. His letters are rather tedious commentaries on legal cases of trifling interest. I don't recall ever reading an exciting letter of Marshall.

Of Salmon P. Chase the opposite is true. Chase's early letters from Ohio, when one manages to decipher the wretched script, often turn out to be denunciations of slavery or impassioned appeals for justice. The piquant touch in Chase's great career comes from the constant dirty tricks he played on Lincoln. Said one senator at the time: "There is rank treason in the President's cabinet."

177

My dear Sir

I shall be greatly flattered by the visit you mention and will receive it with much pleasure

Yours truly

J Marshall

Nov. 14th 1831

John Marshall. Handwritten note signed

Melville W. Fuller,

Nov. 2, 1892 –

Melville W. Fuller

If it is at all possible consistently with the public interests to give him a contract to be fulfilled in Ohio or elsewhere I hope you will do so.

Yours truly

S P Chase

Salmon P. Chase. Handwritten note signed

Oliv Ellsworth

Oliver Ellsworth

James Kent

Joseph Story

Joseph Story

Some wag wrote of Chase: "His face is familiar to all Americans through its presence on the ten thousand dollar bill."

There are four justices of this century whose genius and influence have awesomely affected the Supreme Court—Brandeis, Cardozo, Frankfurter and Holmes. Brandeis was the first Jew ever appointed to the Court (1916) and was considered for many years a radical. His letters, nearly always handwritten, are models of clarity and brevity. Seldom do they run over a page. They have a Lincolnesque quality of simplicity that makes them very appealing.

Perhaps the most influential man ever to serve on the Supreme Court was Oliver Wendell Holmes, Jr., whose limpid literary style gave force to his judicial opinions. The vitality of the man is captured in his letters, many of which are urbane and clever.

In 1929, as a boy of fourteen, I had committed to memory some of the famous poems of Oliver Wendell Holmes, Sr., father of the justice. I wrote to the son, then nearly ninety years old but still active on the Court, and asked him which of his

Sincerely yours,

Felix Frankfurter

Felix Frankfurter

With Every Good Wish

Louis D. Brandeis

Louis D. Brandeis

March 21st 1923

Supreme Court of the United States.
Washington, D.C.

My dear Senator

I have yours of March 17, St Patrick's day, asking that I give an autograph letter to Mr. Albert A. Mortimer of Chicago. I have no such letter and must make one which I hastly do.

With best wishes

Sincerely yours

Hon. ....
U.S. Senate.

Wm H Taft

William Howard Taft. Handwritten letter signed as chief justice

To see so far as one may, and to feel, the great forces that are behind every detail — for that makes all the difference between philosophy and gossip, between great action and small; the least wavelet of the Atlantic ocean is mightier than one of Buzzard's Bay — to hammer out as compact and solid a piece of work as one can, to try to make it first rate, and to leave it unadvertised.

Oliver Wendell Holmes, Jr. Handwritten quotation signed

Andrew Hamilton

Jno Peter Zenger

John Peter Zenger

James Alexander. Assisted Hamilton at Zenger's trial

Very Truly
Clarence Darrow

Clarence Darrow

John T. Scopes

John T. Scopes. Defended by Darrow in the "monkey" trial

---

father's poems he liked best. Though quite infirm, he took the time to reply:

My dear boy,

Your question will have to go unanswered for several reasons, one of which is enough. I do not know. I think you are right in liking "The One Hoss Shay."

Sincerely yours
Oliver Wendell Holmes

Several lawyers who were never members of the Court merit mention. There was the cagey Andrew Hamilton of Philadelphia, defender of John Peter Zenger, New York printer, in the celebrated freedom of the press trial in 1735. Hamilton's great victory in the courtroom, in which Zenger was acquitted of libel against the king, gave the world a new expression: "Get a Philadelphia lawyer." Equally adroit and eloquent was the craggy-faced Clarence Darrow, a crusading attorney who never shunned a tough case and whose withering cross-examinations struck terror into his courtroom opponents.

As might be expected, anything signed by Andrew Hamilton or his associate, James Alexander, is seldom encountered, but letters of their modern counterpart Darrow turn up frequently and are invariably outspoken and pungent.

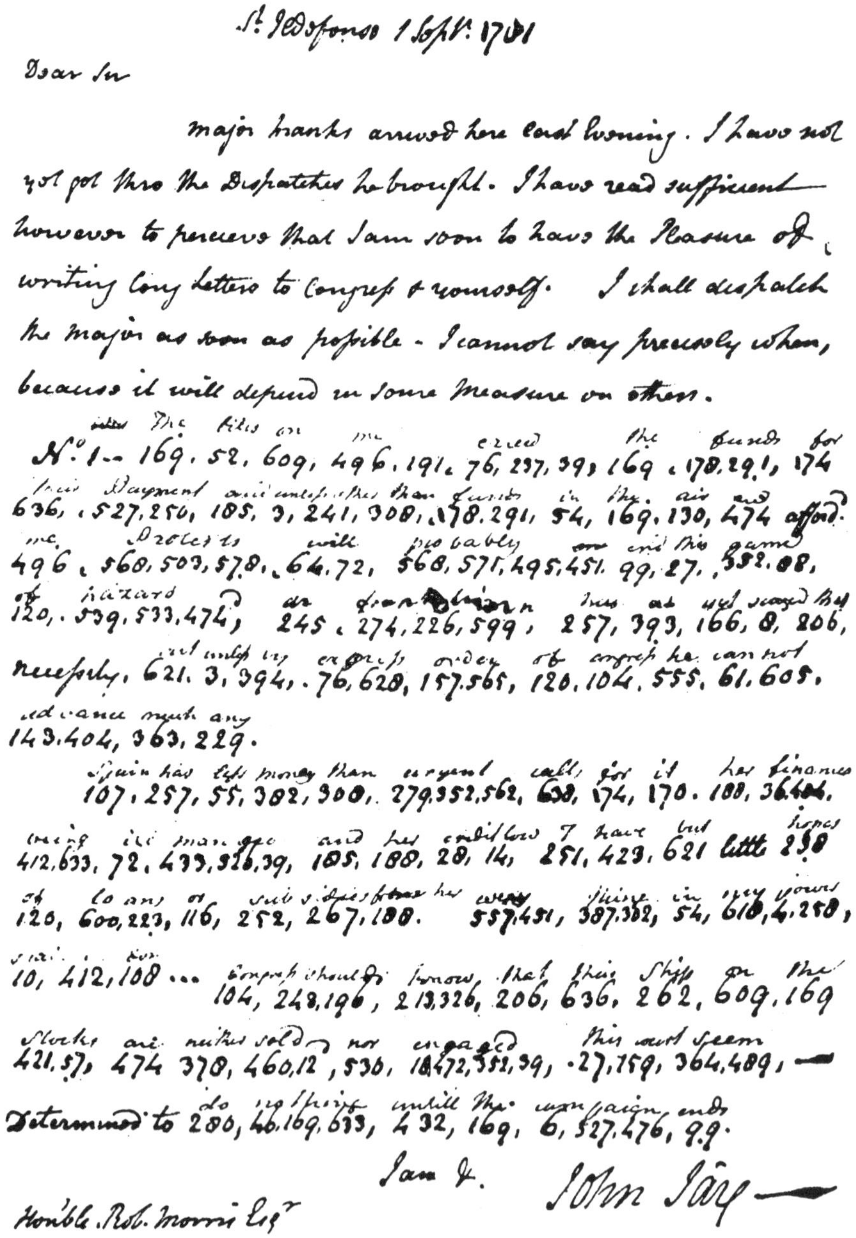

St. Ildefonso 1 Sept. 1781

Dear Sir

Major Franks arrived here last Evening. I have not yet got thro the Dispatches he brought. I have read sufficient however to perceive that I am soon to have the Pleasure of writing long Letters to Congress & yourself. I shall dispatch the Major as soon as possible — I cannot say precisely when, because it will depend in some Measure on others.

No. 1 — 169. 52, 609, 496. 191. 76, 237, 391 169. 178.29.1, 174
636, 527, 250, 185, 3, 241, 308, 178.291, 54, 169, 130, 474 afford
496, 560, 503, 578, 64.72, 568, 571, 495, 451, 99, 27, 352.88,
120, 539, 533, 474, 245, 274, 226, 599, 257, 393, 166, 8, 206,
necessity, 621. 3, 394, 76, 620, 157.565, 120, 104, 555, 61.605.
143.404, 363, 229.
107, 257, 55, 382, 300, 279, 352, 562, 638, 174, 170. 188, 364.
412, 633, 72, 433, 326, 39, 105, 188, 28, 14, 251, 423, 621 little 238
120, 600, 223, 116, 252, 267, 188. 557, 451, 387, 352, 54, 610, 4, 250,
10, 412, 108 … 104, 248, 196, 213, 326, 206, 636, 262, 609, 169
421, 57, 474 370, 460, 12, 530, 18472, 352, 39, 27, 159, 364, 489,
Determined to 280, 46.169, 633, 432, 169, 6, 327, 476, 99.

I am &c. John Jay

Hon'ble Rob. Morris Esq.

John Jay. Handwritten letter, mostly in code, about European politics, signed and addressed to Robert Morris

John Marshall

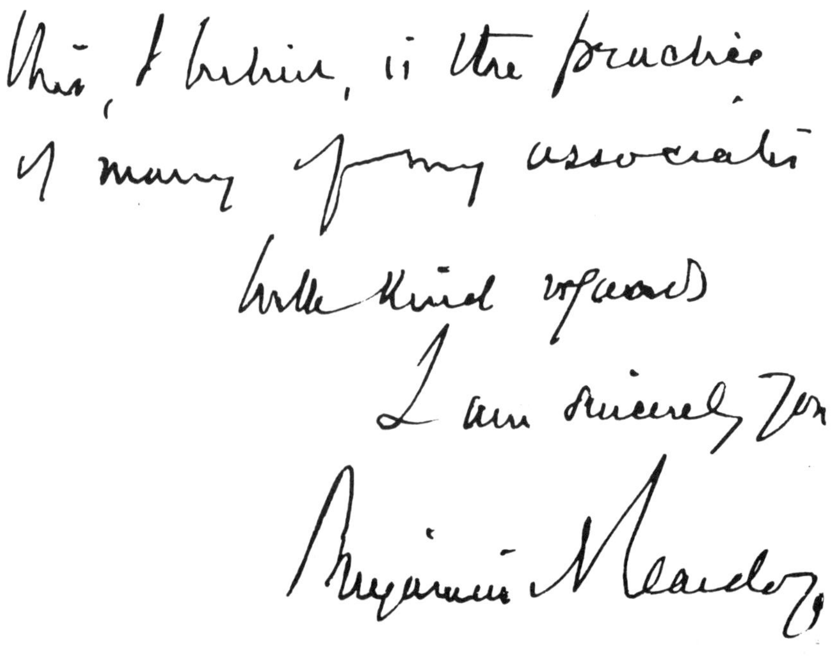

This, I believe, is the practice
of many of my associates
With kind regards
I am sincerely yours
Benjamin N. Cardozo

Benjamin Cardozo. Last four lines of a handwritten letter signed

Supreme Court of the United States
Washington 25, D. C.

CHAMBERS OF
THE CHIEF JUSTICE

Aug 25 '69

My dear Miss Wenger

No one quotation can really express a life philosophy but one which impressed me deeply, especially since it came from J. Robert Oppenheimer is this

"I believe the strength and soundness of Christian sensibility have changed the world at least as much as technological development."

Cordially

Warren E Burger

Warren E. Burger. Handwritten letter signed about his philosophy of life

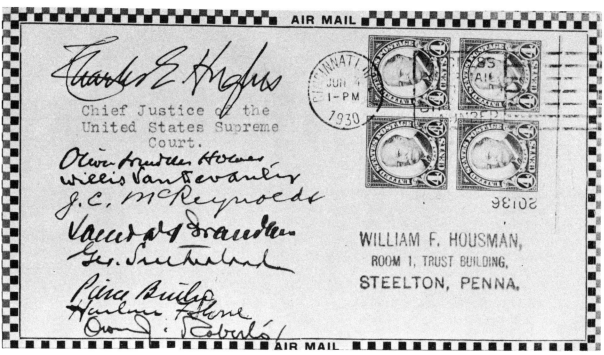

Charles E. Hughes and the Supreme Court. First-day cover signed. Signers include Oliver Wendell Holmes, Jr., Louis D. Brandeis, Pierce Butler, Harlan F. Stone and Owen J. Roberts.

Louis D. Brandeis. Handwritten letter signed about Franklin D. Roosevelt's inaugural address

Chief Justice Edward D. White. Conclusion of a handwritten letter signed

PEAKS AND PITS
27 OF THE PRESIDENCY

William McKinley. Signature and one line in his hand

General Nelson A. Miles

Very truly,

William McKinley. Early signature (1892)

President William McKinley pointed to a map of the Pacific. "Miles," he said to the general at his side, "the future of America is tied to this hemisphere. Every day Japan gets more powerful. One of these days she will challenge us with her great navy. Perhaps not in our lifetimes, but we must be ready. Otherwise she may strike direct at our Western coast from California to Alaska."

"Do you have anything in mind, sir?" asked Nelson Miles, aware that the McKinley Tariff Act had already forced Hawaii to cede Pearl Harbor to the United States in return for duty-free exports.

"We need more than just Pearl Harbor," said McKinley. "We need a ring of front-line defenses against a possible Japanese attack."

A few months later, on April 25, 1898, using the sinking of the battleship *Maine* as a pretext, McKinley asked Congress to declare war on Spain.

In a series of bold strokes, the American navy brought Spain to terms. The defeated nation ceded the Philippine Islands and Guam to the United States, and as a result of American victories in the Pacific, Hawaii was annexed on August 12, 1898. The defense ring was complete.

Often criticized by liberal historians as an "imperialist," McKinley certainly contributed to saving America forty-three years later, for the Japanese surprise attack on December 7, 1941, which destroyed our navy at Pearl Harbor and led to the capture of the Philippines, would instead have fallen upon Los Angeles and San Francisco.

I once sold a secret memorandum in which McKinley commented on the dangers to America of Japan's growing naval power.

Long after he became famous, McKinley continued to sign "Jr." after his name. His letters are plentiful and remarkably uninteresting, the most staidly pedestrian of any President's. His early legal briefs as prosecuting attorney of Stark County, Ohio, are occasionally amusing, for he wrote many indictments against persons accused of keeping houses of ill repute.

McKinley is one of eight Presidents to go to the White House from Ohio. Virginia claims one of these, William Henry Harrison, as a native son, although Harrison lived most of his life in Ohio and was clerk of Hamilton County, Ohio, when elected President.

Of all our great Presidents, none is more appealing than the little tailor from Tennessee, Andrew Johnson, who stood his ground against a vindictive Congress hungry for vengeance against the South. The bullying and threats of Congress did not deter Johnson from carrying out Lincoln's policy of binding up the wounds. He escaped impeachment by only a single vote. But to him goes much of the credit for preserving the Union during the fearful post-bellum years.

Johnson did not learn to read and write until he was in his teens. His young wife, Eliza McCardle, coached him by candlelight. Several early tailor bills of Johnson have passed through my hands, crudely penned, with even his own signature misspelled. Throughout his life Johnson continued to write in a labored script, as though he were still learning the alphabet, but his letters are full of vitality. Johnson was not a suave politician like Lincoln, but he was equally incorruptible. He was the first President to sign documents with a stamped signature. Some say that this delegation of authority to a printer's die was the result of an injury to his hand, but I am inclined to think the printed signature was merely a neat dodge to escape the drudgery of constantly scribbling his name.

Johnson's letters invariably reflect his sincerity and integrity. One of the finest I ever owned explained his view of the presidency:

I never was and never expect to be an aspirant to the presidency of the United States. . . . A man who will abandon principle and the support of sound measures to attain the presidency ought not to be entrusted by the people for he will betray them.

Among modern Presidents, my favorite is not the urbane and handsome Kennedy or the amiable General Dwight D. Eisenhower, but the feisty, hard-punching man from Missouri, Harry S Truman. To Truman fell the tough decisions to drop

U. S. Grant. Photograph signed as lieutenant general

Eliza McCardle Johnson

Andrew Johnson. Handwritten letter signed

Warren G. Harding

James Buchanan

the atomic bomb on the Japanese, by which act thousands of American lives were saved, and to relieve from command the aggressive General Douglas MacArthur, then on the verge of attacking China and perhaps starting a third world war.

Truman's letters are vigorous and outspoken, often rich in humor or tinctured with sarcasm. His letters lack the erudition of Jefferson's and the terse beauty of Lincoln's, but they are the most readable of any President's since John Adams.

Who can forget his famous scorching of the music critic who ventured to ridicule the singing of his daughter, Margaret, or the letter in which he declared, "I would not appoint John L. Lewis dogcatcher."

Were we to measure the failures among Presidents by the corruption in their administrations, surely Grant, Harding and Nixon would top the list. But a presidential failure must be judged by the serious damage his administration inflicts upon the nation and to my mind only two Presidents qualify: James Buchanan, who in early 1861 should have put down the Southern insurrection and jailed its leaders, but by his indecision made it possible for the new Confederacy to mount a prolonged war against the Union; and Woodrow Wilson, a college professor and dilettante of history who unnecessarily involved us in a terrible European conflict, helped to pave the way for Hitler with the League of Nations, and committed future Democratic Presidents to a policy of military meddling in European and Pacific affairs. The tragic involvement of the United States in the Vietnam war was a direct outgrowth of Wilson's foreign policy.

Not long after the end of World War I, his peace plans thwarted by the Allies in Europe, Wilson suffered a serious stroke that affected his mind. I once owned a volume of photographs of women in underwear treasured by Wilson in his last years. The former President had cut them from magazines, pasted them in a scrapbook and annotated them with semi-naughty remarks in a quavery hand.

Buchanan and Wilson were adroit penmen, their scripts neat and precise and free of embellishment. But seldom does either rise above the commonplace in his letters and both were masters of the platitudinous elaboration of the insignificant obvious.

Jan 19, 1953.

Dear Mr. Fleming:

I want to change our joint account to my name and give Mrs Truman power of attorney to sign checks.

It is a legal procedure that has become necessary now.

Sincerely yours
Harry Truman

Please give Miss Conway the necessary papers & cards.

Harry S Truman. Handwritten letter signed on his last full day
as President, giving his wife power of attorney to sign checks

90 CHURCH STREET, ROOM 1303
NEW YORK 7, NEW YORK

14 April 1961

Dear Mr. McSweeney:

Thank you so much for sending me your April
11th editorial. It moved me deeply. I only hope that you have
not done me too much honor.

Our failure to see the war in Korea through to
victory was a major defeat for the free world. With success within
our easy grasp we allowed the situation to degenerate into a military
stalemate. The ultimate result will amount to a complete defeat
for our interests. Victory in Korea would have deprived Red China
of the means to wage global war for generations to come. The
failure to accomplish that victory has permitted it to grow into
a military colossus which threatens all of Asia and may even become
the balance of military power in the world. If this happens it
will jeopardize freedom on all continents. It is quite possible
that future historians may regard the almost pathetic failure of
Washington to understand the situation which existed in the Far
East as the most crucial mistake of this century.

With renewed appreciation to you,

Most cordially,

Douglas MacArthur

DOUGLAS MacARTHUR.

Mr. John J. McSweeney, Editor,
"Times-Leader The Evening News",
Wilkes-Barre, Pennsylvania.

Douglas MacArthur. Letter signed, defending his position in
opposing Truman's stalemate in Korea

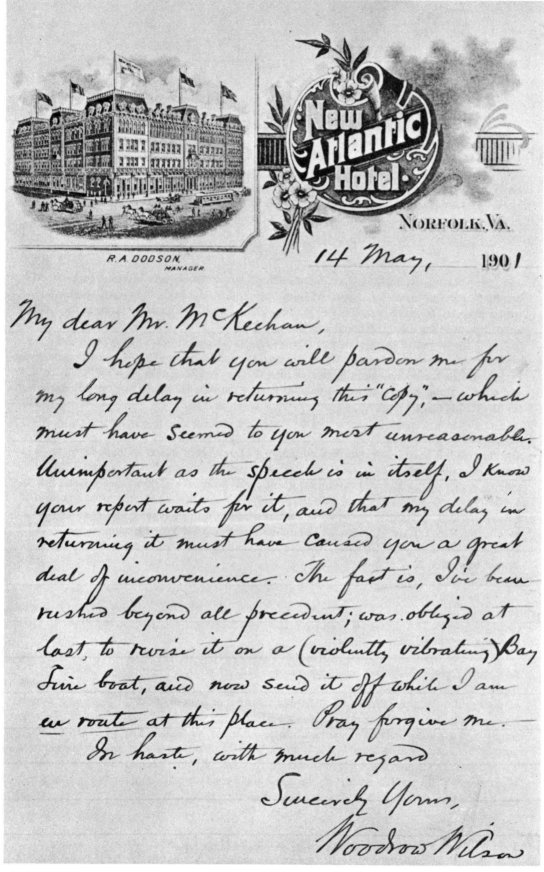

New Atlantic Hotel

NORFOLK, VA.

R.A. DODSON, MANAGER

14 May, 1901

My dear Mr. McKechan,

I hope that you will pardon me for my long delay in returning this "Copy", — which must have seemed to you most unreasonable. Unimportant as the speech is in itself, I know your report waits for it, and that my delay in returning it must have caused you a great deal of inconvenience. The fact is, I've been rushed beyond all precedent; was obliged at last, to revise it on a (violently vibrating) Bay Line boat, and now send it off while I am en route at this place. Pray forgive me. —

In haste, with much regard

Sincerely Yours,

Woodrow Wilson

Woodrow Wilson. Handwritten letter signed, a tautological apology for his delay in sending a speech to his correspondent

THEY GATHERED
28 TO SIGN

The history of any nation is the history of its affirmers and dissenters. Whenever a group of these people assembles in a large room they invariably sign something, usually a proclamation or a manifesto.

On August 2, 1776, in the Old State House at Philadelphia, a gathering of dissidents signed a sheepskin which shook the world—the Declaration of Independence.

"King George can read that clear across the sea," said the president of the Continental Congress as he scrawled his bold "John Hancock" and added an arrogant paraph.

Others lined up to pledge their fortunes and their sacred honor.

"We must all hang together," said the seventy-year-old Benjamin Franklin, "or assuredly we will all hang separately."

Franklin had the alert mind of a young man and was still courting the ladies, even advising his young nephew on the choice of a mistress. Franklin's many letters, indited in the neat, clear script which he popularized in the New World, are as daring and vigorous as his signature.

Thomas Jefferson was there too, a tall man with flaming red hair, his face constantly flushed from wine. He was, some said, three sheets to the wind when he composed the Declaration. But the owner of the finest wine cellar in Virginia was also the wielder of the most powerful pen in Virginia. The thousands of fascinating letters that poured from his quill reveal a keen Renaissance mind. Jefferson's interests ranged from sheep raising and Indian history to Anglo-Saxon poetry and parliamentary practice.

Among other giants in the hall were John Adams, pompous as he was brilliant, but certainly the most exciting letter writer of his age. I never saw a letter of Adams, in that fine, lucid hand of his, without relishing the verbal pyrotechnics. His erudite epistles vary from the insulting to the incendiary. He was capable of anything and guilty of everything except treason and dullness. His cousin Samuel Adams was a correspondent of the same kidney, but he expressed himself with less vehemence.

Every man of the fifty-six who signed the Declaration of

Benjamin Franklin

Samuel Adams

THE WHITE HOUSE
WASHINGTON

August 9, 1974

Dear Mr. Secretary:

I hereby resign the Office of President of the United States.

Sincerely,

Richard Nixon

11.35 AM

HK

The Honorable Henry A. Kissinger
The Secretary of State
Washington, D.C. 20520

Richard M. Nixon. Typed letter of resignation signed

Independence merits a biography and I wish I had world enough and time to write them all, but here I shall mention just one other, the only signer who achieved great fame solely because of the rarity of his signature—Button Gwinnett of Georgia. Nine months after Gwinnett affixed his name to the Declaration, a bullet from the pistol of General Lachlan McIntosh snuffed out his life in a duel.

Recently a young and wealthy philographer told me, "I plan to start a collection of 'signers.' Can you give me any advice?"

"Certainly," I said. "Set aside seventy-five thousand dollars for Button Gwinnett. Then pray every night that you will get a chance to buy one at that bargain price."

Twelve years after the Declaration was signed, some of the same patriots were still around to put their signatures on another great American document, the Constitution. The curvaceous script of the first civilized American, Ben Franklin, had lost little of its gusto, but there was now a new and very bold signature, that of the convention's president, George Washington. Little Jamie Madison also put his tidy, unobtrusive signature on the document he had worked so hard to create. So did Washington's former aide and colonel of artillery, Alexander Hamilton.

About a century earlier, in 1693, the most eminent men of the Massachusetts Bay Colony had gathered to pledge their political troth to King William and Queen Mary of England. Some of the signers of this oath had just attained worldwide notoriety for condemning and executing nineteen of their fellow Americans as witches. Five of the infamous signers were Samuel Sewall (who recanted), Bartholomew Gedney, John Hathorne (forebear of Nathaniel with a w), Jonathan Corwin

Abraham Lincoln

Abraham Lincoln

THE WHITE HOUSE
WASHINGTON

Lyndon B. Johnson

Lyndon B. Johnson. White House card signed

G. Washington — Presid.
and deputy from Virginia

John Langdon
Nicholas Gilman

Nathaniel Gorham
Rufus King

W. Sam. Johnson
Roger Sherman

Alexander Hamilton

Wil: Livingston
David Brearley
W. Paterson
Jona: Dayton

B. Franklin
Thomas Mifflin
Rob. Morris

W.. Blount
Rich. Dobbs Spaight.
Hu Williamson

Geo Clymer
Tho. FitzSimons
Jared Ingersoll
James Wilson.
Gouv Morris

Geo. Read
Gunning Bedford jun
John Dickinson
Richard Bassett
Jaco: Broom
James McHenry

Dan of St Tho Jenifer
Dan. Carroll
John Blair —
James Madison Jr.

J. Rutledge
Charles Cotesworth Pinckney
Charles Pinckney
Pierce Butler.
William Few
Abr Baldwin

William Jackson

Signatures of the signers of the Constitution

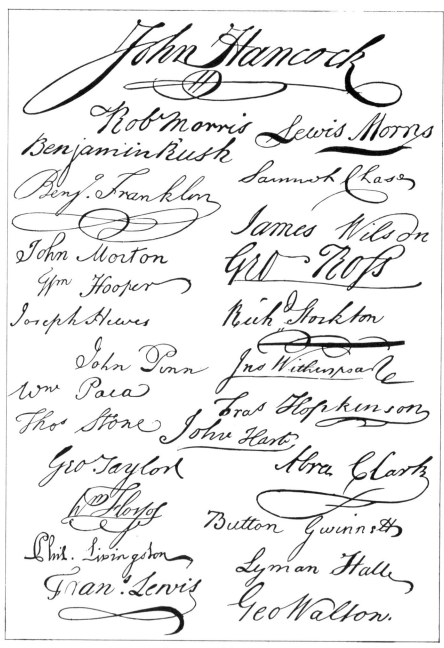

Signatures of the signers of the Declaration of Independence

and Governor William Phips, who approved the witchcraft bill. Here too, appear the signatures of Governor Thomas Danforth of Massachusetts Bay, John Walley, who in 1689 led an expedition against the French and Indians in Canada.

Occasionally the solitary signature of a powerful man can change the course of history.

"If I am to be remembered at all," said Lincoln when he signed the Emancipation Proclamation in 1863, "it will be for this document."

Lyndon Johnson might have echoed Lincoln's comment when he put his pen to the Civil Rights bill, implementing Lincoln's proclamation of a century earlier.

But the most remarkable single-signature paper of modern times—Nixon's resignation from the office of President—contains but one brief sentence.

Francis Lightfoot Lee
Carter Braxton Benj Harrison
Casar Rodney Ths Nelson jr
Geo Read Matthew Thornton
Thos M: Kean Step Hopkins
Edward Rutledge William Ellery
Roger Sherman
Ths Hayward jun
Thomas Lynch Junr
Charles Carroll of Carrollton
Arthur Middleton
Geo Clymer
George Wythe Jas Smith
Sam a Huntington
Richard Henry Lee Wm Williams
Josiah Bartlett Oliver Wolcott
Wm Whipple John Adams
Saml Adams Robt Treat Paine
Th Jefferson Elbridge Gerry

Signatures of the signers of the Declaration of Independence (continued)

Signatures of the signers of the Plymouth Patent, including
(lower left) the celebrated colonizer Sir Ferdinando Gorges

Dear Sir,

The Bearer having been certain of the new Ministry are disposed to... here, I add the same to suggest that of the new Ministry are disposed to... enter into a General Treaty of Peace, Mr Laurens being set at liberty et Liberty may receive such Propositions as they shall think fit to make relative to Time, Place, or any other Particulars, and come hither with them. He is acquainted that we have full Powers to treat therewith, and has the Courage promised in our Commission to ratify and confirm, &c. — I am

Yours most affectionately
ever,

B. Franklin

Benjamin Franklin. Handwritten letter signed about the possibility of a treaty of peace with Great Britain

---

Quincy June 11. 1815:

B. Rush

"Watchman! What of the Night? To what hour of the Evening are we advanced? How many hours remain before day break? Have you a repeating Watch that can strike the hour and the quarter of an hour in the darkest hour of Sablest night?

Rochefoucault, Condorcet, Rodespiene Brisot, Danton, Orleans, Buonaparte, Pitt, Fox, Burk, Alexander, Georges Louis, Charles, Francisco Fredericks are but Puppets: they are but Bubbles. The real Struggle is not between them. They are no more... than Chaff in the Wind, or than Froth on the Surface of the Sea. The fundamental Conflict is between two Systems of Religion and government.

The War of Religion lasts thirty Years, from 1618 to 1648. Will you date this War from 1775 or from 1793? If from the latter Period, it has been only 22 years; eight more are wanting make thirty. And Quœstions whether Superstition or a rational Religion and Atheism Absolute Monarchy or mixed representative government shall prevail, will

John Adams

John Adams. First page and signature from a handwritten letter about the struggle for power in England and France. "The fundamental conflict is between two Systems of Religion and government."

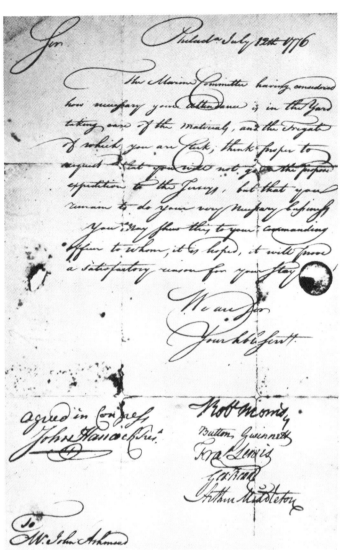

Button Gwinnett. Letter signed by Gwinnett and five other signers of the Declaration. This celebrated letter, dated in July 1776, fetched $51,000 at auction in 1927.

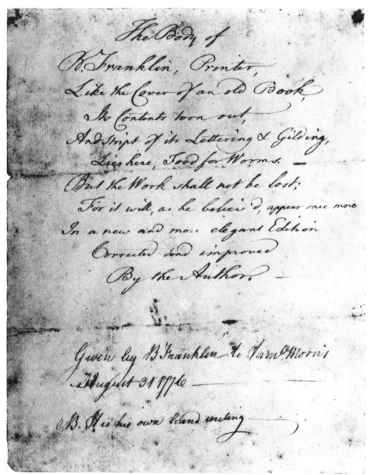

Benjamin Franklin. Handwritten epitaph

John Adams. Signature late in life (1819)

A TRUE COPY

OF THE

O A T H S

That are appointed by Act of Parliament, made in the First Year of Their present Majesties Reign; to be Taken instead of the Oaths of Supremacy and Allegiance, and the Declaration appointed to be made, Repeated and Subscribed

I *A. B.* do sincerely Promise and Swear, That I will be Faithful, and bear true Allegiance to Their Majesties, King *W I L L I A M* and Queen *M A R Y.* *So help me God,* &c.

I *A. B.* do Swear, That I do from my Heart Abhor, Detest, and Abjure, as Impious and Heretical, that Damnable Doctrine and Position, *That Princes Excommunicated or Deprived by the Pope, or any Authority of the See of* Rome, *may be Deposed or Murthered by their Subjects, or any other whatsoever.*

And I do Declare, That no Foreign Prince, Person, Prelate, State, or Potentate, hath, or ought to have any Jurisdiction, Power, Superiority, Preeminence, or Authority Ecclesiastical or Spiritual within this Realm.

So help me God, &c.

I *A. B. do solemnly and sincerely in the presence of God, profess, testifie and declare, that I do believe that in the Sacrament of the Lords Supper, there is not any Transubstantiation of the Elements of Bread and Wine into the Body and Blood of Christ, at or after the Consecration thereof, by any person whatsoever, and that the Invocation or adoration of the Virgin Mary or any other Saint, and the sacrifice of the Mass as they are now used in the Church of* Rome, *are Superstitious and Idolatrous. And I do solemnly in the presence of God, profess, testifie and declare, that I do make this Declaration and every part thereof in the plain and ordinary sense of the words read unto me, as they are commonly understood by* English *Protestants, without any Evasion, Equivocation or mental Reservation whatsoever, and without any Dispensation already granted me for this purpose by the Pope, or any Authority or Person whatsoever, or without any hope of any such Dispensation from any Person or Authority whatsoever, or without thinking that I am or can be acquitted, before God or Man, or absolved of this Declaration or any part thereof, although the Pope or any other Person or Persons or Power whatsoever should dispence with, or annul the same or declare that it was null and void from the beginning.*

Oath of allegiance to William and Mary, signed by the leading citizens in Massachusetts Bay

Adopted unanimously by the Congress of the Confederate States of South Carolina, Georgia, Florida, Alabama, Mississippi, Louisiana and Texas sitting at the Capitol, in the City of Montgomery, Alabama, on the Eleventh day of March, in the year Eighteen Hundred and Sixty one

Howell Cobb
President of the Congress.

4 Alabama
Richard W. Walker
Robt. H. Smith
Colin J. McRae
William P. Chilton
Stephen F. Hale
David P. Lewis
Tho. Fearn
Jno. Gill Shorter
J. L. M. Curry

3 Florida
Jackson Morton
Jas. Patton Anderson
Jas. B. Owens

Texas
John Hemphill
Thomas N. Waul
John H. Reagan
Williamson S. Oldham
Louis T. Wigfall
John Gregg
William Beck Ochiltree

2 Georgia
R. Toombs
Francis S. Bartow
Martin J. Crawford
Alexander H. Stephens
Benjamin H. Hill
Thos. R. R. Cobb.
E. A. Nisbet
Augustus R. Wright
A. H. Kenan

6 Louisiana
John Perkins Jr.
Alex. de Clouet
Charles M. Conrad
Duncan F. Kenner
Henry Marshall
Edward Sparrow

1. South Carolina
R. Barnwell Rhett
C. G. Memminger.
Wm. Porcher Miles.
James Chesnut Jr.
R. W. Barnwell
William W. Boyce
Lawrence M. Keitt
T. J. Withers

5 Mississippi
Alex M. Clayton
James T. Harrison
William S. Barry
W. S. Wilson
Walker Brooke
W. P. Harris
J. A. P. Campbell

Constitution of the Confederate States of America (last page), signed by the Confederate congress

WITH PEN
AND BRUSH **29**

Mark Twain was searching for an artist. Not just any artist. What he wanted was a genius who could bring vibrantly to life the characters in his new novel, *Huckleberry Finn.* There wasn't an artist in the world who wouldn't have sheared a camel to get the job, but Mark had his eye on an unknown who was making commercial sketches. "I can not recall that man's name," he wrote. "There is a Kemble on 'Life,' but is he the man who illustrated the applying of electrical protectors to door-knobs, door-mats &c . . . 4 or 5 weeks ago? That is the man I want to try."

The artist was Edward W. Kemble, age twenty-three, who had never before illustrated a book. His first sketch of Huck Finn was a failure, but Mark coached him along until he had Huck "most rattling good."

If you doubt Kemble's skill, take a look at his drawing of Huck, standing with a good-natured grin and holding his rifle and a slain rabbit. It is the frontispiece to all the early editions of *Huckleberry Finn.*

Kemble's letters are usually about art, and once in a while they are ornamented with delectable sketches. I commend them to all collectors with good taste and slim purses.

I have always been partial to Western art. Borein, Remington and Russell are among my favorites. In September 1937, at the start of the college year in West Los Angeles, I was helping my out-of-town girl friend to find a suitable lodging where she could get a room with board for thirty-five dollars a month. We drove to a tiny bungalow in Westwood which offered such accommodations. A pleasant elderly woman answered the door and showed us into a humble living room furnished with a threadbare carpet and dilapidated furniture. But the walls glowed with beautiful paintings, at least half a dozen large canvases, all depicting cowboys and Indians. The colors gleamed like fire and I could feel the warmth penetrate my body.

"My God!" I said, in a whisper. "These are original paintings by Charlie Russell. They're worth a fortune, at least five thousand dollars each."

The woman overheard me. "Charles M. Russell was my

E. W. Kemble. Self-portrait of himself making the drawings for *Huckleberry Finn* while the office was being moved

Charles M. Russell. Sketch of a steer's skull signed

Frederic Remington. Sketch of a king on a bucking horse signed

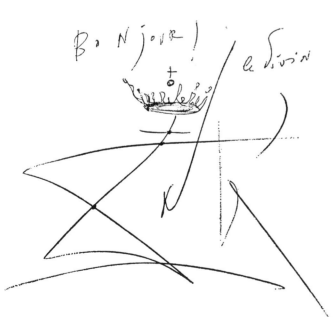

Salvador Dali. Signature adorned with a crown

brother," she said. "He gave me these paintings years ago and of course I will never part with them."

Russell's sister told me she had many letters from her celebrated brother, also not for sale. I have often wondered where they ended up. A few years ago I sold Russell's correspondence with his friend Frank Linderman, a noted authority on the Plains Indians. Russell had little formal education and his letters are full of delightful misspellings. In offering to illustrate a book of Linderman's, Russell wrote: "if Scriberners like the storys its a sinch they will pay for the pictures so when ever thing say its ago Il start the pictures. . . . Il do the work and you can have seven hundred years to pay in."

The letters of John James Audubon, the naturalist and bird artist, are not uncommon, but they are so keenly sought by philographers that they appear to be rare. Many of his notes, written in a swift, fluent hand, describe his adventures while pursuing animal and bird skins. The greatest discovery of Audubon letters and paintings was made at the turn of the century by a Philadelphia book dealer, A. Roggenburger, and his associate, Billy Murray, who stumbled into an acquaintance with the son of Edward Harris, close friend of Audubon.

Billy started the ball rolling [wrote Roggenburger] by getting five of the original watercolors of Audubon's birds. I don't mean the folio prints, but the watercolors themselves, painted and signed by J. J. Audubon. All genuine and he paid $5.00 each for them and sold them for $10.00 each. Between the two of us we bought at different times ninety-five of them, sold them all at the same price.

We also bought about 65 letters for twenty-five cents each and sold them for seventy-five cents. These were all about the book [*Birds of America*] and hunting.

Today a single painting would be a roaring bargain at twenty-five thousand dollars and a good letter of Audubon easily fetches fifteen hundred dollars.

Among artists there are many eccentrics. Dali, for instance, will often sign books for admirers, but he insists upon pocketing the owner's pen. Louis M. Eilshemius, a New York artist who died in poverty in 1941, constantly proclaimed his own

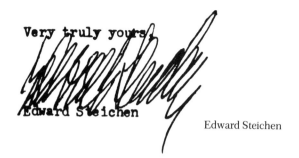

Very truly yours,

Edward Steichen

Edward Steichen

Louis M. Eilshemius. Unpublished sketch, signed with initials, from the top of one of his letters

genius. Many of his half-crazed letters, bitterly complaining about his neglect, were signed "Mahatma." Frequently Eilshemius prefaced his erratic notes with pleasant sketches that are real works of art.

Albert P. Ryder, the great marine artist who lived and died in dusty obscurity, left very few letters, but those I have run across were as strange and compelling as his paintings. Not long ago I sold a poem in his hand, "The Flying Dutchman," on which subject Ryder also painted a masterpiece. The poem reveals that Ryder wisely eschewed the pen for the brush:

> Who hath seen the Phantom Ship,
> Her lordly rise and lowly dip,
> Carusing [cruising] o'er the lonesome main
> No port shall know her keel again.

Three years ago, shortly before his death, I met Alexander Calder. He was weaving about in an alcoholic haze, like one of his own mobiles, having consumed several bottles of champagne. His conversation was made up of disjointed fragments. Most of Calder's letters, usually signed "Sandy," concern his celebrated fluid artistry and the proper ways to hang and light it.

Photography has only recently come into vogue as an art form. Fresh interest is now focused on the letters of the great pioneer photographers—Brady, Muybridge, Steichen and others. Letters of the myopic Mathew Brady are so rare that I have seen but one in thirty years. Most of the notes that bear his signature were penned and signed for him by amanuenses. Even rarer are letters of his skilled assistants, Alexander Gardner and Timothy O'Sullivan.

The great master of psychedelic art, Winsor McCay, introduced Little Nemo to the world in the first decade of this century. McCay's letters are extremely scarce and are passionately sought by collectors of early comics. Much more abundant are notes of the two big O's—R. F. Outcault (Buster Brown) and Frederick Burr Opper (Happy Hooligan). Original comic strips by these and other early cartoonists are now regarded as a decorative art form.

Eadweard Muybridge, inventor of motion pictures

Mathew B. Brady

Stanford White

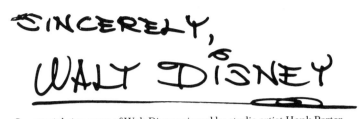

Secretarial signature of Walt Disney signed by studio artist Hank Porter

Secretarial signature of Walt Disney, probably by Hank Porter

Secretarial signature of Walt Disney signed by studio artist Bob Moore

Authentic signature of Walt Disney

Secretarial signature of Walt Disney signed by studio artist

Secretarial signature of Walt Disney, probably by
Floyd Gottfredson

Frank Lloyd Wright

The acknowledged king of comic art, Walt Disney, had a fine, flourishing moniker composed of curlicues and quite illegible. His studio assistants who drew the comic strips and movie cartoons used artistically printed signatures. All fastidiously lettered or printed signatures of Disney must be viewed with caution, for it is doubtful that Disney signed any of them. This important discovery was made by my good friend Charles W. Sachs, of Beverly Hills, California.

Perhaps the most innovative architect since Christopher Wren was Frank Lloyd Wright, who changed the whole tone and direction of architecture. Wright's letters, even on the subject of buildings, are seldom interesting. So eager are collectors for anything bearing his signature, however, that even the dullest epistles quickly change hands at autograph bourses.

It is not possible to stroll through New York City without running across at least one of the graceful, baroque structures designed by Stanford White. A Gay Nineties swinger, White was shot and killed by playboy Harry K. Thaw in a dispute over the affections of the actress Evelyn Nesbit. White's letters are seldom exciting and have·not stirred the cupidity of philographers despite his dramatic demise.

April 17 1919

Friend Frank
    I got both your letters
and picture of trapper and all the storys
and they sound good to me of corse I will
make the pictures but I think your foolish
to offer me pay for the Illustrations on body
else do it and if Scriberners like
the storys its a sinch they will pay
for the pictures so when ever they say its
ago Il start the pictures of corse if
you want to pay for them Il do the work
and you can have seven hundred years to pay
in that old trapper is surtenly a bright
eyed old sport old dad time has been
good to him
    I just got back from Miles City had
a good time but thair isent many of the
old time cow men left I met many
folks that asked after you I wish
you had with air Ted Olive was with us
a special train that packed the bunch
and we slept on the cars they tell me that
this state is dry but that train and
Miles town was dripping wet
    I would like to be up thair with you
but thairs no chance till later
        with best whishes from us all
            to you all your friend
                        C M Russell

Charles M. Russell. Handwritten letter signed to Frank
Linderman about making some illustrations

Winsor McCay. Original drawing signed of Little Nemo

Frederick Burr Opper. Original drawing signed of Happy
Hooligan

London March 30th 1836

My Dear Harlan. —
        The inclosed was sent to me a few
evenings ago, and I understand from Yarrel
that it is a letter of thanks for your Book. —
I had hoped that it was your Diploma from
the Zoological, but Yarrel says that no deaths
have occurred, and that you must wait until
one takes place. — I have heard that you had
sent your Book to Mr King, alias the Noble
Lord of Kingsborough, but he will not bite.
and this I could have told you. Havel has
been obliged to enter a suit against him for
accounts unpaid since many Years. —
        on the 5th of Next Month No 79 & 60. go
to New York along with the Title page of the thing
Vol. I dare say you have received and read the
3d Vol. of Biog. — with best regards from
all to all, I remain yours in truly
                        John J. Audubon

To R. Harlan M. D.
    & & &
    Philadelphia

John J. Audubon. Handwritten letter signed, mentioning his
books

[Albert P. Ryder's manuscript poem, handwritten:]

Who hath seen the Phantom Ship,
Her lordly rise and lowly dip,
Careering o'er the lonesome main
No port shall know her keel again.

But how about that hopeless soul
Doomed forever on that ship to roll,
With grief claims her despairing own
And reason hath it ever flown
As in the loneliness around
Is a sort of joy found
And one wild ecstasy, into another flow
As onward that fateful ship doth go.

But no, Hark! Help! Help Vanderdecken cries,
Help; Help, on the ship he flies;
Ah, woe is in that ~~fearful~~ *awful* sight,
The sailor finds there ~~eternal~~ night,
'neath the waters he shall ever sleep
And ocean ~~shall~~ *will* the secret keep.

[vertically, upper right:] Poem from the John Gellatz
Family Statuman.
Being by the painter's hand
Albert P. Ryder

Albert P. Ryder. Manuscript poem signed (at upper right, vertically), about the Flying Dutchman

Sidney Smith. Original sketch signed of Andy Gump

[card, handwritten:] Yours Truly
Bill Nye
Feb 18 – 1888

[handwritten note:] I'll sneak in here by Bill Nye who I would like to have met. This is the best cast I was ever in, Will Rogers.

[Alexander Calder's handwritten letter:]

27 Mar 50

Dear Curt
    If Berggruen is a buddy of yours I will treat him as gently as possible. I am taking things over, and hope that Maeght will buy some, outright — the others will be mine, after the show. And perhaps Heinzie + I can agree on something at that time.
    Will you tell him to look me up c/o Lefebvre Foinet 19 rue Vavin
    They may have to go to England first
    Did you find the Stallion? And has "Blue Feather" come back from L.A.? + whaca bout those S.F. guys?   Sandy

Alexander Calder. Handwritten letter signed "Sandy"

[R. F. Outcault drawing, handwritten:] Most Sincerely Yours
Tige.
And R. F. Outcault
Dec 7th 1905.

R. F. Outcault. Original drawing signed of Tige, Buster Brown's dog. With a signature of Bill Nye in the upper left and a handwritten note signed of Will Rogers: "This is the best cast I was ever in."

Walter Gropius, architect

Charles Willson Peale

Rudolph Dirks. Original drawing signed of the "Katzenjammer Kids"

Edward Hicks, primitive artist

William Thornton, architect; worked on U. S. Capitol

Margaret Bourke-White

Benjamin H. Latrobe, architect; designed parts of the Capitol and the White House

Frederick Law Olmsted, architect; designed Central Park in New York; worked on Capitol grounds

Charles Bulfinch, architect; worked on U. S. Capitol

Daniel Chester French

James Montgomery Flagg

Thomas Hart Benton. Original sketch of a pumpkin signed

Dear Laurent: Pardon the day's
delay. I hope it will not have
inconvenienced you greatly. —
— — I also hope enclosed will
be acceptable.
It is a true registration of
my feelings.
Sincerely
Alfred Stieglitz —

May 6/22

Alfred Stieglitz. Handwritten letter signed

To make enduring photographs,
one must learn to see with one's
mind's eye, for the heart and the mind
are the true lens of the camera"

Yousuf Karsh
1970

Yousuf Karsh. Handwritten quotation signed

Ỹ Pirate Bold.

It is not because of his life of adventure and daring that I admire this one of my favorite heroes; nor is it because of blowing winds nor blue ocean nor balmy islands which he knew so well; nor is it because of gold he spent nor treasure he hid. He was a man who knew his own mind and what he wanted *Howard Pyle*

Howard Pyle. Original sketch signed of a pirate and a frigate, with a characterization of "my favorite heroes"

Lyonel Feininger

Lyonel Feininger

Maxfield Parrish

Maxfield Parrish

Lorado Taft, sculptor

F. O. C. Darley, illustrator

W. W. Story, sculptor

Benjamin West

William Dunlap, artist; dramatist; historian

Samuel F. B. Morse

Portrait of Washington

There should be one in the Capitol of acknow-
-ledged resemblance — By its size & character
it should produce emotion. What American
can look on his countenance & not sympathize on
his exalted patriotism?

The Picture now offered is equally an Histor-
-ical work commemorating interesting events —
The resolution of Washington in the Attack on
York town & the assistance of Lafayette &c.

Benjamin West. Handwritten document, describing his ideas
about a portrait of Washington

N. C. Wyeth

Sep.r 1839

Thomas Sully

Boston Dec.r 14. 1805 Rec.d of Isaac P. Davis
One hundred Dollars in full for a Portrait
of Washington to be painted by me —
Gilbert Stuart

Gilbert Stuart. Handwritten receipt signed, acknowledging a
payment of $100 in full for a portrait of Washington

Washington Hunt

John Singer Sargent

*Yours truly
A. B. Frost.*

A. B. Frost. Original sketch signed

*Boston June 20. 1806. For Value received, I promise
to pay to Mr Isaac P Davis or order, One Thousand
dollars in Sixty days, with customary Grace. —
Charles Bulfinch*

Charles Bulfinch. Handwritten note signed

*I along with you
Yours Joseph Pennell
at marys wedding*

Joseph Pennell. Self-portrait signed, depicting himself at a wedding

Childe Hassam

Childe Hassam

George Grosz

George Grosz

Washington Allston

Washington Allston

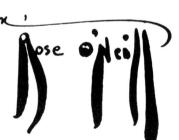

*Yours with enthusiasm,
and Kewpish love
for all children
and child-lovers,* *Rose O'Neill*

Rose O'Neill. Handwritten note signed, about Kewpies

Vendredi 29 Décembre

Monsieur,

J'ai eu d'empêchements pour vous faire par venir ma cotisation pour le déjeuner Apollinaire dans le délai marqué sur la souche, mais, Max Jacob m'a dit hier soir qu'il serait en core le temps si je vous envoyait les sept ronds aujourd'hui ainsi je vous envoie le mandat corres pondant avec mes saluta tions les plus empressés

Diego M Rivera
26 rue du Départ.

Dans le cas où il serait trop tard je me permets de vous porter sur ma carte demain par suit si cela ne vous dérange pas trop

Diego Rivera. Handwritten letter signed in French

Edwin A. Abbey

Will James, Western artist

Henry Moore

Horatio Greenough, sculptor

Asher B. Durand, engraver and painter

John Singleton Copley

N.Y. Feby 2/90.
1512 Broadway.

My Dear Clarke

Very sorry I u
unable to attend your "Slag".
Wednesday, had previous engage
Thanks for kind consideration

Yours
F.S. Church

Frederick S. Church. Handwritten letter signed, with sketch
of the lady and the tiger

Respectfully your
most Obt Servt

J. Vanderlyn

John Vanderlyn

Andy Warhol

Andy Warhol

With pndul regards
affectionately yours
Mary Cassatt

Mary Cassatt

Charles Addams

W. W. Denslow, illustrator of *Oz* books; sea horse signature

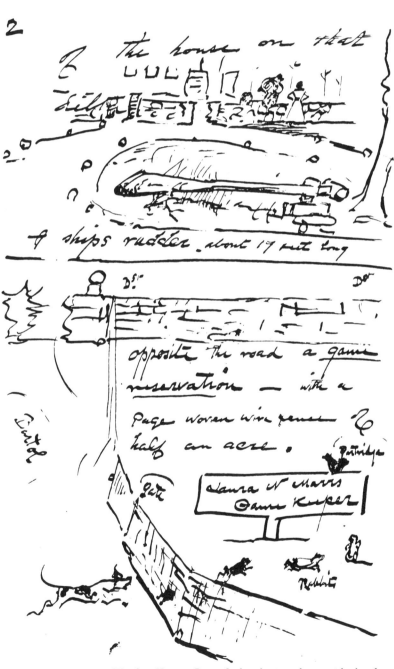

Winslow Homer

Winslow Homer. Page of a handwritten letter with sketches giving directions

John Sartain   John Sartain

Hiram Powers   Hiram Powers

Rembrandt Peale   Rembrandt Peale

Norman Rockwell

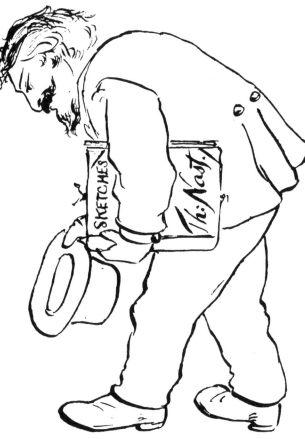

Thomas Nast. Self-portrait signed

Norman Rockwell. Sketch of a dog signed

*Buffalo Club.
London.   Aug 2. 88.*

*Dear Sir. I find a note from you written
long ago — during my absence in Italy —
I have great pleasure in answering it and
sending you the autograph you ask for
Very faithfully yours
J. A. McN. Whistler*

James McNeill Whistler. Handwritten letter signed with his
regular signature and butterfly signature (at left of his name)

H. Inman

Henry Inman

John Trumbull. Printed receipt, filled out and signed, for two
of his most famous prints

Rockwell Kent

Rockwell Kent

Alexander Wilson, bird artist

St. Memin

St. Memin, profile artist

3 Washington Square North, New York
May 8, 1963

Dear Mr. Steadman:

You must know that I appreciate
the very handsome exhibition of my work
and the fine catalogue that you have
arranged for the University of Arizona.

The quotations from some of my writing,
which were written many years ago, seem
still pertinent to much of the painting of
to-day. At least I still believe in what I
have said.

I should like to have seen the show,
but that was not possible.

Sincerely,
Edward Hopper

Edward Hopper. Handwritten letter signed about an exhibition of his work

Grandma Moses

Grandma Moses

I'll give you something to copy
if you like, & after a while you can
find out some new friend or several
of them, who will give you good
advice.
Who was it who first told
you of me?
I hope to hear that you are
coming soon
Yours truly

A H Wyant

A. H. Wyant. Handwritten note signed

Gordon Grant. Sketch of a boat signed

with kind regards and
wishing you great success

Geo T Bellows.

George T. Bellows. Handwritten note signed

Charles Dana Gibson

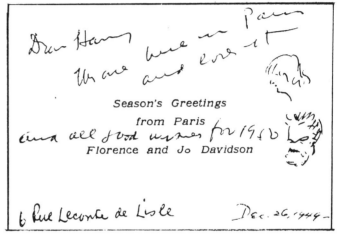

Jo Davidson. Handwritten note signed with a sketch of his
wife and a self-portrait

Robert Ripley, "Believe It Or Not" artist

Tudor Jenks. Self-portrait signed

THE CELLULOID
SERAPHIM **30**

It was my spectacular good fortune some years ago to uncover half a dozen boyhood letters of Rudolph Valentino (Rodolfo Guglielmi), penned in his beautiful Italian script to a close friend. Writing from school, Valentino complained about being locked in a dark closet as a punishment for bad conduct. At fifteen, he was already girl-crazy. He had a visiting card to leave with the chorus girls he was courting. Rudolph picked up a social disease at sixteen and wrote: "From now on, I'm going out only with nice girls."

Years ago, in company with other philographers, I disdained to handle autographs of movie stars and considered them of very little value. I know now that I made a terrible mistake. Once I turned down with elevated nose a handwritten letter of Humphrey Bogart, in which he apologized for accidentally ramming another boat with his yacht. On another occasion I was even stupider. I refused to buy a collection of intimate notes of Archibald Leach, later known as Cary Grant, in which the young actor discussed his struggles for recognition and his inability to make a living.

Not long ago a vivacious young man burst into my gallery and announced, "I want to start a collection of autographs! I'd like to go in for something culturally worthwhile, but I also want a good investment. What do you recommend?"

I said, "Movie stars."

"You must be kidding. I thought you'd suggest Presidents or signers of the Declaration of Independence. But movie stars!"

Just that morning I had bought an early letter of Will H. Hays, president of the Motion Picture Producers and Distributors of America, Inc. Dated 1922, long before talking or color films, the letter was prophetic. I handed it to the young man to read:

I have come to visualize the motion picture as a great, unbelievably great, three-fold instrument for good.

In the first place, it can and will *fill a necessity*—the necessity for entertainment.

In the second place, it can and will *instruct*—which is indeed a precious power.

Rudolph Valentino

Humphrey Bogart

Cary Grant

Will H. Hays

Naturalization Service, Washington, D. C.,

(Signature of Applicant)

Greta Garbo

Marilyn Monroe. Signed as "Norma Jean," her own name

Instead of collecting autographs work to make your own interesting to other people!

D.W. Griffith

D. W. Griffith. Handwritten note signed about autograph collecting

In the third place, the motion picture can do more, I believe, than any other existing agency to *unite the peoples of the world*—to bring understanding not only between man and man but between nation and nation. . . .

The influence of the motion picture on our national life is indeed limitless—the influence on our taste, our conduct, our aspirations, our youth and its consequent immeasurable influence on our future. . . .

Then I told my visitor, "Hays never realized that television would someday bring the motion picture and its stars into every home and make it the most powerful cultural medium of all time."

I went on to remind him that today the movies are recognized as a great art form—the most significant new art form since the year 1623, when two actors named Heming and Condell published the fugitive plays of one William Shakespeare. Until then, plays were considered merely as popular entertainment for the masses. They were performed and forgotten. But from 1623 on, drama was regarded as a great art form.

Already in the field of motion picture collecting, I informed the novice collector, a handwritten letter of Greta Garbo is worth as much as a handwritten letter of Lincoln; a letter of Marilyn Monroe is worth as much as a letter of Robert Morris, famed signer of the Declaration of Independence and financier of the Revolution.

I concluded: "Collect Presidents or signers, if you wish, but I predict that during the next ten years the values of movie stars will increase faster than anything else in the area of philography."

Of special interest to historians of the movies and photography are the letters of the noted directors and cameramen. Rarest of all, perhaps, are the documents of D. W. Griffith, creator of the "close-up," who did so much to revolutionize the film industry.

Frank Sinatra

Lillian Gish

Frank Sinatra. Variant signature

Jack Benny

Greetings

Gloria Swanson

Robert Taylor

Montgomery Clift

Gary Cooper

Pola Negri

Eddie Cantor

William S. Hart

Claudette Colbert

W. C. Fields

To the one and only Leonora,
The girl you wish you'd met before.
I could go on at length with more
But that would make you poets sore.

With apologies to
Edgar Allan Poe.

Bebe Daniels. Handwritten quatrain signed

Cordially yours,
William Powell

William Powell

I'm an American ham, who loves Canadian bacon

Cordially
Groucho Marx

Groucho Marx. Handwritten epigram signed: "I'm an American ham, who loves Canadian bacon"

Errol Flynn

All Mits good

James Cagney

Judy Garland

All my best,
Jayne Mansfield

Jayne Mansfield

Joan Crawford

Gene Kelly

Gene Kelly

Betty Grable

Betty Grable

Carole Lombard (Gable)

Cesar Romero

Cesar Romero

Harpo Marx

Good luck
Clark Gable

Clark Gable

Judy Garland

Judy Garland. Early signature, when a child star

Tom Mix

Take it Easy
and God Bless
Broderick Crawford

Broderick Crawford

All the best

Ray Bolger

Bette Davis

June 5, 1958.

Bette Davis

Tallulah Bankhead

Best Wishes
Jean Harlow

Jean Harlow. Authentic signature

Sincerely Yours,
Robert Montgomery

Robert Montgomery

Gratefully Yours-
Jean Harlow

Jean Harlow. Signature penned for Harlow by her mother, "Mama Jean," who signed virtually all letters and photographs that bear her daughter's name

Jimmy Durante

With every good.
wish.

Charles Boyer

Charles Boyer

Best

Judy Holliday

Judy Holliday

Ed Wynn
11/14/57

Me Too!!

Keenan Wynn
1958

Ed Wynn and Keenan Wynn

all Good Wishes
Wallace Beery

Wallace Beery

Marlon Brando

Marlon Brando

Bud Abbott

Lou Costello

Bud Abbott and Lou Costello

Sydney Greenstreet

Sydney Greenstreet

Sincerely always:

Stan Laurel.

Stan Laurel.

Stan Laurel

Oliver Hardy

Oliver Hardy

Marlene Dietrich

Ronald Colman

Anthony Quinn

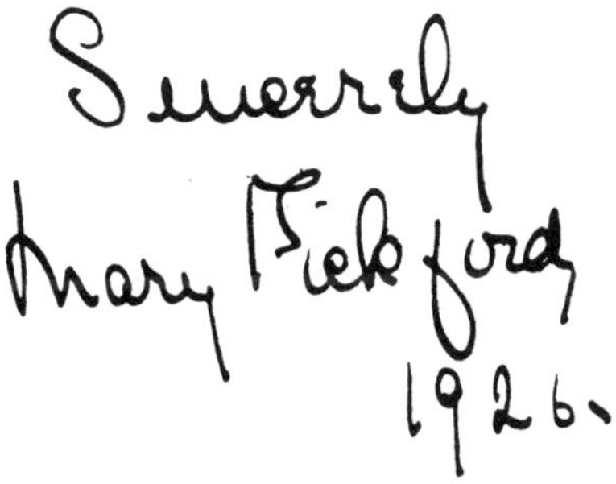

Mary Pickford

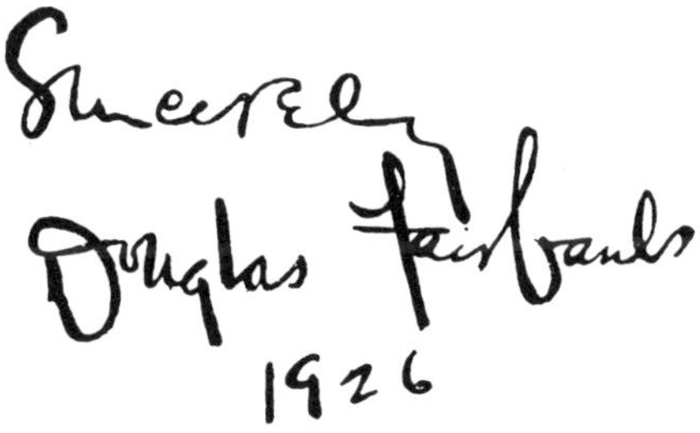

Douglas Fairbanks

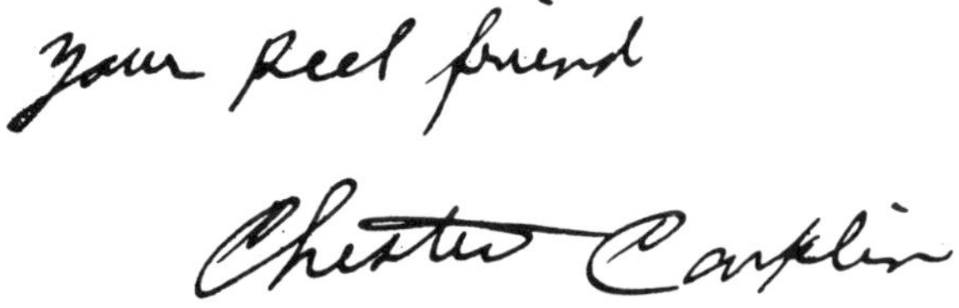

Chester Conklin

Tyrone Power

James Dean

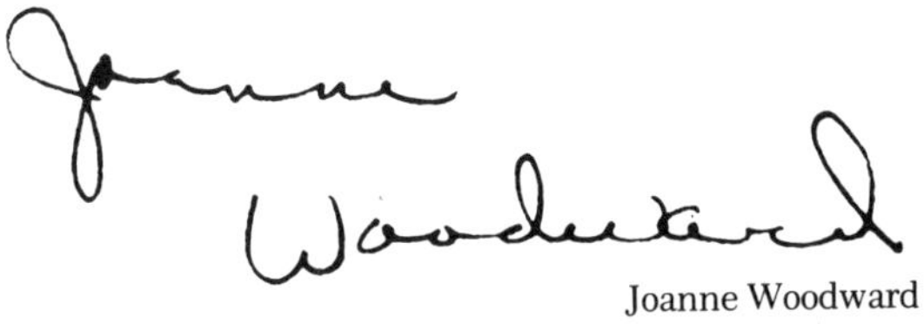

Joanne Woodward

Marion Davies

Paul Newman

Jimmy Stewart

Richard Burton

Best Wishes
Grace Kelly

Grace Kelly

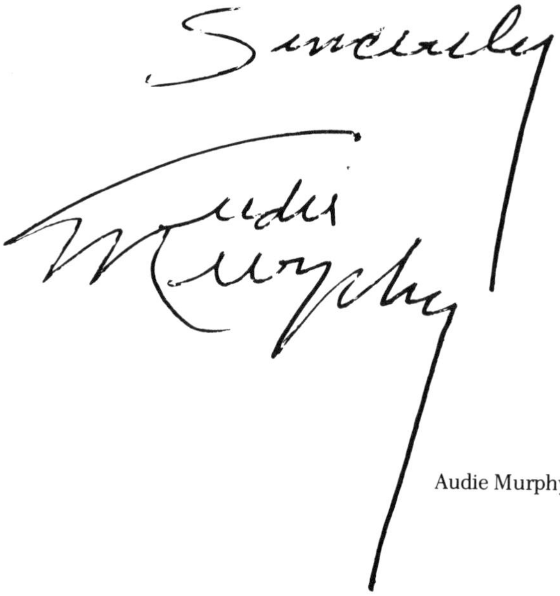

Sincerely

Audie Murphy

Elizabeth Taylor

Love

Faye Dunaway

Orson Welles

Mabel Normand

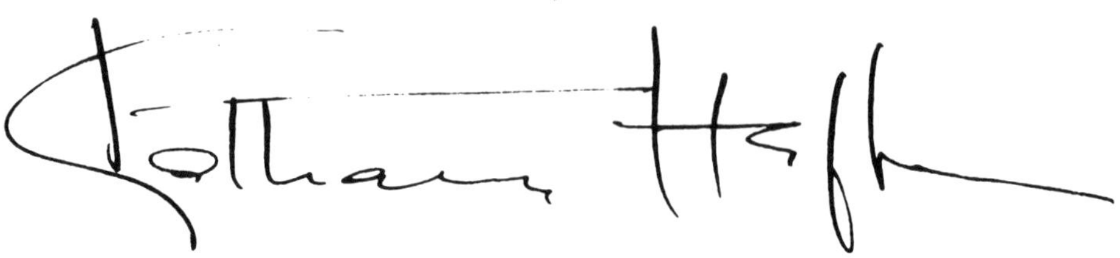

Katharine Hepburn

Ernie Kovacs

Paul Muni

Charles Laughton

Sal Mineo

Mary Martin

Buster Keaton

Best Wishes
Russ Columbo

Russ Columbo

Perry Como

Bing Crosby

Fanny Brice

Fredric March

Clifton Webb

Sincerely
[signature] Ella Fitzgerald

[signature] David O. Selznick

[signature] Chico Marx

Sincerely
[signature] John Ford

[signature] Otto Preminger

I hope you
will never die untill
I kill you
Sid Grauman

Sid Grauman. Handwritten note signed

[signature] Adolph Zukor

[signature] Flo Ziegfeld

[signature] Mack Sennett

[signature] William Wyler

Cordially yours,

[signature] Samuel Goldwyn

President.

[signature] Carl Laemmle

Billy Rose

Billy Rose

Greetings from Hollywood and Cecil B. deMille

Cecil B. deMille

Hattie McDaniel

Hattie McDaniel

Sincerely, Elvis Presley

Elvis Presley

Sol Hurok

Sol Hurok

May _____, 1933 Al Jolson

[EACH PASSENGER MUST SIGN]
[A SEPARATE DECLARATION]

Al Jolson

Florence Vidor

Florence Vidor

Gene Autry

Gene Autry

All My Best, Sammy Davis

Sammy Davis, Jr.

Sincerely Yours Roscoe Fatty Arbuckle

Fatty Arbuckle

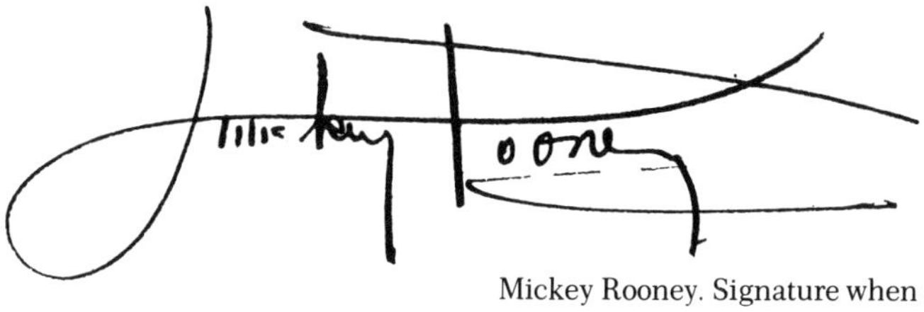

Mickey Rooney. Signature when a child star

Hal Roach

Frank Capra

Mickey Rooney, as a young man

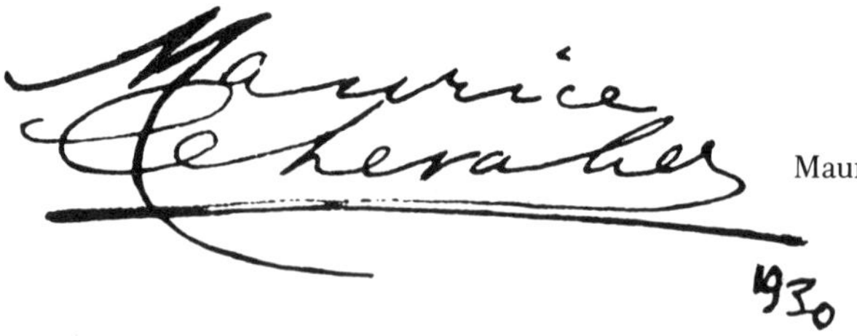

Sincerely,
Fred Astaire

Vincent Price

Pearl Bailey

John Garfield

Maurice Chevalier

Peter Lorre

Jeanette MacDonald

Béla Lugosi

Béla Lugosi

Christopher Plummer

Christopher Plummer

George Reeves

George Reeves

Basil Rathbone
MEMBER'S SIGNATURE

Basil Rathbone

Nigel Bruce

Nigel Bruce

Boris Karloff

Boris Karloff

Lon Chaney, Sr. Original sketch by Margery Brown, signed by Chaney

Warner Oland

Warner Oland

King Vidor

King Vidor

Houghton - Mich.
April 22/17

Mr Isaiah Bowman
American Geo Society
New York —

Dear Sir —

I enclose here with signed
card to be used in connection
for my proposal for fellowship.
The clipping that Mrs
Hubbard enclosed to you must
have been from some
Toronto paper.

Pearl White

George Raft

Darryl F. Zanuck

Randolph Scott

Warm regards
John Wayne

I am enclosing a notice from the Royal Geographical Magazine which gives a fuller statement of my work which you requested from Mrs. Hubbard.

Will, great pleasure acceptable an election to your society.

Sincerely Yours
Robert Flaherty.

Robert J. Flaherty. Canadian motion-picture director; invented the documentary

Laird Cregar

Laird Cregar

George Sanders

George Sanders

Fay Wray

Fay Wray

Mae West

Mae West

Conrad Veidt

Conrad Veidt

HEROES ON HORSEBACK **31**

Philip Kearny

General McClellan studied the "job application" in front of him. "So Phil Kearny wants a commission," he said. "Well, he won't get it from me. I don't want any one-armed officers in my cavalry."

"He's still got a strong right arm," said McClellan's aide. "I've seen him in battle. He rides like the devil and clenches the reins in his teeth. What's more, he's fearless."

"No," said McClellan. "My decision is final."

Refused a commission in the regular army, which he had served brilliantly in the Mexican War, Kearny finally settled for a Civil War appointment as brigadier general in the New Jersey militia.

He was soon an inspiring sight in every skirmish, always at the very front of his troops, waving his saber savagely and, as a fellow officer put it, "holding his bridle in his teeth, with characteristic impetuosity."

At the second battle of Bull Run, he drove back the corps of Stonewall Jackson. At Chantilly, in September 1862, he was shot and killed during a reconnaissance.

Kearny's letters are mostly routine and colorless, but those written during the Mexican War are pungent and interesting. He was a friend of Indian fighter General O. O. Howard, and was present when Howard lost his right arm at the battle of Fair Oaks. Looking up at Kearny after the amputation, Howard quipped, "Well, Kearny, now we can buy our gloves together."

No less colorful was George A. Custer, the famous "boy general" of the Civil War. Custer won his general's appointment at twenty-four because, explained General Alfred Pleasonton, his commanding officer, "I need a young general who is absolutely without fear who can ride with his command straight into the heart of enemy country and Custer is that man."

Custer performed dozens of valorous feats during the war and survived to die eleven years later in a desperate clash with

O. O. Howard

Headquarters 3ª Di. Cav
M.M.D. Dec 8ª/64
The Commissary of the 1ª Brig is
authorized to issue to the bearer
(50) fifty pounds of salt.

G A Custer
Bvt. Maj Genl
Comng 3 Di.

George A. Custer. Handwritten order signed as Civil War general

G E Pickett .

George E. Pickett. Led "Pickett's Charge" at Gettysburg

Phil. H. Sheridan

Philip H. Sheridan

the Sioux Indians at the Little Big Horn.

Few autographs are more appealing than Custer's. His Civil War letters are always interesting, full of piquant details. I never pick up a Custer letter without a little thrill of expectation. And I've never been disappointed.

Many years ago I acquired a collection of seventeen torrid love letters written when Custer was a youth to his first sweetheart, Mollie J. Holland of Cadiz, Ohio. Mollie had cut some passages from the letters and blotted out others, but what remained was enough to reveal a sizzling romance. In one letter, Custer asked: "When are we going to get into that trundle bed?" In another, he wrote: "My dear I have been trying to invent some plan by which we could have that take place which we have talked about so much." Many of the letters, written when Custer was a schoolteacher before he went to West Point, are signed, "Your devoted love Bachelor Boy." On December 15, 1856, writing from "My Schoolhouse" in faded ink made from the frontier pokeberry juice, Custer apologized for "that occurrence in the kitchen," vowing that he did not mean "to act dishonorably toward you, for I swear by all I hold sacred that before I would be guilty of such a base act, I would undergo any torment." In later letters, penned from West Point, Custer describes how he was thrown from his horse when he attempted a jump and how he and other classmates smuggled girls into the dormitories.

The excitement of Philip H. Sheridan's great cavalry career is reflected in his correspondence of war date. Some of his letters written during the Indian campaigns after the Civil War capture the agonies and joys of the frontier years. In a letter to

I have but one motive in these matters and that is duty to our country, which I know you will recognise as paramount to everything else.

Most Respectfully
& Truly Yours
J.E.B. Stuart.
Major Gen'l

Jeb Stuart. Handwritten note signed: "I have but one motive in these matters and that is duty to our country. . . ."

Custer congratulating him on his victory over Black Kettle's village, Sheridan wrote: "The battle of the Washita River [November 27, 1868] is the most complete and successful of all our Indian battles & was fought in such unfortunate weather & circumstances as to reflect the highest credit on yourself & Regiment."

The Confederacy had many great cavalry leaders, the most romantic of whom was the young and handsome Jeb Stuart, killed in action at thirty-one. Stuart was bold and brilliant in battle. He adored women and flirted outrageously in his correspondence with the young rebel girls who fell in love with him. He was forever exchanging locks of hair with feminine admirers and his sudden death, a terrible blow to the Confederate cause, must also have anguished thousands of fair ladies in the South. I recall a letter in which he wrote to a young woman: "A mystic chord binds kindred natures even though never met."

Almost a century earlier, a fellow Virginian, Henry ("Light Horse Harry") Lee, dashing cavalry leader, played havoc with the British forces in North Carolina and Virginia. A close friend of Washington, Lee authored the famous epitaph "First in war, first in peace, and first in the hearts of his countrymen." Lee was a prolific correspondent and peppered his associates with interesting letters. Documents signed by him as governor of Virginia appear in the most modest of autograph collections.

Another famed cavalry officer of the Revolution was Colonel William Washington, a distant relative of George. Colonel Washington loved saber-to-saber encounters with the British foe and on one occasion he clashed in a fierce duel with Colonel Banastre Tarleton in which both men were wounded. Colonel Washington's letters are rather hard to find, but they repay the effort, for they are invariably exciting.

More than a hundred years later, the Spanish-American War (1898) produced an audacious cavalry officer who led a bully charge up San Juan Hill in Cuba. This heroic American

John H. Morgan. Confederate cavalry raider

Colonel William Washington

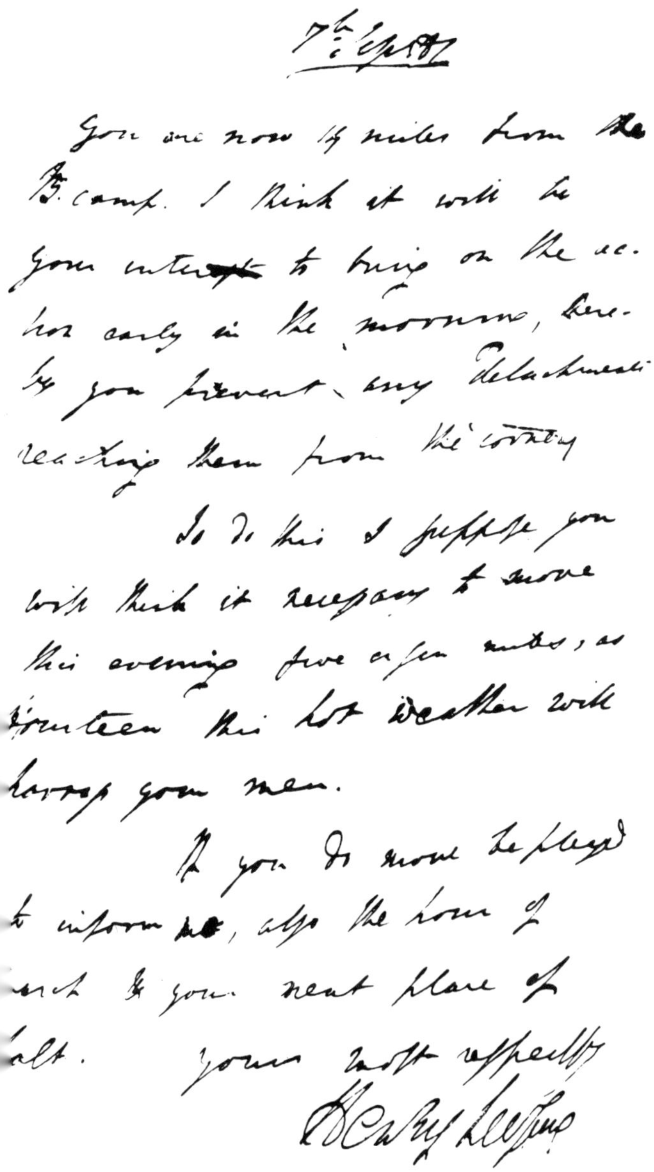
You are now 14 miles from the B. camp. I think it will be your interest to bring on the action early in the morning, because you prevent any detachments reaching them from the country.

To do this I suppose you will think it necessary to move this evening five or six miles, as fourteen this hot weather will harrass your men.

If you do move be pleased to inform me, also the hour of march & your next place of halt.

yours most respectfully
Henry Lee Junr

Henry Lee. Handwritten letter signed on military maneuvers

George S. Patton, Jr.

assault by the Rough Riders made Colonel Theodore Roosevelt famous and carried him right into the White House. Roosevelt's letters are always interesting. Teddy never pulled his punches. He said what he thought, and what he thought always packed a wallop. Most of his letters were typed, but Roosevelt often altered the text in ink or penned additional comments so that many of his notes have the zesty flavor of original manuscripts.

The last of the great cavalry leaders—General George S. Patton—began his career on horseback and wound up in a tank. Patton subscribed to the Nazi theory that "anything goes in war." Some of the things that "went" with Patton were viewed with alarm and often anger by the American infantry. Whenever Patton took prisoners, which was infrequent, he forced them to dig a pit and then machine-gunned them into it. Word got around among the Nazi soldiers that Americans were slaughtering prisoners and this made it tough on the infantry who had to "mop up" after Patton, whose rapid pursuit of the retreating enemy forced him to by-pass many strongly defended positions. Our infantry discovered that an entrenched foe that is afraid to surrender can be costly to defeat.

Patton was a collector of old weapons, especially pistols, and he acquired a superb collection of rarities by looting German museums, a practice followed earlier by Hermann Goering. But Patton was less subtle than Goering. Usually he did not enter museums by the front door, but simply drove his tank through the walls.

Patton's letters are invariably exciting. At the end of World War II, I was a sergeant in the Air Corps, stationed in Belgium. I ran across a file of letters at headquarters from Patton to General Hoyt S. Vandenberg, commenting on tactical bombing by the Ninth Air Force. The letters were marked "Secret" and had not been declassified. The temptation to slip them into my pocket was great, but I resisted. I have always regretted that I did not yield to the devil's cajolery, for two weeks later an order came from higher headquarters to burn all the files.

of it I want the pleasure of Miss Mollies company to the party let me know in your next, I would have asked you about it yesterday but you know how mixed up we were but if I do not hear of it and you have the offer of someone elses company do not refuse for my sake but use your own pleasure,

I do not know when that party at Hopedale will take place now I do not expect it will be soon though but I will see you soon and then we can talk about it.

Mollie you need not be afraid of me falling in love with that Smiley Girl if I do

George A. Custer. Handwritten page from an early love letter to Mollie J. Holland, Cadiz, Ohio, 1856: "Mollie you need not be afraid of me falling in love with that Smiley Girl . . ."

Colonel John S. Mosby. Signed photograph

Jeb Stuart. Handwritten letter signed

John S. Mosby, Confederate raider, known as "the Grey Ghost." Handwritten letter signed about the battle of Bull Run, explaining that the Union commander, McDowell, had made a serious error, "but there was no Napoleon on our side to take advantage of it."

We stand for enforcement of the law and for obedience to the law; our government is a government of orderly liberty equally alien to tyranny and to anarchy; and its foundation stone is the observance of the law, alike by the people and by their public servants. We hold ever before us as the all-important end of policy and administration the reign of peace at home and throughout the world; of peace, which comes only by doing justice.

Theodore Roosevelt

Theodore Roosevelt. Handwritten statement signed on his political creed as President

HAWAII: THE
32 PARADISE ISLANDS

King Kamehameha I

Captain James Cook

John Montagu, fourth earl of Sandwich

"Surrender or leap!"

This was the cry of King Kamehameha of Hawaii and his warriors as they drove their enemies to the cliffs of the huge mountain Nuuanu Pali on the Hawaiian island of Oahu. Most of the cornered men, aware of Kamehameha's cruelty, jumped to their deaths.

By this fierce battle in 1795, Kamehameha the Great won control of Oahu and became the first king to rule all the islands of Hawaii. Kamehameha looked like a savage and acted like a savage, but he was also an astute diplomat. He knew how to fight but not how to write, and the tiny X with which he signed his name belied his great physical strength.

The kingdom ruled by Kamehameha was originally called the Sandwich Islands by its discoverer, Captain James Cook, whose brawling sailors quickly corrupted the natives. The very islanders who originally hailed Cook as a god later clubbed him to death in a brawl.

Hawaii's story, one of high adventure, murder, rollicking monarchs, ruthless conquest and beautiful women, is dramatically recorded in the few letters and documents that survive the tumultuous years of the nineteenth century.

After Kamehameha's death in 1819, the royal parade continued with the vacillating drunk, King Kamehameha II, also known as Liholiho, under whose inept reign, and that of his successor, King Kamehameha III, Hawaii was transformed from a palm tree paradise into a land ravaged by syphilis, vandalism and drunkenness. After five Kamehamehas, the last two of whom were excellent kings, Hawaii got its first elected monarch, Lunalilo, an uncouth but charming alcoholic who was a patron of literature and art. During his reign the spread of leprosy throughout Hawaii was so alarming that the king established a board of health and several leper colonies.

Seldom encountered are letters of Father Damien, a Belgian priest who, hearing of the terrible condition of the lepers on the Hawaiian island of Molokai, volunteered to live and work among the victims of this loathsome disease. Father Damien helped the lepers to build a system of water pipes, thus

Kamehameha V (Lot)

King Kamehameha II (Liholiho)

Kamehameha III

Kalakaua

Kamehameha IV

Lunalilo

providing fresh water. He tended the sick and dressed their ulcers. He comforted the dying and buried the dead, and at last, after twelve years of heroic effort, he fell victim to the disease. Photographs of him taken just before his death show a sad and beautiful face corroded by the marks of his fatal illness. His disfigured, almost fleshless hands with their big-knuckled, bony fingers dangle nearly helpless from his sleeves.

A month before he died, Father Damien wrote to an old friend in Belgium, Sister Ignatius, that even his own family seemed to regard him as contaminated: "They treat me as if they were ashamed of my having caught this disease. . . . I strive to bear courageously the terrible burden which the good Lord has seen fit to lay upon me."

Almost to the moment of his death, Father Damien kept on working for those even more helpless than himself. Father Damien may never be canonized, for his leprous bones have not performed the requisite three miracles. Besides, the Catholic Church prefers to make saints of hysterical peasant women who have "visions" or bleed mysteriously on holy days. Father Damien has no need of such sainthood. If there is a God and there is a heaven, I have no doubt that this great man sits at God's right and drinks celestial wine from a goblet of gold.

When Father Damien died on April 15, 1889, the ruler of Hawaii was Lunalilo's successor, Kalakaua, known as "the Merry Monarch." Kalakaua could and often did polish off five bottles of champagne in an afternoon.

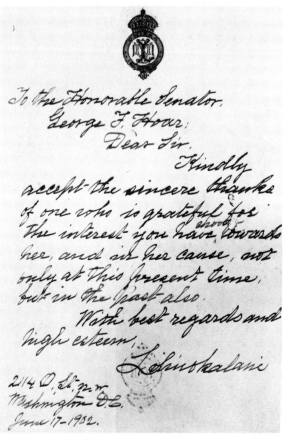

Queen Liliuokalani

but a huaaiwa little town in an out of the way place, but it bids fair to become a large city hereafter on account of its good situation & healthy climate. Her English letters are full of nothing but the Fenian subject, & I have one from Lady Agnes Courtenay who says a large of troops including some of the Guards have gone to Ireland today to quell the disturbance. It is time this long letter drew to a conclusion & do so now with hopes of its finding your Majesty well. I am yours very faithfully Emma

Emma, queen of Kamehameha IV

Kapiolani, queen of Kalakaua

Sanford B. Dole

Recently a young collector showed up in my gallery with that expression of mingled joy and eagerness which bespeaks a new interest in life. "I've just started to collect the autographs of Hawaiian monarchs," he exclaimed. "And guess who's the first in my collection?"

"Kalakaua."

He looked astonished at my detective skill. "How did you know?"

"Very simply," I explained, suppressing a little smile of triumph. "Kalakaua's autograph is fairly common. He was a fluent penman and traveled widely in America, signing his name for all who asked. He is only hard to find in handwritten letters."

"That is a very clever deduction," said my visitor, "and for your sake I wish it were correct. I do not have Kalakaua's signature, but I have a letter written by his sister, Queen Lil."

Despite the plenitude of his royal scrawl, Kalakaua did not put his dying wishes on paper. Instead he whispered them dramatically into the recording trumpet of an Edison phonograph, leaving his kingdom to his sister, Queen Liliuokalani, the last royal ruler of Hawaii. A pleasant and talented woman, Queen Lil composed the beautiful farewell song "Aloha Oe."

The first president of Hawaii was Sanford B. Dole, head of the great pineapple empire, who led a successful revolt against Queen Lil. Dole apparently enjoyed making money, for most of his letters deal with financial schemes. It was during Dole's presidency, on June 4, 1900, that Hawaii was annexed as a territory by the United States.

Kalawao July 21th 1886

F H Hayselden Secretary of the Board of Health

Dear Sir

Please have the kindness to send me by
next Monday Steamer if she comes around here
50 boxes of - Kai Gio Kioso Joku Yaku - bath medeci
50 boxes of Sei Kets - wren pills
50 packages of Decoction Hichiyou bark
10 pound of Bicarb Sodium . . . .
This is all for the introduction of the Japanese treatment

Should the Steamer not come over here next week
you want to send by her - to be landed at Kaunak
a Small Supply of each, Say 5 boxes - packages and
2 pounds of Soda - with a request to M Meyer
to send it down immediatly
By filling this order without postponing
you will greatly oblige you afflicted friend and Serv

J Damien cath ps

PS Wanted 2 outlets to be fitted in the botiom of bath tobs
and 2 Small Termometers - Farenheid

Father Joseph Damien. Handwritten letter signed, ordering
medical supplies "for the introduction of the Japanese treatment [of leprosy]." Dated 1886, the letter is subscribed "your
afflicted friend and servt."

Iolani Palace
Honolulu February 12 1874

To His Excellency
     P. Nahaolelua
President of the Legislative Assembly
of the Hawaiian Islands,

Sir:

I have received at the hand
of your Committee the Certificate of
my Election to-day by the Legislative
Assembly as Successor to the Throne
of the Hawaiian Islands,

I wish to express to the Legislative
Assembly through you my thanks for this
highest mark of their Confidence and
to say that I accept the Royal Trust

Kalakaua

Kalakaua. Handwritten letter signed, Honolulu, 1874, accepting the certificate of his election "to the Throne of the Hawaiian Islands . . . I accept the Royal Trust."

SOME
BLACK POETS **33**

The story of black authorship in America began at a Boston slave auction.

In 1761 John Wheatley went to market to buy a cheap servant as a companion for his wife and was the successful bidder on a slender, frightened little African girl about seven years old, just off a slave ship and clothed only in a fragment of dirty carpet.

Mrs. Wheatley named the girl Phillis and soon discovered that her husband had picked up a bargain. Phillis was uncommonly bright. She learned to read and write with ease and by the age of fourteen was studying Latin and composing verses.

Phillis specialized in elegies and no acquaintance or celebrity died without a barrage of heroic couplets to commemorate his passing.

Most of Phillis's occasional verse is a slavish imitation of Alexander Pope. In one poem she described her kidnapping as a small child:

> I, young in life, by seeming cruel fate,
> Was snatched from Afric's fancied happy seat.
> What pangs excruciating must molest
> What sorrows labour in my parents' breast! . . .
> Such, such my case. And can I then but pray
> Others may never feel tyrannic sway?

At nineteen, frail Phillis, by then a member of the Wheatley family, traveled to London for her health. There she was lionized and had her verses published. It was the zenith of her brief life. After the death of her mistress, she married a clever but shiftless free Negro and died in poverty.

Phillis Wheatley's letters and manuscripts are extremely uncommon and for the past quarter century I have searched vainly for even the merest scratch from her quill. If you relish literary delicacies, I advise you to join me in the quest, for I can imagine no more intriguing fragment of black Americana than a letter or manuscript of Phillis Wheatley.

Refreshingly abundant (by comparison, only) are the letters and manuscripts of Paul Laurence Dunbar, the poet laureate of Dayton, Ohio. Before and after he wrote his dialect poems,

I am very affectionately your Friend
Phillis Wheatley
Boston March 21. 1774.

Phillis Wheatley. Last line of a handwritten letter signed

On Going

A grave is all too weak a thing
   To hold my fancy long;
I'll bear a blossom with the spring,
   Or be a blackbird's song—

Countee Cullen

Countee Cullen. Handwritten quatrain signed

Paul Laurence Dunbar.

Paul Laurence Dunbar

Gwendolyn Brooks

Gwendolyn Brooks

among the finest in English, Dunbar was an elevator operator. His literary output was enormous and reflects a longing for the tranquillity of plantation life and a feeling of restless apprehension over emancipation.

Dunbar died at thirty-four but bequeathed to posterity a precious legacy of manuscript poems, penned in a fastidious, very legible hand. Some years ago, Mrs. Harry Belafonte, wife of the black actor, asked me to suggest an appropriate gift for her husband.

"Why not a manuscript poem of Paul Laurence Dunbar?" I said. "He is the first great black poet of America and I, for one, still read his poems with pleasure."

Mrs. Belafonte agreed and bought from me a signed poem of Dunbar, framed with a photograph of the handsome, youthful poet.

Among more recent black poets, Countee Cullen, James Weldon Johnson and Langston Hughes come to mind. Cullen's letters are very scarce and those of Johnson, an intellectual, are freighted with thoughts about the future of black authorship.

Langston Hughes wrote in a large, rounded script, always in green ink. So prized are his manuscripts that he has attained the ultimate honor: his signed typescripts have been extensively forged for sale to unsuspecting collectors.

19 May 1961

Dear Miss Turner:

I'm very glad to hear that you could use the material I sent you, and I do look forward to seeing the book. Please note that my address, after June 1st, will be Portland, Connecticut.

Sincerely,
Richard Wilbur.

Richard Wilbur. Handwritten note signed

Langston Hughes. Handwritten note signed

James Weldon Johnson. Last page of a handwritten letter signed in which he discusses the future of black literature: ". . . it appears that the scales are turning, and Negro writers of prose are becoming more and more important. It may be expected that in the next decade . . . they will supersede the writers of poetry both in output and significance."

THE
SEA HAWKS 34

"An English frigate is now in sight from my deck," wrote Captain James Lawrence on June 1, 1813. "I have sent a pilot boat out to reconoiter. . . . I am in hopes to give a good account of her before night."

The enemy frigate turned out to be the *Shannon*, commanded by Captain Philip Broke, who had previously sent a cavalier challenge to Lawrence. Although his men were poorly trained in gunnery, Lawrence sailed in the *Chesapeake* to meet Broke. Soon the vessels closed in combat. The *Shannon* fired a deadly broadside at fifty yards and Lawrence fell, mortally wounded. Broke led a boarding party and was struck on the head by a musket stock and severely injured.

Dying, Lawrence whispered his last words: "Don't give up the ship." A few minutes later his crew surrendered. Although Lawrence's judgment and leadership were egregiously at fault, he won immortality with his five dying words. Had he lived, he might have been court-martialed and cashiered.

Lawrence's letters are seldom encountered and deal mainly, as one might expect, with routine naval matters.

The War of 1812, in which Lawrence lost his life, was mostly fought at sea and the roster of heroes is impressive: Oliver Hazard Perry ("We have met the enemy and they are ours"), Thomas Macdonough, Stephen Decatur, David Porter and William Bainbridge, to name but a few. For the most part, their letters are not as exciting as their spectacular adventures before the mast.

Sailing without waiting for orders, Captain Isaac Hull took the *Constitution* to sea, and six hundred miles from Boston ran into the British frigate *Guerrière*. The vessels maneuvered for position.

Moses Smith, a gunner on the *Constitution*, wrote that "an eighteen-pound shot came through us, striking just abaft the breech of the gun to which I belonged. The splinters flew in all directions. We immediately picked up the shot and put it in the mouth of long Tom, a large gun on deck, and sent it home again with our respects."

A Yankee gunner saw a cannonball bounce off the *Constitution*'s oak planking and shouted, "Her sides are made of iron."

Captain James Lawrence

David Porter

Isaac Hull

an English Frigate is now in sight from my deck, I have sent a pilot boat out to reconnoitre, and should she be alone I am in hopes to give a good account of her before night,

Edward Preble

John Rodgers

John Barry Capt.

Thus the famous frigate won the name "Old Ironsides." After many victories, including the total defeat of the *Guerrière*, the old ship was sentenced to be scrapped in 1830, but a twenty-one-year-old medical student, Oliver Wendell Holmes, wrote a stirring poem that roused the nation to save her.

Few people know that John Paul Jones, the naval hero of the Revolution who captured the British man-of-war *Serapis* in a fierce battle by moonlight, was also a poet. Jones's adventurous life, during which he shipped in the slave trade and killed at least one man in a brawl, reached its romantic peak when as a victorious sea captain he was feted by the belles of Paris. For them, and for liberty, he wrote adulatory verses. I once possessed a panegyric in his hand which began:

> Insulted Freedom bled; I felt her cause
> And drew my sword to Vindicate her Laws.
> My zeal still prompts, ambitious to pursue
> The Foes ye Fair! of Liberty & you.

Jones's letters, penned in a neat script with an enormous signature, were often full of brimstone. He was a feisty little Scotsman who spent his entire brief life spoiling for a fight. His notes are much prized and fetch astronomic prices whenever they are put on the block.

The Civil War furnished a spate of picturesque sea dogs,

We have met the enemy and they are ours:
Two Ships, two Brigs one
Schooner & one Sloop.

Yours, with great respect and esteem

O H Perry.

Oliver H. Perry. Handwritten dispatch signed to the secretary of the navy describing his victory over the British at Lake Erie: "We have met the enemy and they are ours."

Isaac Chauncey

Isaac Chauncey

Chs Stewart

Charles Stewart

His Britannic Majesty's Ship
Shannon off Boston   June 1813

Sir,

As the Chesapeake appears now ready for Sea, I request you will do me the favor to meet the Shannon with her, Ship to Ship, to try the fortune of our respective Flags,

Captain Philip Broke. Original manuscript challenge to Captain James Lawrence of the American ship *Chesapeake* to meet the British vessel *Shannon* in a sea battle

chief among whom was Admiral David G. Farragut. Letters of this determined leader, famed for his expletive defiance of enemy mines (then known as torpedoes), are abundant and often exciting. The same may be said for other naval heroes of the War Between the States, such as David D. Porter and Raphael Semmes.

For some reason I cannot explain, the letters of the sea commanders of the Spanish-American War have never appealed to philographers. There is no more interest in Admiral George Dewey than if the battle of Manila Bay had been fought in a bathtub. Even Richmond P. Hobson's incredible feat of almost corking up the entire Spanish fleet at Santiago by sinking a collier in the harbor's neck does not stir the imagination of collectors. These splendid men, personal heroes of mine, await the wizard's touch of a great historian.

D. G. Farragut

David G. Farragut

George Dewey

Admiral George Dewey

as that fully
your ob. Ser.

T. Macdonough

Thomas Macdonough

Joshua Barney

Joshua Barney

O better that her shattered hulk
   Should sink beneath the wave;
Her thunders shook the mighty deep,
   And there should be her grave;
Nail to the mast her holy flag,
   Set every threadbare sail,
And give her to the god of storms,
   The lightning and the gale!

Oliver Wendell Holmes
Boston Jan. 21st 1865.

Oliver Wendell Holmes. Last stanza of his famous poem on *Old Ironsides*, written out and signed. This dramatic poem roused public indignation against the scrapping of the celebrated ship.

J Toucey

Isaac Toucey

M C Perry

Matthew C. Perry

H. Paulding

Hiram Paulding

United States naval cipher used in the War of 1812. With the present sophisticated equipment, a cryptographer could break this code in two minutes.

TW. Tingey

Thomas Tingey

R. P. Hobson

Richmond P. Hobson

Dahlgren

John A. Dahlgren

Raphael Semmes

John L. Worden

Uriah P. Levy, credited with abolishing corporal punishment in the navy

Richard Dale, second in command under John Paul Jones

Thomas Truxton

William T. Sampson

John Paul Jones. Handwritten letter signed, about a medal awarded to him by Congress and $2,000 sent to him by Thomas Jefferson

John Paul Jones. Early signature, *Jno. Paul* (1773), before he killed a man in a brawl and added *Jones* to his name

Old Ironsides commanders. Among the celebrated names are William Bainbridge (upper right), Isaac Hull and Charles Morris (under Bainbridge), who was an officer on *Old Ironsides* when it defeated the *Guerrière*.

William S. Sims

David D. Porter

The words as I remember were "Kill Japs,
Kill Japs, Kill more Japs" and we surely
did.
    All good things to you—
      W.F. Halsey
        Fleet Admiral, U.S. Navy

Admiral W. F. ("Bull") Halsey. Handwritten statement signed: "The words . . . were 'Kill Japs, Kill Japs, Kill more Japs' and we surely did."

FLAG SHIP *Hartford*
WESTERN GULF BLOCKADING SQUADRON

Mobile Bay Augt. 9th 1864

Dear Commodore,
    I sent you all the Prisoners from Fort Gaines but I had not sight to pen a line — all my little vessels have arrived and that is 3 more, & one the finest has been burnt by the unaccountable conduct of the Captain trying to run in with the squadron when we passed the Forts — & she was run on shore & destroyed — But ah! a sad fate was that of poor Craven & his officers & crew — She disappeared in a moment — but we paid them for it in the end as well as we could.

David G. Farragut. First page of a handwritten letter from Mobile Bay, 1864: "I sent you all the prisoners . . ."

"Today I'm going to show you my greatest treasure," said my new friend, a prominent Los Angeles philographer.

I was only seventeen and a senior at Beverly Hills High School, but I was already fascinated by California history and autograph collecting, even though I was too poor to afford even a twenty-five-cent signature.

As we entered my friend's Beverly Hills mansion I was awestruck by the beautiful paintings and sumptuous Oriental rugs, into which my worn tennis shoes sank ankle deep. Each room was full of rare and beautiful antique furniture. Ascending the wide carpeted stairs to his study, I felt sure that "his greatest treasure," whatever it might be, would not compare with his sumptuous residence.

His study was like a museum. On the walls were original sketches by Delacroix and Vernet, with a dazzling display of rare weapons and crossed rapiers.

From a drawer in his desk he took a sheet of yellowed paper and placed it gently in my hands.

"It is the baptismal certificate, written and signed by Father Junípero Serra, of the first white child ever born in California."

I was very familiar with the career of Father Serra, founder of San Diego and other cities in California. I still recall my tremendous excitement when I held this precious document, an almost electrical current going through my fingers. While the owner was not looking, I reverently placed a kiss upon the signature of the great colonizer.

Serra's letters and documents, written in an attractive script in Spanish, all concern life at the missions. His autographs and those of his friend and biographer, Palou, are very difficult to come by.

The love of the Spaniards for the rococo is evident in their signatures, always adorned with paraphs or rubrics, those gallant terminal flourishes full of verve and originality. No signature was legal without a rubric; and a rubric by itself, without the writer's name, was considered a legal signature.

The signatures of the early explorers, the viceroys of New Spain, and the military commandants and governors of

Father Junípero Serra. Handwritten document signed, 1775

Gaspar de Portolá

Fernando de Rivera y Moncada

Joseph Antonio Rengel

Pedro de Nava

Alexandro Malaspino

Stephen W. Kearny. Seized Los Angeles, January 1847

California present an astonishing array of beautiful scripts. Some of the signatures are almost works of art. Even a routine legal document of early California may be a "period piece" of great calligraphic beauty.

The Spanish governors of California are a romantic lot, some honest, some corrupt, some brilliant, some stupid, but all of them appointed by the king of Spain to pump as much wealth as possible out of the new and impoverished province. Even after the United States took over California in 1848, the most valuable products were hides and tallow until a bearded man named Jim Marshall, working at John Sutter's mill, spotted a bright glitter while digging a mill race. At first Marshall thought it was an opal. When he picked it up, the gleam of pure gold sent chills through him. He mounted his horse and galloped to Sutter's office.

"We're rich! We're rich!" he cried, with a mad look in his eye.

Sutter saw the crazy look and had a momentary impulse to reach for his rifle. Then Marshall cast a fistful of virgin gold scales on his table.

"I was fairly thunderstruck," wrote Sutter later.

To Marshall he said, "Keep this a secret, Jim." The two men rode to the spot of the discovery. With his penknife, Sutter pried an ounce-and-a-half nugget from a small rock.

But even before they got back to the mill the secret was out

[John A. Sutter signature — complimentary handwritten close in French]

John A. Sutter. Complimentary handwritten close signed from a letter in French

[Fernando de Rivera y Moncada handwritten subscription]

Fernando de Rivera y Moncada. Handwritten subscription signed from a letter

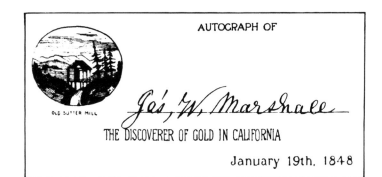

James W. Marshall

[Jacobo Ugarte y Loyola signature]

Jacobo Ugarte y Loyola

[John A. Sutter signature — complimentary handwritten close in German]

John A. Sutter. Complimentary handwritten close signed from a letter in German

[José de la Guerra y Noviega signature]

José de la Guerra y Noviega

[Commodore Robert F. Stockton signature]

Commodore Robert F. Stockton. Helped to conquer California

and their Indian workers were dancing with joy and shouting, "*Oro! Oro!*"

James Marshall's halting signature turns up only on ornate cards picturing Sutter's mill, which he signed for a "contribution," usually fifty cents or a dollar, much later in life when he was down on his uppers. I never saw a letter of Marshall. John A. Sutter, his boss, a clever Swiss entrepreneur operating under a Spanish land grant, peppered California with interesting letters in English, Spanish, French and German. He had his deft hand in everything and owned many shops and·a fort in addition to his mill. He even traded with the Indians for furs. The discovery of gold on his land destroyed him. His property was overrun by prospectors and much of it was seized by the government. Most of the letters written late in his life speak of his efforts to get some compensation or a pension to rescue him from destitution.

Take gunpowder and bullets, mix with a train of covered wagons and a band of hostile redskins. Add rampaging buffalo and a touch of desert sun and cholera. There you have the recipe for the great overland gold rush.

Indian Agency of New Helvetia
May, 22ᵈ 1847.

Cornelio Chief of the Shonomney tribe has presented himself here, on my request, to receive my Orders and Instructions.

The said Chief promised faithfully, that he and his tribe will in future have nothing more to do with Horsestealing, nor trading horses with the Horsethiefs; therefore I request the Commanding Officer of the expedition against the horsethiefs, to not molest the Shonomney tribe, as they are willing to obey the Orders of the Government. The Shonomney tribe could be very usefull by assisting to subdue the hostile Chausilles & Potoiaches on the River Merced, which two tribes dont like to abstain from horse stealing nor do they like to surrender and enter in friendly relations with me.

Sutter
Sub Agent for the Indians on & near the Sacramento & San Joaquin Rivers.

John A. Sutter. Handwritten document signed, introducing a Shonomney Indian chief

Francisco Palou

The journals and diaries kept by travelers to El Dorado are among the most dramatic and suspenseful in history. Most of the entries were penned by campfire in the evening.

Some years ago a rather overstuffed, dowdy woman entered my gallery with a small package wrapped in newspapers under her arm.

"I found this in our garage," she explained. "If it has any value at all I want to sell it."

She opened the package and handed me a small manuscript book bound in battered calfskin, an overland journal kept by a traveler to California in 1849.

The first page I looked at put me in the middle of an Indian attack on a circle of covered wagons.

"This is worth at least a thousand dollars, possibly a great deal more," I said. "Leave it with me overnight and I can give you a better idea after I read it."

The woman's face turned pasty. "Give it back!" she cried. And clutching the old journal to her portly bosom, she fled, half stumbling, half running, from my gallery.

I never saw her again. But she has no doubt joined the pathetic throng of valuable-document owners who travel restlessly from dealer to dealer, year after year, forever in quest of the "right" price and forever believing that everyone seeks to cheat them out of their priceless treasures.

Juan Bautista Zappa, missionary

Luis de Velasco, father of New Spain (1550–1564)

Francisco Venegas (1810–1813)

Antonio María Bucarely y Ursúa (1771–1779)

El Cavallero De Croix (1766–1771)

Marqués de Branciforte (1794–1798)

Juan de Padilla, el Conde de Revillo Gigedo (1789–1794)

Miguel José de Azana (1798–1800)

Martín de Mayorga (1779–1783)

Felix de Marquina (1800–1803)

Josef de Iturrigaray (1803–1808)

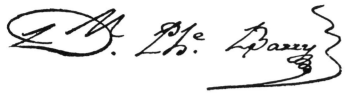

M. Phelipe Barry (1770–1775)

Diego Berica (1794–1800)

Phelipe de Neve (1775–1782)

Josef Argüello (1814–1815)

Pedro Fages (1782–1791)

Pablo Vicente de Sola (1815–1822)

Joseph Antonio de Romeu (1791–1792)

José María de Echeandía (1825–1833)

José Joaquín Arrillaga (1792–1794; 1800–1804)

José Figueroa (1833–1835)

José Castro (1835–1836)

Juan Bautista Alvarado (1836–1842)

Mariano Chico (1836)

Pío Pico (1832; 1845–1846)

Manuel Micheltorena (1842–1845)

ACKNOWLEDGMENTS

For the enthusiastic help and cooperation accorded me by the philographers of America I wish to express my deepest gratitude. No author ever had more friendly assistance.

For permission to reproduce facsimiles or publish material I am grateful to Dr. David Light of Miami Beach, Florida; Morris Login, an old friend in the Bronx; John Taylor of McLean, Virginia, a noted authority on presidential autographs; Michael Reese II of South San Francisco, an expert on Confederate signatures; Florence Persons of New York, for several choice items from her collection of black Americana; Creighton C. Hart of Kansas City, owner of a remarkable letter of Jesse James; Doug Beckett and Robert Kuhn, both generous friends of San Francisco; W. J. Gillard of Wayne, New Jersey, for the use of Chief Joseph's signature; Martin Riskin of New York; Richard D. Sinchak of Warren, Ohio; Richard Calow of New York; Steve Barnett of Provo, Utah, for his immense assistance in providing rare Mormon autographs; and my daughter, Carolyn Brooks Hamilton, for the loan of her Lon Chaney signed portrait.

Others who helped were D. N. Diedrich of Ball State University, Muncie, Indiana, who allowed me to reproduce his handsome transcript of "America the Beautiful"; Colonel Walter Pforzheimer of Washington, D.C., who provided facsimiles of Rose Greenhow from his espionage collection; Drew Eliot of New York for several rare theatrical autographs; Irving Wallace, the celebrated author, for autographs of Jim Thorpe and Frederick Douglass from his personal archives; Tal Kanigher of Burbank, California, for permission to use rare signatures from his Western collection; Lionel A. Aucoin of Spencer, Massachusetts, for many interesting musical items; Brent F. Ashworth of Provo, Utah, who provided me with some rare, almost unique, facsimiles from his great collection of Western autographs; and James J. Fuld of New York, who furnished a facsimile of the rare signature of Scott Joplin.

Especially am I indebted to the libraries and museums that cooperated in this work, and I wish to thank the University of Texas at Austin for permission to use materials from the Dienst Papers, the Johnson Papers and the Austin Papers, all in the

Barker Texas History Center; the Draper Collection of the Wisconsin Historical Society; the Alderman Library and the C. Waller Barrett Library at the University of Virginia in Charlottesville; the Lew Wallace Papers at the Indiana Historical Society for their courtesy in allowing me to reproduce a rare letter of Billy the Kid; the Fall River Historical Society for a facsimile letter of Lizzie Borden; the Society of California Pioneers for the use of Emperor Norton material; the publishers of *California Calligraphy,* Romona, California, who munificently allowed me to borrow some of the flamboyant signatures of the early explorers and governors; and Agnes C. Conrad, the state archivist of Hawaii, for ferreting out and making copies for me of rare autographs from the Hawaiian Archives in Honolulu.

The unpublished sketch of the Alamo by Edward Everett on page 174 is included courtesy of the Amon Carter Museum, Fort Worth; gift of Mrs. Anne Burnett Tandy in memory of Thomas Lloyd Burnett.

A special paragraph of thanks goes to my very old and dear friend Professor Howard J. Pollman of East Lansing, Michigan (we were boys together in Los Angeles, California), who went to extraordinary lengths to obtain rare facsimiles for this book and offered constant encouragement and valuable help.

I am also greatly indebted to the Swann Galleries, Inc., an outstanding New York auction house and specialists in rare books and autographs, for permission to use facsimiles from their catalogues; Bruce Gimelson of Chalfont, Pennsylvania, an old friend who permitted me to reproduce illustrations from his auction catalogues; and especially to the great auction firm of Sotheby Parke Bernet, which generously granted permission to use whatever illustrations I wished from its magnificent catalogues.

In many ways, my indebtedness to fellow dealers surpasses all others. Nancy L. McGlashan of New York provided the text of an unpublished letter of Stonewall Jackson's widow and James Lowe, an old friend, also of New York, made a special effort to furnish me with a letter of Edward Everett Hale. Other dealers who graciously provided help or advice were Jeff

Marsh of Fort Lauderdale, Florida; Conway Barker of Dallas, Texas; my good friend and autograph expert Herman Darvick of Rockville Centre, New York; Thomas L. Parry of Raleigh, North Carolina; David Battan of Fresno, California; my old friend Charles W. Sachs of *The Scriptorium* in Beverly Hills, California; and Rosejeanne Slifer of New York, a dear friend who furnished unusual examples of Frederick Douglass's handwriting.

I owe a heavy debt to my long-time friend Robert F. Batchelder of Ambler, Pennsylvania, for advice and the loan of material; Paul C. Richards, the celebrated expert and dealer of Templeton, Massachusetts, whose prolific catalogues are always a pleasure to read; Gordon T. Banks and Goodspeed's Book Shop of Boston, Massachusetts; H. Keith Thompson, Jr. my close friend and executive vice president of Hamilton Galleries, for his encouragement and aid; and to my friends and associates Neale Lanigan, Jr., of Fairfield Village, Pennsylvania, and James Camner of Plainsboro, New Jersey, whose jointly written, monumental catalogue on movie star autographs was both a source and an inspiration to me, as it will be to thousands of philographers in the future.

My thanks are due to Random House, Inc., New York, for permission to reproduce self-sketches of William Saroyan, Erica Jong, Gregory Corso and Laurence Ferlinghetti from Burt Britton's *Self-Portrait: Book People Picture Themselves.*

Finally, I must mention my enormous indebtedness to my close friends Diana and Kenneth W. Rendell of Newton, Massachusetts, great autograph experts whose matchless catalogues provided me with many facsimiles, and Mary A. Benjamin, publisher of the renowned "The Collector" and one of the world's greatest autograph dealers, who magnanimously opened her files to me without reserve and went to special trouble to furnish me with rare and unusual facsimiles.

Lastly, I want to thank Harold Grove, my editor at Harper & Row, who permitted and even encouraged me to express my opinions freely and without restraint in my comments on history and literature, and my wife, Diane, whose constant encouragement and reading and rereading of the manuscript, always with the proffer of dozens of valuable suggestions, vastly improved this book.

INDEX

Page numbers in italics refer to illustrations.

About the Author

A collector for over half a century, Charles Hamilton is the world's foremost authority on autographs. His impact on philography, or the science of autograph collecting, has been enormous. As an amateur sleuth, Hamilton has tracked down and helped send to prison fourteen manuscript forgers and thieves. In 1963 he established the first American auction gallery devoted exclusively to autographs. A scholar with a penchant for the dramatic, Hamilton's frequent clashes with the FBI and Secret Service and his constant, amazing discoveries in the field of rare documents have made front-page news all over the world.

In addition to writing twelve books, eight of them about autographs, Hamilton has published two pamphlets of sonnets. His favorite authors are the ancient Latin poets and historians. He also collects volumes on snakes, insects and withcraft.

"Autograph letters and manuscripts are the raw stuff of history," says Hamilton. "Without them we would have no literature, no music, no recorded culture."

Hamilton was born in Ludington, Michigan, and grew up in Flint, where he was the neighborhood bad boy. After his father's death he moved with his family to Los Angeles and earned a master's degree in English at U.C.L.A. Hamilton served four years in the Army Air Corps, then worked as an office manager and copywriter before turning to philography in 1952. He now lives with his wife, Diane, and their four children in New York City, where he directs his world-famous auction gallery.